FRUIT, FIBER, AND FIRE

FRUIT, FIBER, AND FIRE

A History of
Modern Agriculture
in New Mexico

WILLIAM R. CARLETON

University of Nebraska Press
Lincoln

Library of Congress Cataloging-in-Publication Data
Names: Carleton, William R., author.
Title: Fruit, fiber, and fire: a history of modern agriculture in New Mexico / William R. Carleton.
Description: Lincoln: University of Nebraska Press, [2021] | Includes bibliographical references and index.
Identifiers: LCCN 2020042839
ISBN 9781496216168 (hardback)
ISBN 9781496226969 (epub)
ISBN 9781496226976 (mobi)
ISBN 9781496226983 (pdf)
Subjects: LCSH: Agriculture—New Mexico—History—20th century. | Apples—New Mexico—History—20th century. | Cotton—New Mexico—History—20th century. | Peppers—New Mexico—History—20th century.
Classification: LCC S451.N6 C375 2021 | DDC 338.109789—dc23
LC record available at https://lccn.loc.gov/2020042839

Set in Fanwood Text by Laura Buis.

Contents

Preface

In the fall of 2007 I cleared out an overgrown half-acre twenty miles north of Albuquerque of willows, elms, and various annual weeds, and planted a few rows of garlic that I planned to sell the following summer. Though full of energy, earnestness, and enthusiasm, I lacked an intimate knowledge of the landscape and faced a steep learning curve on how to grow vegetables there. Over the course of several sweaty months and years, I eventually expanded the garden and learned the ins and outs of managing a small farm business. As I sought to learn how to grow vegetables in the arid climate, my mind often wandered to the region's agricultural history. How have other farmers done it? What did they grow, and why? Though I gleaned what I could from a small number of lay books, I could not find a scholarly history of recent commercial agriculture in New Mexico that could answer many of my questions. This project, in part, sprang from the seed of that quest. My hope is that within these pages lie some useful details for local farmers and local food advocates, that I provide some kindling for their further research, and that I offer them an overall sense of how rich and diverse an agricultural history this region has experienced over the long twentieth century.

This book, however, strives to tell a history that will interest many more people than just the curious farmers out there. My intended audience goes well beyond the farming community to include all those interested in the broader cultural and environmental history of the twentieth-century New Mexico borderlands and how that history fits into even broader national and global narratives.

To tell this story I have relied on the help of a long list of people. First, to all those who read and commented on previous drafts of this book, I owe an enormous debt of gratitude. I especially want to thank my dissertation adviser, Virginia Scharff, and my dissertation committee members, Samuel Truett, Luis Campos, and Jared Farmer. Without their input and support this book would not have happened. I am grateful, too, to the two anonymous reviewers who provided highly instructive and helpful comments. This is a better book because of the time they took.

Individual chapters have also been strengthened by a host of generous scholars. I owe all the members of the "Food Across Borders" symposium, sponsored by the William P. Clements Center for Southwest Studies at Southern Methodist University, much thanks for their input on chapter 5. I would also like to thank the members of the 2015 Western History Dissertation Workshop hosted at Yale University, and the members of the 2015 Workshop on the History of the Environment, Agriculture, Technology, and Science hosted at the University of Colorado–Boulder, all of whom provided challenging insights for chapters 1 and 2, respectively. I also remain grateful to Dr. Deborah Fitzgerald, who provided comments on what became chapter 3 for a panel at the 2016 American Society for Environmental History annual meeting in Chicago.

Many others have helped along the way. Many thanks for all the help from archivists at the Center for Southwest Research, at NMSU, and at the New Mexico Farm and Ranch Heritage Museum; and to Gordon Tooley, who spent a fruitful day with me early in my research planting trees, talking apples, and sharing articles from his personal library. I am grateful to the crew at the *New Mexico Historical Review*, under the leadership of Dr. Durwood Ball, for the camaraderie and support they provided along the way. I am highly indebted to Bridget Barry and the entire editorial team at the University of Nebraska Press, and to Vicki Low for such thoughtful and careful copy edits. Thank you, as well, to Marisa Thompson, who let me crash in her guestroom for all those research visits to Las Cruces. Most of all, I am grateful for my family, who helped me along in too many ways to count.

FRUIT, FIBER, AND FIRE

Introduction

As perhaps you have noticed, it has become difficult to dissociate New Mexico from its iconic chile pepper. For many, the very notion of New Mexico might bring to mind the smell of roasting green chiles in the fall, the sight of red chile wreaths and *ristras* hanging beside adobe walls, or the burn in the chest from a pungent dish of carne adovada. Today the ubiquitous imagery of the chile—emblazoned on license plates and billboards, on airport T-shirts and souvenir shop mugs—has become so identified with New Mexico that it nearly serves as a synonym for the state. But, as the following pages reveal, such unequivocal status has taken time to develop; along the way, other crops have held reign over the Land of Enchantment. This is a history of how these shifting crops reflect deeper change, and how the iconic crops of long-ago harvests can, through careful attention, continue to bear valuable lessons on the greater historical narratives of our past.

At the core of my decision to hone in on specific crops is my conviction that to understand the history of a people, we must understand the history of the plants that have sustained them. In New Mexico perhaps no crops have defined the people and their landscape in the industrial era more than apples, cotton, and chile. These crops together illustrate how agriculture has spurred migrations of plants and people, and, in turn, shaped the culture of the place. The physical origins, the shifting cultural meanings, and the environmental and market requirements of these three iconic plants all broadly point to the convergence in New Mexico of larger regions—the Mexican North, the American Northeast, and the American South—and of diverse regional attitudes toward industry in agriculture.

These three crops, all industrialized at different times in the twentieth century and in very different ways, help shed light on the nonlinear, interwoven, and contested path of agricultural modernization in New Mexico. As these pages will demonstrate, for much of the twentieth century modernization did not simply radiate from cities into their hinterlands; rather, the broad project of modernity, and resistance to it, has often originated in farm fields, at agricultural festivals, and in agrarian stories. This historical examination of apples, chile, and cotton in New Mexico helps illuminate the many, and often surprising, ways that New Mexicans have embraced, eschewed, appropriated, or fought modernity over the long twentieth century.

Many recent monographs have focused on a diverse array of crops, from corn to wheat, bananas to pecans, all over the world. The best of these have illustrated, to varying degrees, the coproductive relationships between agricultural production and consumption, the role of culture in shaping the natural world, the ways crops can both reify and defy borders, and the complex consequences a single plant can have on a landscape and society.[1] Several historians have emphasized how crops, as they become icons, embody myths of the people who cultivate, consume, and celebrate them. William Thomas Okie argues that the Georgia peach, for example, "is at the center of a myth, an imaginative pattern, a belief-embodying, meaning-shaping history"; Cindy Ott explains how the ubiquitous Halloween pumpkin became a site where "the American agrarian myth . . . found expression."[2] This book draws from the many useful approaches these histories provide to offer its own unique contribution by examining in depth the interdependencies and relationships between industrial and nonindustrial systems. These crops, their farmers, and their attendant industries together reveal an agricultural and cultural history of New Mexico that sheds new light on New Mexicans' relationship to modernity, race, nation, and the environment.

To tell this history, I have divided the book into six chapters. I devote two chapters to each crop, and each chapter approaches the crop's history from different historical lenses. Though each chapter carries its own conclusions, common to all is the broad question of how modernity, in the form of agricultural industrialization, took shape in the New Mexico borderlands. When scholars have investigated the history of industrial agriculture, a term that many use but few define, many have focused on technological advances, such as tractors or synthetic fertilizers and pesticides, or on biological advances, such as hybrid seed breeding. As historian Deborah Fitzgerald has invaluably articulated, by the 1920s an "industrial ideal," larger than any single technological innovation, had emerged in the United States that brought to the forefront efficient, large-scale production under specialized labor models.[3] As historians have begun to emphasize, this shift in agricultural industry involved more than efficiency-minded innovations in production; it also involved appropriating old myths into new forms of storytelling, specifically designed to spur consumer demand and support the increased yields made possible by innovations in production.

Storytelling, in the form of advertising, as Douglas Sackman has pointed out, "responded to the crisis brought about by the advent of mass production" and helped shape modern agriculture into "a form of imperialism . . . composed of both land and images." Agrarian storytelling, which took many forms beyond advertising, helped shape an agricultural imperialism by defining not just what agricultural products Americans should and shouldn't buy but also core cultural attitudes of national identity, race, and citizenship. Agrarian stories in the United States have long celebrated a democratic republic composed of white, male, landowning farmers, writing out all others as subservient and unentitled. "Studying agrarian narratives," as historian Sarah Wald explains, "helps identify the cultural logic through which various groups are written into and out of the nation."[4] With an eye on both land and image, this book investigates how the introduction of industrial agriculture, built on science, technology, and innovative storytelling, shaped not only the physical landscape of New Mexico's irrigated valleys but also the cultural landscape, through the particular crops growers planted and the stories that grew alongside them.

Storytelling played an essential role in agricultural modernization in the long twentieth century, in part by defining notions of progress. "Modernity," suggests Frederick Cooper, can be thought of as a "representation, as the end point of a certain narrative of progress, which creates its own starting point (tradition) as it defines itself by its end point."[5] In the case of modern agriculture, agrarian stories often present a teleology that situates agriculturalists either in the nostalgic "traditional" past or in the ever-improving modern present. At times, as this book explores, stories of industrial agriculture embrace elements of "tradition" in the quest toward an ever-improving modern goal.[6] This embrace—itself a response to latent, popular anxieties over modernity—nonetheless helps solidify a core story of a general progression from one element of a binary, tradition, to the other, modernity, and ultimately serves to validate the modern project.

This book challenges this dichotomous narrative of agricultural modernization from a variety of angles, including cultural mixings and introductions of seeds and technologies, to investigate the modern reliance on a diverse set of alternative agricultural systems. This approach echoes recent shifts in agrarian scholarship. "Seeds," historian Courtney Fullilove has recently argued, can "challenge us to reconsider linear or progressive models of innovation, and of history as a form of storytelling about the past." Indeed, a careful examination of the history of seeds defies conventional teleologies of modern agriculture precisely because, as scholars such as Jack Kloppenburg and Noel Kingsbury have shown, modern agriculturalists in the global North have consistently relied upon seeds from small farmers in the global South.[7] With deep irony, then, modern agricultural industry has relied on the embedded labor of countless generations of nonmodern farmers that the genes of these seeds reflect. Yet seeds are only one of many cultural artifacts that can help reveal the interwoven relationships between agricultural industry and the very types of agricultural systems that industry aims to supplant. This book travels from farmworker fiestas to agricultural fairs, from research stations to small cooperatives, from abandoned apple orchards to fields where geese weed cotton, all in search of threads of the diverse agricultural systems interwoven into the fabric of our agricultural past that modern storytelling has missed.

A central premise to this investigation is that there is neither a single form of industrial agriculture nor a single form of traditional agriculture; rather, many ever-changing approaches of agriculture have existed in tandem, often influencing each other in surprising ways. Through examining how various approaches to agriculture have relied upon, benefited from, or challenged each other, we see that simple dichotomies between industrial and nonindustrial agriculture disappear. In their place emerges a more nuanced portrait of an ever-changing, creative agricultural landscape that defies the teleological narratives of progress or of inevitable and ever-increasing resource and labor exploitation that often accompany discussions of agricultural industrialization. Agricultural industrialization in the twentieth century, this book shows, followed a nonlinear and highly contingent path.

Philosopher Bruno Latour has argued that we have never been modern. In his framework, as we retrospectively acknowledge the processes of hybridization that have shaped the modern project toward ideals of purity, we see that the project has in fact never been pure and we have never therefore been as modern as we had conceived. We might as easily declare that our agriculture has never been industrial. Despite popular images of industrial agriculture as an ever-progressing, ever-modernizing monolithic form, agriculture in the modern era has in fact been a dynamic hybridity of systems, a hybridity that survives only with the survival of agricultural systems seemingly opposed to, or at least located well beyond the fence lines of, industry. These systems, which predate notions of modern industry, have not only survived within the shadows of industry but have also in some cases been essential to it.

To illustrate this winding and hybridizing path of industrialization, I begin with two chapters that examine the history of apples in New Mexico. "Assessing the meaning of the apple," writes historian William Kerrigan, "a fruit . . . enshrined as a cultural symbol, in American history is also no simple task."[8] The first two chapters tackle this challenge by examining the aspiring apple districts of New Mexico over the course of roughly a century, beginning with how commercial horticulture shaped New Mexico's cultural and environmental landscape in the decades surrounding statehood in 1912. Through an examination of booster literature, newspaper articles, governor reports, horticultural board records, and other primary documents, chapter 1 investigates how New Mexico boosters, growers, and scientists used various meanings of the apple—heavily laden with notions of Anglo morality, virtue, and nation—to entice white immigrants to settle and modernize the region. I examine, too, how the commercial apple brought not only deeply entrenched myths but also virulent moths that reworked the physical and cultural landscape. The eradication of the codling moth required cooperation among growers that swiftly led to coercive pesticide laws and cultural critiques, leaving little room for alternative approaches to horticulture. Together these myths and moths help explain how the early industrial apple in New Mexico represented a widespread and at times coercive effort, only partially successful, to fundamentally reorder and homogenize the physical and cultural landscape of the territory in the name of modernity, profit, and nation.

In chapter 2, I follow the history of apples into northern New Mexico at mid-twentieth century. I compare the stories of two markedly different apple-growing ventures. First, I examine the history of James Webb Young, an influential advertising executive who moved to a remote canyon near Cochiti Pueblo and developed a hugely successful orchard business through his marketing acumen. Under the persona of "Old Jim Young," he developed a "champagne apple" that became the focal point of family pilgrimages to the orchard even long after he had passed away. Second, I examine an apple cooperative in Chimayó that, in the wake of Reies Tijerina's "Courthouse Raid" in Tierra Amarilla in 1967 and the region's broader social turmoil, became a centerpiece for a less radical, state-driven counterstrategy to revive northern New Mexico economically. Though the cooperative very nearly succeeded, it ultimately failed due to problems with management, outside competition, and several environmental setbacks, including a devastating freeze in 1971. Together, these histories of apple growers reveal northern New Mexico to be a complex site of competing visions for the cultural identity of the state, its relationship to modernity and colonialism, and to the rest of the nation—themes that continued to converge late into the twentieth century.

From apples, I move to cotton. Between the world wars, the global empire of industrial cotton spread into newly irrigated lands of southern New Mexico and far west Texas and reshaped regional cultural, socioeconomic, and environmental connections. Chapter 3 examines how cotton's arrival spurred new migrations among farmers and farmworkers, led to new and stronger regional alliances among growers, and strengthened ties between the land-grant colleges and growers throughout the borderlands. As cotton set in motion migrations of diverse people and genetic material into the region, it paradoxically led to increased homogenization in the fields themselves as farmers organized to plant the same single variety of cotton, often in large, monocropped fields that left little room for soil-building, rotational crops. Yet this homogenization was neither foreordained nor complete; rather, industrialization followed a contingent, ever-changing, and contested path. The history of New Mexico's many early cotton farms, themselves ever-evolving composites of diverse growing systems, reveals how one-crop farming during this time often belied early logics of industrialism and relied, both directly and indirectly, on more diverse farms of all sizes.

In New Mexico, as well as throughout west and south Texas, Southern-style paternalism often aligned with emerging doctrines of scientific management and ideals of industrial efficiency to create a new landscape of interwar New Mexico that highlights the changing ideals of industrial agriculture throughout the nation. Chapter 4 examines the nuances and contingencies of this industrial ideal by focusing on one of the largest and most successful cotton farms in the region, Stahmann Farms. Over the course of roughly four decades, from the founding of the farm in 1926 to the farm's last cotton crop in the late 1960s, Stahmann Farms gained success by embracing a diversified crop regime and paternalistic labor structure that upended simple narratives depicting agricultural industrialization as a linear path toward monoculture and ever more exploitative labor practices. Stahmann Farms embraced a paternalistic approach to industrial agriculture that featured flexibility for extensive crop diversification and intricate cultural negotiations with the farm's workers.

The success of Stahmann Farms came not simply from its crop choices but also from its spatial and cultural geography. The borderlands farm benefited from its proximity to Mexico in several ways; in turn, a thread of *mexicanidad* was woven through the culture of the farm. The transnational threads of cotton on Stahmann Farms come as little surprise; global historians such as Sven Beckhardt have adeptly illustrated the workings of a cotton empire, rooted in financial centers in Europe, that connected vast stretches of the globe for centuries.[9] Yet broad-sweep commodity histories often miss how local actors, broadly influenced by the workings of a global cotton empire, spun their own interregional webs of cotton that had tremendous impacts on the regional landscape. In the pages that follow, I take a more on-the-ground approach that views the myriad interregional exchanges facilitated by the cotton economy in the New Mexico borderlands. The borderlands are not simply a remote region worked upon by forces created by actors in distant cities; they are a site of intricate, interwoven connections—at once transnational and local—that crossed geopolitical, cultural, and environmental borders in ways that significantly shaped the southern New Mexico cotton economy and the broader New Mexico borderlands.

The final two chapters focus on the state's most iconic crop, the chile pepper. Chapter 5 examines the first chile pepper, developed at New Mexico's land-grant college in the early twentieth century, and its breeder, Dr. Fabián García. The "number 9 chile," as García called the pepper he bred, was more than simply the first scientific and industrial chile pepper; it embodied a pan-Hispanic and nationally inclusive vision for New Mexico that encouraged cultural transformations both within and beyond the New Mexico borderlands. García's efforts transformed more than the chile's genetics; his efforts represented the first major step in transforming the idea of the chile into a modern crop that the nation as a whole could more readily consume. García's number 9 chile illustrates how breeding for industrial traits involved crafting new definitions of place, identity, and citizenship. Perhaps better than any other single crop variety, the number 9 chile sheds light on the intersections among modernity, race, and nation within the wider agricultural and cultural network of the early twentieth-century U.S.-Mexico borderlands.

The final chapter traces the history of the chile pepper into the current century by examining not only subsequent breeding efforts to shape the chile but also the many efforts to reimagine the chile through its stories. The modern chile is more than a selectively bred chile; it is a carefully told chile. The narratives of the industrial chile, and the counternarratives that often surround the state's native chiles, once again reveal how modernity continues to be contested in the fields and kitchens of the state. The history of the chile in New Mexico, like the state's histories of apples and cotton, reflects an American agricultural past rife with myths, fables, pageantry, and, occasionally, outright lies. Rather than an exercise to merely "expose the dirty underbelly" (to borrow William Thomas Okie's words) of agrarian stories, this chapter, as throughout the book, investigates storytelling to better understand the process of agricultural modernization in New Mexico and the efforts to resist it.[10]

Altogether, this is a history of modern agriculture that focuses on its extremities to better understand the heart. The local stories matter; they represent lives filled with meaningful struggles, lessons, and successes. Yet I intend this to be more than simply a local history. The implications of how agriculture industrialized in New Mexico stretch well beyond the state's irrigated fields and speak to the greater process of modernization in the long twentieth century. "We need a history of agriculture," Courtney Fullilove implores, "that shifts focus from institutions of research to the broad field of agrarian knowledge on which they drew. It should fasten changes in material environments to the systems of knowledge deployed to describe and transform them. And it should identify the contingency and variety of environmental decision making at local, regional, national, and international scales."[11] The following pages provide one such history by seeking out the many systems of knowledge in our recent agricultural past, whether in the seeds themselves or in the broader culture of farmers and farmworkers. In the process, seemingly inconsequential marginalia—maybe a farmworker's meal, a small orchard's advertisement campaign, or a long-gone chile seed—add up to an agricultural past with diverse cultural influences, many possible futures, and competing visions for how to feed and clothe ourselves that remain relevant as we continue to reimagine the crops of our future.

ONE

Apples

1

Before There Were Aliens, There Were Apples

Myths, Moths, and Modernity in New Mexico's Early Commercial Orchards

Roughly three and a half decades after her father gunned down the most famous outlaw in America, Elizabeth Garrett immortalized her beloved New Mexico in what would soon become the official state song. Her father would no doubt have appreciated the horticultural paradise the song depicts. Pat Garrett, whose landholdings included an orchard of over eight hundred apple and peach trees, had spent and lost a fortune trying to dam the Pecos River near Roswell in an effort to create a lucrative agricultural valley. His daughter's portrayal of a "Nuevo Mejico" filled with rugged sierras, fiery-hearted "Montezumas," and "dotted with fertile valleys" captured the mythic ideal shared by her father and many other eastern newcomers alike. At the heart of the vision was a familiar and thoroughly "American" crop; the smell of apple blossoms, not roasting green chile, filled the breezes of the visionaries' minds.[1]

Those four decades between Pat Garrett's first fruit tree and the state's official adoption his daughter's blossom-filled song witnessed rapid agricultural industrialization that profoundly shaped the physical and cultural landscape of New Mexico. Fruit in general, and apples in particular, initially led the way. Apples brought in more money and were grown in more parts of the territory than any other crop, apart from grain or hay, in the decades surrounding the turn of the twentieth century.[2] But even more than with crops such as alfalfa, wheat, or corn, apples required a highly industrialized landscape—physically and culturally—to grow profitably in a competitive regional and national market. Apple production relied on major irrigation and rail systems; modern technology to grow, market, process, pack, and ship; cooperation among growers; and federal and local governmental support in the form of land-grant college research, tax-funded horticultural boards, and spraying laws. While investors and farmers experimented with other industrial crops, including sugar beets, sweet sorghum, and even canaigre, no horticultural crop was planted more widely in New Mexico than the apple.[3] In nearly every narrow mountain hamlet and broad irrigated valley alike, farmers gave apples a try.

No crop represented cultural change more than the apple. Yet, perhaps because the industry proved shorter-lived and less economically significant compared to other regions, historians have largely ignored the role of early industrial horticulture in New Mexico despite its significant cultural impacts on the region. The apple carried deep cultural meanings as a symbol of Anglo morality, virtue, and nation. Apples also required commercial growers to adopt the most modern technologies—involving irrigation, tillage, smudging, and pesticides—and therefore represented a force of modernization. The early industrial apple in New Mexico represents a widespread, pervasive, and at times coercive effort, only partially successful, to reorder and homogenize the physical and cultural landscape of the territory in the name of modernity, profit, and nation.

The Cosmopolitan Fruit

In the late nineteenth century many apple varieties took a cross-country journey that reflected larger migrations and transformations. Industrialization was changing where and how apples were produced, and who was producing them. Home orchards, mostly in the East, gave way to specialized commercial orchards, largely in the West. These newer, more western districts—or "fruit belts"—all vied for a share of the enormous national, and even international, market. Commercial western orchards were often large, flat fields with reliable irrigation, fertile soil, and, initially, an environment free of many pests common in the East. To offset the added costs of irrigation and long-distance rail charges, growers increasingly specialized in monocultures of a few varieties, grown and managed according to the most scientific methods of the day; they were supported by major infrastructure projects, such as the railroads, irrigation projects, and agricultural colleges. No longer a profitable side venture for the diversified small farm, fruit growing became a big industry requiring full-time commitment and a fair amount of capital to get started. A competitive fruit grower was at the forefront of modern agricultural science and industrialization.[4]

The United States was the world's top apple producer in the late nineteenth century. Several major fruit-growing sections of the country—including the Intermountain West, from southern New Mexico through Colorado and Utah—vied for supremacy during the four decades surrounding the turn of the twentieth century. High apple prices in the late 1880s spurred heavy plantings, which led to lower prices for much of the 1890s, exacerbated by the Panic of 1893, which swept the nation. By the turn of the century, however, as prices once again rose, throughout the West new orchards were planted, while throughout the East, old and inefficient ones were removed.[5] For newly arrived settlers throughout the irrigated reaches of the mountainous West, a ready eastern market connected by a newly laid railroad, new irrigation technologies, extremely optimistic estimates of water supply, and the absence of virulent pests inspired hope that the apple industry would succeed.

Apples were not new to territorial New Mexico. Seedling varieties with Spanish origins had been grown in New Mexico since at least the early seventeenth century. Sometime in the 1850s, Archbishop Jean Baptiste Lamy imported apples from east of the Mississippi for his renowned orchard in Santa Fe; in 1859 John Clark planted apples from Missouri at Los Luceros in Rio Arriba County.[6] By the 1870s apples from these and a few other orchards were highly praised as far away as Colorado. Much more common in New Mexico in the 1870s, however, were the "native" apples that commentators variously described as "sweet and leathery," a "bitter sweet native apple the size of a plum," and a "small sweet variety of very little value."[7] Newcomers from the East viewed these seedling apples as inferior in quality but nonetheless proof of the territory's good soil and fruit-growing conditions.

Some of the earliest commercial orchards were planted with local consumption in mind, particularly near mining communities. But soon the railroad made more distant markets available. Wealthy local businessmen planted the most successful early orchards.[8] Although initially commercial orchards faced neighbors' skepticism, tales of success quickly spread around the territory and beyond. Locals initially dubbed Manley M. Chase's orchard in Colfax County "Chase's Folly," for example, but when Chase's trees matured and he began shipping apples into Texas, Oklahoma, and Colorado, eventually taking gold at the Chicago World's Fair, the laughter abated. By 1910, looking back on his sixty-five-acre orchard's success, Chase could declare that "beyond any question . . . this is as good a fruit country as any of the famous fruit-growing districts of Colorado or the Northwest, and it has some advantages over them." In fact, he added, "In my judgment there is no better paying crop to be grown in Colfax County."[9]

Such tales of success were fodder for local boosters. Throughout the territory pamphlets and articles declared New Mexico ripe for becoming the next great apple-growing region of the country. Land developers (often organized into "orchard companies") and individual settlers planted commercial orchards in nearly every irrigated valley of the territory, from Mimbres to Cimarron, Las

Cruces to Taos, and scattered points between and throughout. The success of apples, though predictably overblown by local boosters, was nonetheless quite real. "Apples are the most important orchard fruit in the United States, and they are also the most cosmopolitan," state horticulturalist Fabián García declared in 1910, and "undoubtedly the most important orchard fruit in New Mexico."[10] While growers had early success with the cosmopolitan fruit throughout the territory, only two districts—the Farmington and Roswell districts—developed into large, regionally and nationally significant apple-growing regions. In both districts, in opposite corners of the state, white settlers had arrived to remote outposts of the irrigated West with horticultural visions of virtue, health, science, and profit.

The Land of the Big Red Apple

In the mid-1870s John Chisum's apple orchard must have been a remarkable, if not unsettling, sight to the Hispanos in nearby Plaza de Missouri. Though not enormous by industrial standards, the cattle baron's new orchard of 1,500 fruit trees in long, neatly ordered rows nonetheless intimated major changes for villagers and their surrounding landscape. Many of the local residents would eventually find work building, and rebuilding, the irrigation infrastructure for a horticultural vision that targeted new settlers and largely excluded them.[11] Over the course of roughly three decades—1890 to 1920—the Pecos Valley fruit district developed from cattle-raising country of mostly creosote, grama, and acacia into an irrigated, more homogenous landscape that produced a significant portion of the entire Mountain West's apple crop. People came to call the Pecos Valley, along with the San Juan Valley, the "land of the Big Red Apple."

Despite the hopeful moniker and the thousands of carloads of apples shipped out of state, both valleys fell short of the apple-growing dominance investors and growers had envisioned. Many factors— among them an overestimated water supply, long distances, tenacious pests, early frosts, floods, and increased competition from elsewhere—stifled the effort to transform the region into a commercial horticultural center. In the Pecos Valley, success came sooner than in the San Juan Valley, but left sooner, too. Some growers left the valley entirely, while many others switched from apples to an old staple of the South that by the 1920s had swept across the southern reaches of the irrigated West.

While Chisum's was one of the first orchards in the region, Charles Eddy and Pat Garrett first developed the vision of an irrigated agricultural mecca of white settlers in the Pecos Valley. Eddy, originally from New York state, recruited capitalists from Chicago and Colorado Springs to undertake the monumental task of controlling the Pecos. Their principal recruit, Colorado mining baron James Hagerman, soon became instrumental in creating what he and Eddy envisioned as a grand agricultural center. With deep pockets extending to New York, Chicago, and Colorado, and with the aid of the newly passed Desert Land Act, Eddy devoted his efforts toward securing the money, water, land, and settlers needed for "a model community in the desert."[12]

Developing the area meant first attracting investors, but soon it also meant attracting farmers. By 1891 Hagerman explained that he wanted "steady, industrious, frugal people—people who understand farming and fruit growing and are not afraid to work and do not expect to make a fortune in one or two years." Hagerman and other investors, such as fellow easterners-turned-westerners Francis Tracy and Charles Greene (editor of the *Santa Fe New Mexican*), hoped to make money by raising fruit themselves and by selling improved land already planted with fruit trees. They organized the Pecos Orchard Company in 1892, and planted over half a million fruit trees in their first two years. Charles Greene supervised the company from Chicago, as well as another company, the Pecos Irrigated Company, which also planned to sell off subdivided sections with irrigated, newly planted orchards.[13]

Fruit was central to investors' pitches to attract the "right" kind of people to settle the valley. Boosters specifically sought potential settlers from Colorado, St. Louis, Louisiana, and eastern states, and even from European countries such as Denmark, Italy, and Switzerland. In 1892 alone Hagerman spent $55,000 to recruit immigrants. Advertisements boasted that the area, with the "richest," most extensive cropland in the Southwest, would surely make a modest fortune for the industrious and patient grower. "It is generally conceded that there is no line of business that will bring as large returns on the investment as will a bearing orchard in the fertile valleys of the West," a typical booster tract stated. "Visit the Roswell district yourself and confirm these statements."[14] Stephan Bogener writes that most of the "'unbiased' valley citizens who had grown fruit trees and vines" quoted in booster tracts "were intimately connected with land sales and irrigation in the valley."[15] While other products constituted more of the railway cargo, the Pecos Valley Railroad advertised itself as the "Fruit-Belt Route" to entice further immigration to the valley.

Contrary to the boosters' claims, many newly arrived farmers struggled. Many arrived just before a devastating flood wiped out irrigation infrastructure in 1894, and just before the various nationwide economic crises of the 1890s set in. A Swiss contingent of largely inexperienced farmers returned to Switzerland after only two years in New Mexico. To respond to farmers' troubles, investors such as Hagerman formed the Pecos Valley Orchard Company in 1894, aided by nationally renowned pomologist Parker Earle. Missouri-based nursery Stark Brothers, the largest in the country, traded stock for trees. Hagerman spent nearly $100,000 on the orchard, planting nearly a thousand acres in trees. After experimenting with a wide range of potential commercial crops, such as sugar beets, cotton, and canaigre, Hagerman was convinced that only fruit, and especially apples, were profitable in the valley. His large orchard soon became well known throughout the region. When Hagerman refused to sell his entire apple crop, on the trees, for $65,000 in 1902, and instead elected to pick, pack, and ship the fruit himself, newspapers and industry reports took his success as a sign of the valley's economic promise.[16]

While growers continued to plant more apples in the northern end of the valley, the southern end near Eddy (later Carlsbad) struggled. Plagued by poorer soils, more saline water, leaky irrigation infrastructure, and damage from another devastating flood in 1904, the southern section shifted away from fruits. The northern section, however, near Roswell and Hagerman, continued to grow apples. In 1892 Nathan Jaffa discovered a massive artesian aquifer beneath Roswell that produced, initially at least, an abundance of water from self-pressurized wells. Boosted by this unique and reliable water source, and by relatively richer soils than further south, the area rapidly grew into a significant apple producer.[17]

A strong regional market developed. Growers tapped into a large Texas market, where they were usually able to sell their Jonathan apple crop at least two weeks before the same variety ripened in the Pacific Northwest, the main competition for the New Mexico industry.[18] These advantages were enough to overcome the state's relative distance from other national markets, damage from occasionally devastating spring frosts, and a long growing season that allowed for four broods of codling moths, the insect pest most devastating to apples.[19] By 1920 the Roswell area had become a major apple-growing district in the Mountain West.[20] New Mexico apples thrived initially because they took advantage of their national isolation by serving nearby regional markets.

In the opposite corner of the state, newcomer horticapitalists likewise developed an apple industry by serving a regional market. Like Roswell the Farmington District was settled by mostly white easterners enticed by the dream of healthy horticultural pursuits. Whereas the Pecos River wound through the heart of "Little Texas," where early landowners often came from southern states (some had even fought for the Confederacy) and sold their apples to southern markets, San Juan County settlers were mostly northerners who had arrived via Colorado and shipped their apples through Colorado markets to points further north and east. "The tide of immigration thus far is mostly from Missouri, Colorado, Kansas, Nebraska, Iowa, Texas, Oklahoma and the Northwest," a booster tract from 1906 reported. As in Roswell and throughout the West, whiteness was emphasized. "The people are law-abiding, thrifty, industrious and energetic," the tract continued. "Only one-tenth of the people of San Juan County are of Spanish or Mexican parentage, and these live apart in one settlement. They are intelligent and honest, many of them speak both English and Spanish and are well off financially."[21]

Unlike in Roswell, the lack of a rail connection was perhaps the biggest obstacle for San Juan growers. Before 1903 all fruit had to be hauled by cart to Durango, Colorado. After the rails came, apples still had to be loaded to a standard-gauge boxcar in Farmington, then to a narrow-gauge car in Durango, and back to a standard-gauge car east of the Rockies. The result was high handling charges that made competitive pricing more difficult. While the big orchards were shipping fruit to both coasts and even Europe, the majority of commercial apples grown in San Juan during the first decades of the industry went through Durango.[22] A smaller percentage went to markets in eastern Arizona and parts of western New Mexico.[23] Often the San Juan crop was sold and marketed as Colorado apples, a fact that local boosters continually pointed out had largely helped the Colorado brand. Like the Pecos growers, the early orchardists initially benefited from a pest-free environment that produced worm-free apples well after California fruit was gaining a bad reputation for blemished fruit. Such an advantage, however, did not last long.

Just as in Roswell, apples spurred land speculation. An advertisement for the Bloomfield Orchard Co. boasted "280 acres set to trees last spring—row upon row of trees planted with the accuracy of a mosaic."[24] The area's largest orchard—Sunnyside Ranch— exemplifies this pattern. In 1880 William Locke planted eighty-four acres in fruit trees—including eighty varieties of apples—shipped by rail from the East, then by wagon to Farmington. Locke reported to Governor Bradford Prince in 1890 that he had roughly twelve thousand trees in his orchard, by far the largest in the area.[25] As in Roswell, growers embraced industrial farming early. "The people generally have dropped off the old style of farming," Locke wrote to Governor Prince in 1891, "and added the more modern facilities for doing this work." Locke sold the orchard to W. N. Kight, who ten years later once again put the orchard on the market, this time subdivided into five- to forty-acre tracts.[26]

Proximity to the Navajo and Ute reservations also differentiated the Farmington experience. Navajos provided labor in the orchards but also an important market for the produce. A booster tract in 1906 explained that "the New Mexico portion of the great Navajo Reservation, with its almost 2,000 Indians, furnishes a valuable home market for San Juan County products. These regenerated Red Men own immense herds of sheep and goats and carry on an ever increasing manufacture of world famous Navajo blankets, the annual wool, pelt and blanket sales representing heavy revenues." Here Navajos are treated as an asset: they are "peaceable, industrious, and far advanced in their civilization" and "rarely leave of the reservation." They are "self-supporting." The "Utes, too, are peaceable and in many instances industrious." Indians' "regeneration" is emphasized, as is their contribution as a market.[27]

This rosy description of Native populations shows how the industry relied on them in myriad ways. The Hyde Exploration Company, for example, which was responsible for excavating Chaco Canyon, also ran a large orchard. Navajos would sometimes pick apples for the company, in addition to providing the sales outlet for lower-grade apples.[28]

The Reordered Landscape

To profitably grow an apple in New Mexico for a consumer in Texas in 1900, a typical grower needed a lot of help. He (most, but not all, growers were men) needed help from his fellow growers nearby, from his hired workers, and from his wife and kids. He needed help, too, from the local college, from the horticultural board, and from political leaders. He needed a good source of irrigation, adequate roads, and access to a railroad. In short he needed an entire region that was on board with the project. The commercial apple-grower was not the homesteader taking a stand with a spring-fed small orchard in a remote canyon two days from the nearest post office; he was tied into regional markets and needed to be in a region with significant support and subsidies for his project. Once he had that, he could get to work reordering his land into an efficient farm system.

First, the land needed to be cleared. The galleta, blue and black gramas, saltbush, Mormon tea, shadscale, and Indian ricegrass of the San Juan Tablelands; and the creosote bush, acacia, gyp grama, tarbush, and saltbush of the Pecos valley Chihuahuan desert all had to be cleared to make way for one species.[29] Once cleared, a grower would have been wise to plant the cleared land with a leguminous cover crop, such as alfalfa, for a year or two to build humus and soil fertility. If the orchard were planted on speculation, however, this step would often be skipped. Either way the grower then had to select good trees to plant.

A good orchard needed strong, reliable trees grafted to good rootstock. Most growers, not skilled in the specialized art of grafting, purchased grafted trees from a nursery. A San Juan County booster tract reported that "one or two large nurseries are needed. There is a big demand for fruit trees and shrubbery, and thousands of dollars' worth is shipped in from a distance every year."[30] Often these nurseries were in the East, though there were some noted grafters in the West, particularly in Colorado, where no doubt some of the Farmington District trees were sourced.[31] Once the grafted trees were purchased, they needed to be planted correctly in the most efficient pattern and spacing possible.

Clearing the land and replacing the native vegetation with ordered rows of a single species led not only to homogenization in the form of monoculture; the monoculture itself became more homogenized. Whereas it was not uncommon in the 1880s to hear of large orchards with sixty or more varieties of apples, within a couple decades most orchards had only five or six varieties in production. It became more profitable to grow a few popular varieties that could be sent in bulk rail shipments, alone or combined with other farmers' apples of the same variety.[32] Furthermore the land-grant college had experiment stations that took the onus of experimentation from the farmer to the professional researcher. The net result was not only an agricultural landscape of increasingly similar farms growing larger amounts of the same few varieties but also a consolidation of knowledge production into the central institution of the college.[33]

Western commercial orchardists strove to increase efficiency in all facets of their operation. Efficient irrigation often meant digging furrows where the new trees would be planted; orchardists only irrigated in the planted furrows for the first two years, which significantly saved both water and time. In older orchards growers would often irrigate through furrows plowed between rows. Often, beginning growers intercropped young orchards with market crops such as celery, sweet potatoes, and strawberries as a way of making money off the land before trees began to bear fruit and while leaf cover was still thin enough to let sufficient sunlight through. Other work included manuring, cultivating, and, if pests appeared, spraying. Pollination was also key; growers often either kept bees or hired local beekeepers during the pollination period in spring. Beginning in the early twentieth century, smudging (the practice of burning fuel in orchard heaters on spring nights when a freeze was possible) became standard practice. The apples then had to be picked at peak ripeness; sorted by size, shape, color, and quality; and packed efficiently in a box known as the "western box"— work often performed by women.[34]

The western apple grower was a full-time horticulturalist who employed cutting-edge science and invested a lot of personal labor, hired labor, and capital in equipment to compete on the national markets. The grower relied on a mix of local and extralocal resources to transform nature into an exportable commodity. Expensive technologies catalyzed the trend toward specialized, intensive fruit growing. But of all the industrial adaptations toward the goal of an efficiently homogenous landscape, none was as initially as important as pesticide spraying.

The Industrial Pest

"You will remember always the pink and white of an apple orchard in bloom on a lazy spring day . . . You are drugged by the haunting perfume that will always remain with your memories of nature's most productive flower garden," longtime Farmington resident and apple grower Mary Hudson Brothers wrote in 1938, "but the apple grower, blind to all this beauty, sees in drifting petals only that the time is ripe for the calyx spray."[35] Such unromantic and practical-minded words provide a counternarrative to the blossom-filled breeze of Elizabeth Garrett's state song, capturing the nearly half-century-old industrial reality of New Mexico apple-growing that many casual observers had missed. The codling moth, along with a host of scale insects, propelled horticultural industrialization in late nineteenth- and early twentieth-century New Mexico. Early pesticides saved the emergent industry from immediate economic disaster with an imperfect solution that led to the territory's first compulsory pesticide treadmill, due to increasing moth resistance, and left behind a legacy of contaminated soil. The story of early pesticides in New Mexico illustrates the cultural impact of industrial agriculture, as large growers, legislators, and researchers, in their struggle to control a resistant nature in the name of industry and nation, quickly became a coercive force of modernization.

Sometime in the late 1880s, the codling moth arrived in New Mexico, likely by rail in a box of imported apples, and quickly got to work transforming the ecology of the territory.[36] The moth had been tormenting eastern apple orchards since the 1820s. It had been only a minor problem prior to the advent of large commercial orchards, but, like so many other pests, it thrived on the monocultures that replaced diverse habitat with tracts full of its host species. By the 1870s it had reached California and seriously threatened the emergent industry there. Throughout the West, the industrial pest was fast becoming as ubiquitous in commercial orchards as the sweet smell of apple blossoms. By the turn of the century the moth had arrived in all the major apple-growing districts of New Mexico.[37] Some more isolated areas were spared the moth for another decade or longer, but, eventually, wormy apples could be found in untreated orchards throughout the territory.

For years, even after the moth's appearance, state boosters sold the idea that New Mexico's natural advantages in fruit production included the absence of pests, especially of the codling moth. New Mexico's pest-free atmosphere, sold alongside its tuberculosis-free air, provided an environmental advantage—just like abundant water, rich soil, moderate temperatures, or ample sunlight—that could be exploited and transformed into marketable products. A 1901 Eddy County booster tract, for example, declared erroneously that the dry air of the county meant fruit pests were nonexistent, and that the "'codlin moth' has never yet put in appearance here."[38] An 1898 article from Scranton, Pennsylvania, republished by the Bureau of Immigration, similarly declared that "the high altitude of most of the territory renders dangers from insect pests less than in other sections," and that New Mexico apples harkened back to the taste of childhood before "disreputable worm-eaten and effete apples" made their way into the markets.[39] Perhaps the most emphatic advertisement came in 1900, on the train leaving Durango, carrying one hundred carloads of apples and a sign that read, "All from San Juan County, New Mexico. A Million Apples and Not a Single Worm."[40] Even as late as 1907, a booster tract from Illinois declared that in Colfax County, New Mexico, "trees are absolutely free from disease and insects. Apples are perfect in growing and flavor and free of worms. Spraying has not been necessary in this country."[41] Three years later M. M. Chase reported that Colfax County was remarkably still codling moth–free. "Those insects and parasites which make fruit growing so uncertain and expensive in many localities do not exist here, and so far spraying has not been necessary," Chase reported. "I can say I have never found what is known as a wormy apple in my orchard."[42]

Despite both the real and the exaggerated absences of the moth, wormy apples eventually appeared in orchards, often in huge numbers, throughout the territory. As early as 1891 one observer in Santa Fe claimed to the state entomologist that the codling moth in some parts of New Mexico was "certainly worse than I have ever noticed it in the 'States' anywhere."[43] He described a nearby orchard where "the value of this little 'ranch,' which is wholly devoted to fruit and has hitherto been very profitable to the owner, is reduced one-third, if not one-half, by the mere presence of the Codling Moth."[44] The presence of the moth greatly concerned researchers, growers, speculators, politicians, and everyone interested in the economic development of the territory. Within a few years of the moth's first arrival in the territory, growers throughout the territory and researchers from the newly founded land-grant college joined others around the country in a quest for methods of extermination.

Pesticides provided a relatively new and unproven option. For them to be effective, growers had to coat the trees with poison just as new generations, or broods, of insects were hatching. Growers used two main types of pesticides: arsenates such as London Purple, Paris Green, and, later, the much more effective lead arsenate for "biting insects" like the codling moth; and soaps made from alkalis, resin, kerosene, and even tallow and whale oil for "sucking insects" like scales.[45] Although lead arsenate pesticides proved more effective than the earlier London Purple and Paris Green, many growers and researchers remained skeptical of the practice for the first decade of their introduction. The expense of spraying—not only the capital investment for pressurized spraying equipment but also the added labor of a team of men to spray the orchard four to eight times a year and the added need to space trees far enough apart for machinery, which in some cases meant removing trees—was a major deterrent for smaller growers. The potential health impacts of arsenic sprays were a further concern. As far away as London, newspapers had begun complaining about white, presumably arsenate residue on American apples. Perhaps the single biggest issue concerning spraying was the need for cooperation among all growers. Because moths freely traveled across property lines, spraying was only effective if the neighbors sprayed as well.

The uncertainty, cost, and concerns surrounding pesticides led growers and researchers to experiment with approaches beyond spraying. After several years of observation throughout the territory, several growers, as well as the college's entomologist Theodore Cockerell, considered chemical pesticides such as Paris Green and London Purple "ineffectual," arguing that fighting the pest with living predators was a far better solution.[46] Spraying quite simply was "not the success in the west—and especially the southwest—as it is in the northeast," Cockerell argued; instead, living predators such as "woodpeckers—particularly the 'flicker,' should be encouraged as far as possible, and boys should not be allowed to shoot them." Even better, Cockerell posited, would be to starve the insect by destroying every piece of fruit in the valley for one year: "Whether it is possible to carry out the plan so thoroughly as to get good results . . . obviously depends on the extent to which orchardists are willing or able to co-operate."[47]

Several prominent growers, including strong proponents of spraying, seriously considered the starvation strategy and concluded in 1897 that "there seems no other way at hand to get rid of the pest but to starve it out."[48] The idea remained popular enough that in 1907, following a heavy spring frost that killed most of the apple crop in the Mesilla Valley, horticultural inspectors were hired by the board of commissioners to inspect and kill any surviving fruit in orchards and inspect all incoming shipments of apples. The following year Fabián García reported that "it was impossible to find any wormy apples."[49] "Orchards which two years before were practically destroyed by the codling moth seemed to be absolutely free from any worms in the spring of 1908."[50] The starvation strategy proved successful, but at the ultimately intolerable cost of the valley's entire seasonal harvest. The strategy speaks to the ineffectiveness of early sprays and the willingness of growers and researchers to look beyond sprays as a tactic. It also reveals the socially minded but nonetheless coercive side of industrial agriculture—in the form of mandatory inspections and fruit destruction—even more evident in policies surrounding pesticide sprays.

Despite efforts to develop alternative pest control strategies, by the turn of the century prominent growers, horticultural societies, and the college all advocated spraying as the best solution. One of the first endorsements came from Cockerell's predecessor at the college, C. H. Tyler Townsend, who in 1891 argued at length that arsenate pesticides were safe for human consumption. London newspaper reports about American apples having dangerous arsenic residues, Townsend made clear, were "without a shadow of foundation, [and] were made without doubt in the interest of speculators, and with the sole view of injuring the sale of American apples in the English market." In an effort to drive home his point, he remarked that, given the low levels of pesticide residue on apples, someone would have to "consume several barrels of apples in a sitting in order to obtain a fatal dose."[51] Prominent orchardist Dr. J. H. Bailey in 1894 similarly advocated spraying and declared it safe for human consumption. By 1899, despite Cockerell's doubts, the college officially backed spraying Paris Green over other methods,[52] and by 1902, Fabián García confidently claimed lead arsenate to be the "best and most economical way of fighting the insect." While "many of the large orchardists in this locality have had very little faith in spraying," García continues, "the time is coming when our apple growers will have to spray, if they expect to have any considerable amount of sound fruit."[53] Indeed, within a decade of the moths' arrival, such language of inevitability shaped the discussion around spraying; regardless of an individual's stance on pesticides, the choice not to spray disappeared from commercial fruit-growing districts.

As spraying became the preferred method of extermination, the problem of the codling moth increasingly became a social one. Because the codling moth easily crossed property lines, one neighbor who didn't spray would provide enough host trees to make everyone else's spraying regime effectively pointless. Pesticides thus required cooperation, voluntary or otherwise, to be effective; such cooperation relied on cultural acceptance of both the problem and the solution. Land developers, politicians, researchers, and growers, and anyone else invested in the apple industry and economic development of the territory, all promoted a cultural shift among fruit growers to commit to spraying—and with it the scaled-up agriculture that justified the increased costs of spraying.[54]

Cultural change took a variety of forms. On a rhetorical level, those who chose not to spray were variously derided as stubborn, unprogressive, "slipshod," or selfish. At times the critique was blatantly racialized. For example, Judge J. F. Wielandy of Santa Fe explained to the college entomologist in 1891 that spraying was difficult in his region because "the universal practice in New Mexico, of planting trees too close . . . affords excellent shelter for the moth and every other variety of insects; but there is no argument that could be brought to bear to dispossess a Mexican or so-called 'old-timer' of his preconceived and irrational notions. To undertake this task is absolutely useless."[55] Often, however, cultural critiques extended beyond racial lines. Southern New Mexico ranchwoman Edith Nicholl, for example, argued, "that there are progressive Mexicans and unprogressive Americans may be taken for granted, the latter vastly more numerous than the former. The often unavailing efforts to induce some fruit-growers to take measures for the extirpation of the insect pests which have lately begun to infest our orchards is one proof—nay, one of several—of the existence of the latter."[56]

Diligent pest control, industrial proponents argued, was the responsible, intelligent, and even "patriotic" thing that all growers, regardless of race, needed to embrace for the good of business and the territory. College entomologist Cockerell explained in 1894 that his research was not simply for "the purely self-interested farmer"; it would "lead us to conclusions of importance to the Territory at large" and maybe even be "an honor to its fatherland." New Mexico citizens, he implored, should gladly "look to the future" and consider entomological research, and with it the advances in industrial agriculture it may bring, with "an unselfish feeling, a form of patriotism."[57] The problem of pest control, Cockerell's appeal makes clear, did not simply come down to a lack of commercial farmers, but rather to a lack of future-minded commercial farmers who understood the economic intelligence and the patriotic virtue of science. Impatient self-interest, in other words, threatened the accumulation of scientific knowledge for the larger good of industry. Such an appeal to science in the name of patriotism and the "fatherland" makes clear the inextricable connection between science, industry, and nation in the history of early commercial orchards.

Such lofty rhetorical appeals, however, were undergirded by a much more immediate and forceful tool to impel cultural change: the law and its enforcement apparatus. Nearly as soon as the codling moth arrived, so, too, did legislation compelling growers to exterminate it. Following the example of California, New Mexico and a host of other territories and states developed orchard inspection and spraying laws.[58] The New Mexico legislature passed its first pest control law in 1891, largely in response to early scale infestations and as a preventive action against further pest ingresses. "Being practically in close proximity to southern California," Townsend wrote in reference to the new law in 1891, "it is rather to be wondered at that we have not more of the fruit enemies which abound there, and which may at any time make their appearance within our limits. It is only by the greatest vigilance, and by measures of the utmost precaution on the part of all concerned, that such a contingency can be prevented."[59] The law allowed concerned landowners to petition for the creation of county horticultural boards of commissioners, which would hire inspectors to visit orchards, order owners to promptly spray any infested trees, and issue binding orders if the owner refused. In the rare cases where the owner still refused, the inspector could spray the trees himself at the owner's expense, or even cut down and burn infested trees. If an owner refused to pay for the extermination, a lien against his property would ensue. Within a year of the law's passage, Doña Ana horticultural inspectors enforced spraying of London Purple and Paris Green on all orchards with scales or moths.

Mandatory spray laws help illustrate the state-making role of turn-of-the-century industrial horticulture in New Mexico and elsewhere throughout the West. Similar to state boards of health, which largely only appeared in the United States after the Civil War, and which, in the words of William Novak, represented an "administrative reform . . . in the direction of centralization, professionalization, and uniformity," state horticultural boards represent important, though often overlooked, state-making institutions.[60] Boards of health, which provided legal regulation designed to benefit the *salus populi*, or public good, run counter to popular myths of Western individualism and Turnerian exceptionalism. Though too often overlooked by historians, horticultural boards and their pesticide laws similarly served to regulate society and represented a continuation of *salus populi* policing in the West into the first decade of the twentieth century. These laws illustrate that growers' attempts at agricultural control in the turn-of-the-century West not only meant attempting to control their own farm's environment, but their neighbor's environment, as well. As such these boards not only mark an important step in the emergence of a more industrialized agriculture in the West but also an early example of public commons regulations that illustrate how state-making in the West occurred in rural environs.

Mandatory spraying was hardly met with universal enthusiasm. Although the Doña Ana County Board reported cooperation from growers—"we have not been compelled thus far to resort to the law in compelling fruit growers to spray their orchards but on the contrary we are pleased to report a hearty cooperation of all interested"—their meeting minutes paint a different picture. In the daily records that inspector Barker submitted to the board, for example, he frequently reported serving legal notice to growers who showed reluctance to spray. In one case, after finding scale in local apple grower Marten Lohman's orchard, Barker had the infested trees cut down and burned.[61] A letter from F. N. Page, an orchard owner from Guadalupe County, to Governor Hagerman in 1906 further illustrates resistance to spraying. Page complained about Jose Pablo Sandoval, the president of the county commissioners, who opposed a petition to establish mandatory spraying in the county. Sandoval "opposed the petition on various grounds 'that the county was too poor,'" Page explained, and "'that it was wrong to impose the cost of spraying on the *poor people*,' and various other reasons." Page requested that the governor "write to Don Jose Pablo Sandoval saying to him that it is necessary to spray as a benefit to all the people." Many smaller growers no doubt shared the board president's concern.[62]

Despite opposition, New Mexico's orchard inspection laws certainly led to a further industrialized agricultural landscape in New Mexico. As Mary Hudson Brothers's statement makes clear, spraying became a routine part of apple growing for all commercial orchardists. "The development of spraying led to many changes in the industry," an industry analyst explained in the early 1920s, "the apple grower had to choose between being an intensive orchardist, prepared to spray and produce clean, attractive fruit, or going out of the orchard business."[63] Yet, the story of the moth in New Mexico reveals that such analysis captures only part of the story.

Despite decades of inspections, the codling moth, and the efforts to eradicate its host environments—both in the orchards and in growers' minds—continued with only partial success well into the twentieth century. Sprayings became less effective and more frequent as moths evolved to be more resistant.[64] In southern New Mexico especially, where four broods of the moth developed each year, spray regimens became heavier than in most other apple-growing regions. By 1938, as the college experiment station actively sought alternatives to lead arsenate as a partial response to national residue legislation, their research revealed dangerous levels of lead and arsenic on New Mexico apples.[65] Unsprayed orchards persisted as well, and with them the antagonism toward both the nonindustrial and the sloppy industrial farmers who were blamed for the moths. "Is this the land of the big red apple, or was it only a pipe dream?" a man asked a successful orchardist at a Roswell Rotary Club luncheon in 1923. "No, the big red apple is not a pipe dream," responded the orchardist, "but the average man who tries to grow it is a joke." The average grower, he asserts, does not spray on time, nor cultivate in the spring, irrigate often enough, or grow the best varieties. The moth is not the problem, in other words, the man is: "We need not wonder that trees are being pulled out by the hundreds when we have orchards in the hands of men that ought to be running livery stables."[66]

The story of the codling moth reveals how agro-industrial control of the physical landscape often went hand in hand with control of the social landscape. Industrial pests forced commercial fruit growers to employ cutting-edge technologies based on scientific research; those unwilling or unable to embrace scientific, capital-intensive, industrial farming were pressured—in the name of the country and by law—to change their stance or pick a different crop. The story of the moth also reveals the degree to which the physical nature of a crop shapes the historical impact of agriculture on a place and its cultures. In this case the apple's capacity to host a virulent pest led to social pressures, and even coercion, that created cultural change. Yet, the story of the moth only begins to touch on the cultural history of the early New Mexico apple industry. Newcomers brought with their apples powerful and pervasive cultural meanings. The stories, myths, and ideals that people transcribed onto the apple go just as far as its material attributes—its growing requirements, its pests, its shipping capabilities, and so forth—in explaining how the fruit shaped the landscape where it was planted. The next section explains how these stories—uniquely New Mexican amalgams of the local and extralocal—tapped into larger national myths. Those myths played just as important a role in shaping the landscape as the codling moth and the spray guns that followed.

The Apple as a Cultural Colonizer

Early in the twentieth century, as the big red apple was becoming an industrial force in some of the larger irrigated regions of the territory, people began to pay more attention to a few ancient apple trees that still bore tiny yellow fruits. The Manzano apple orchard, located in the tiny hamlet of Manzano in the mountains just east of Albuquerque, was shrouded with mystery and lore. A Spanish friar had planted the trees sometime prior to the Pueblo Revolt, the popular legend went. They survived a century of neglect before a new wave of Spanish settlers discovered them sometime around 1800 and named the new village in their honor. These were thus the oldest apple trees in the country, and they stood in silent rebuke to the teleology of American conquest. The improbable and science-defying trees—a source of pride, nostalgia, and reverence to many throughout New Mexico—were as loaded with cultural meaning as they were with apples.

One of the first written records of the orchard comes from Lieutenant James W. Abert, who in 1846 was told by "even the oldest inhabitants" of the village that "the trees were old even when the first settlers came."[67] Decades later, villagers told archaeologist Adolf Bandelier that the trees were simply "much older than the recollections of their fathers and grandfathers."[68] Bandelier surmised that the stout trees were at least two hundred years old, likely planted by a Spanish friar. This story was considered the best historical explanation of the orchard for over half a century.

By all accounts the inhabitants of Manzano revered the old trees. "The Manzano people have a deep regard for the grove, which is almost sacred," a journalist reported in 1911. "They will not allow it to be touched."[69] For those outside the mountain hamlet, the reverence was often tinged not only with wonder and pride but also a sense of Progressive Era responsibility and even a note of "imperialist nostalgia." The modern newcomers—colonizers who had brought industry, science, and multitudes of orderly monocultures of commercial apple varieties to the region—memorialized the trees as they poignantly gazed back at the very landscape and people that their colonial presence had transformed. The poignancy often came with a decidedly triumphant note. Commemorations celebrated not only the tenacity of the ancient trees to withstand environmental stress and neglect but also the scientific civilization that had come to appreciate and save the trees. This keenly paternalistic imperialist nostalgia, ripe with Progressive Era faith in modernity, celebrated the age, perseverance, and inevitable passing of these trees, and, by extension, the nonmodern cultures and people of New Mexico.

The concerted effort to take care of and preserve these living monuments began in the early twentieth century, just as the Progressive Era tide of social reform swept across the nation. In 1905 a local development association threw "a working picnic," asking volunteers to come "with their sardines and crackers," camp out, and help "get the work of caring for and protecting the trees started." The picnic was successful enough to become an annual event; three years later it drew over five hundred people to the orchard.[70] Five years later, in 1912, state horticulturalist Fabián García set out, amid a modest amount of media coverage, to take scions from the ancient trees to determine its origins once and for all, and to try to graft the trees to new rootstock and thereby preserve the potentially rare and important genetic stock of the trees.[71] Once again, however, the trees seemed beyond scientific categorization, and García's efforts yielded no conclusions. It was not until 1936 that the newly developed technique of tree-ring analysis abruptly shattered New Mexico's pomological origin story with the news that the trees were likely only planted around 1800.

The old trees were used to promote both tourism in New Mexico and the burgeoning apple industry. Early tourism guides often included the orchards as a destination. In 1907 L. Bradford Prince, New Mexico's former governor and foremost apple enthusiast, now president of the newly formed Apple Congress, urged the organization to use an image of the old trees in its official seal. It is deeply ironic that he would choose the old, "unimproved" Spanish variety to promote an apple industry that was rapidly reducing apple diversity, especially of the seedling type growing in Manzano. But the symbol perfectly promoted New Mexico as a place with deep roots that were at once exotic (planted by the Spanish) and familiar (a European fruit with biblical roots and status as the most American of fruits). Prince even went as far as to declare, tongue-in-cheek, at the beginning of his address to the Apple Congress in 1911, that the apples in fact predated the Spanish altogether. They were none other than living remnants of the Garden of Eden.

Such an outlandish declaration led to an even more outlandish stunt at the American Apple Exposition in Denver in 1911. The exposition generously offered a "handsome wedding present," as well as some apples from the old trees themselves, to any couple that happened to be named Adam and Eve, and who desired to be married at the exposition's auditorium in front of twelve thousand people.[72] Such an event, presciently anticipating the reality television that would come a century later, illustrates the modern core that ran through the Manzano nostalgia. What better way to celebrate these survivors of a bygone era than with a media promotion involving twelve thousand spectators in a state-of-the-art auditorium? The stunt not only bathed the trees in modern spectacle, it managed to take claim of New Mexico's deep history by somehow writing out the very Native and Hispanic forebears that gave that claim validity. The recrafted legend of the ancient apples in Edenic terms paints New Mexico's claim to history and originality in firmly Anglo-digestible terms, a place where the original white man and woman fatefully gazed upon the apples of this immaculately planted paradise.

The ironies of this hypermodern Denver wedding using old, "unimproved" trees to promote New Mexico's rapidly modernizing apple industry certainly run deep. Beneath the many ironies specific to the Edenic wedding lies a deeper irony that pervades the history of industrial agriculture beyond apples. Industrial agriculture, in New Mexico and elsewhere, often relied on nonindustrial agriculture in myriad ways. In this case New Mexico's emergent apple industry used local agriculture, culture, and history to provide a "classy" display at this national exposition and, hopefully, a marketing edge.

Also beneath the sometimes lighthearted story of the Manzano apple orchard's veneration and ironic appropriations lay a very real and not so lighthearted notion of racial and cultural superiority. Just years prior to the first picnic to save Manzano's ancient trees, white newcomers expressed disregard for and, at times, even condemnation of native trees such as those in the Manzano orchard. They considered the small, bittersweet, yellow *manzanas mejicanas*, as many locals called them, to be "unimproved" and an indication of the native population's lack of intelligence, aversion to hard work, and racial inferiority. Edith M. Nicholl's 1896

Observations of a Ranchwoman in New Mexico hardly minces the connections between varieties of apples and race. "The fruit of New Mexico, since being taken hold of and improved upon by Americans, possesses both looks and inward merit," Nicholl explains. Such "improvements," Nicholl makes clear, were directly connected to racial superiority: "The Mexican, unless a superior specimen of his race, is at once too supine intellectually, too lazy physically, and too unintelligent by heredity, to improve upon methods acquired three centuries ago."[73]

To Nicholl, like many others, the existence of old fruit orchards in the territory offered proof of the territory's suitability for fruit culture but not of the existing culture's suitability for fruit-raising. "Needless to say that, while it was the sight of native orchards heavy with fruit which was the impelling motive of the original American settler," she observed, "it is not from the orchard of the native that the magnificent apples, peaches, and other fruits for shipping are culled."[74] F. C. Barker, also in the Mesilla Valley, came to a similar conclusion in 1893 when discussing the possibility of pears doing well in the territory. "As to the soil being suitable for pears we have the very best evidence in the large healthy trees to be found growing in many of the old Mexican gardens," Barker explained. "Unfortunately these old trees are poor varieties. There is a fortune to be made here by any one who will plant out twenty acres of the modern varieties of pears."[75] An otherwise celebratory account of the Manzano orchard in 1911 also echoed this sentiment, concluding that the most significant meaning of the trees was its implications for "the adaptability of the foothill lands of New Mexico to the culture of the great American fruit."[76] For each observer the old trees signified an opportunity for newcomers to turn the natural wealth of New Mexico's soil and climate into material profit.

White settlers imparted meaning to the differences between the *manzanas mejicanas* and their "improved" varieties. Such ideas reflected the settlers' broader beliefs in their racial and cultural superiority, a theme that ran through discourse about apples throughout this period. Newcomers explicitly connected improved varieties of apples with Anglo whiteness. As a Farmington grower argued in 1908, apples were superior to California oranges (their main competitor), because, unlike the orange and its Hispanic origins, the apple was the "native" fruit of the Mayflower pilgrims. Never mind that the apple was in fact not native to New or Old England (it is native to south-central Asia), the apple was so quintessentially Anglo-American in many people's minds that it was simply "native."[77] Some even celebrated the apple for its white body. Employing a common cliché used throughout the country to equate apples to white women's bodies, San Juan apples were "rosy cheeked" and advertised in 1901 as having "a tint as delicate and beautiful as a blush that overspreads a gentle maiden's cheek."[78]

The association of the American apple with Anglo whiteness extended beyond simple notions of heritage or phenotype. The apple came to embody a mix of science, industriousness, and agrarian virtue that many white people considered absent in the native and Hispanic populations. A Roswell resident explained in 1904 that much of the success of his county's fruit-growing section owed to the fact that the newly settled farmers were "good men who understand farming, who fully value every acre or land and every drop of water . . . and who, above all else, are thorough and industrious."[79]

Boosters and politicians used these cultural connotations of the industrial apple—at once Anglo-American, modern, and profitable, and suited to New Mexico soils—to entice would-be white settlers to the region. The New Mexico Bureau of Immigration, founded in 1888 with the explicit purpose of bringing more white people to the territory, often highlighted the region's fruit-growing promise. At the forefront of this early effort to promote apple culture was the New Mexico Horticultural Society, also founded in 1888. With territorial governor L. Bradford Prince at its helm, the society organized fairs and exhibitions showcasing the territory's abundant produce, intended to convey both the natural wealth and the cultural industriousness of the territory. Although other fruits, along with industrial crops such as sugar beets and sorghum, also made the list of displayed crops, apples were by far the most prominently displayed. The display of abundant, unblemished, familiar apples served to promote the modern and Anglo aspect of the territory, and ease easterners' racial anxieties.

Apples were a quintessentially American fruit in a nation that considered fruit growing to be a particularly "pleasurable and interesting pursuit," where a man of modest means could pursue wealth healthfully and virtuously. "Fruit-growing has always attracted city people," two industry analysts reported in 1921, "and in specialized fruit regions to-day are many who, after retirement from business, sought fruit-growing as a healthful vocation and yet one which might be expected to offer fair returns on investment."[80] Boosters ascribed a "certain biblical respectability" and "bourgeois enlightenment" to fruit culture throughout the West. Fruit growing shaped the California Dream, historian Kevin Starr has argued, by encouraging, above all else, a "rural civility" in the West.[81] The early apple districts of New Mexico show how the image of a healthy and harmonious pastoral workscape spread throughout the desert and mountain West. Such images touted the healthy climate and the horticultural potential of the region. No boosters' promotional vision of a western irrigated Eden was complete without dangling fruit.

The dangling fruit for the boosters, of course, was the horticultural settler himself. New Mexico apple districts, like their fruit-growing counterparts in California and throughout the West, sought white emigrants from the eastern United States and Europe to form model communities that competed in national markets with cutting-edge scientific agriculture.[82] Jared Farmer's description of the ideal late nineteenth-century irrigation colony shareholder in California holds true for New Mexico apple districts, as well. This financially independent "agrarian entrepreneur grew luxury crops for profit using the latest technologies and scientific methods," Farmer writes, and "did not like to be called a farmer [but rather] *grower* or *horticulturalist* or, better yet, *rancher*." A letter from an M. E. Dane in the Vermejo Valley to Governor Prince in 1889 echoed this ideal and went a step further, assuring territorial boosters that New Mexico was in fact a superior destination to California for potential settlers. "There are lots of people coming into this valley from the East . . . most of them are people with means. . . . I am very anxious to have them invest and improve here," Dane writes. "We have the productions here to make this superior to California [in] climate, fruits, alfalfa, grains, vegetables, and all kinds of stock."[83] Throughout the West, boosters, politicians, and land developers, who had themselves invested fortunes in irrigation works and rail systems, considered such fruit growers—white, hardworking, and even bourgeois—as value added to their investments that would start farms and businesses, raise families, and attract others like them.[84]

The ideal, however, proved elusive. Percy Hagerman, reflecting in 1934 on his father's investments in the Pecos Valley in the last decade of the nineteenth century, declared in exasperation, "Every other thing that has been tried down here, with the one exception of apple growing in Roswell has proven a failure. I have made up my mind that this country has got to go back to stock raising and depend on that for whatever prosperity it has. That means that it will never be a decent country to live in; no cattle country never is. All the expensive efforts that have been forth to make this a white man's country have been futile and always will be."[85] Hagerman's lament reveals not only the explicit effort to transform the Pecos Valley's racial and cultural landscape through transforming the agricultural landscape but also the limits of those efforts. Roswell failed to become a wholly "white man's country" despite the success of apples.

In the decades surrounding the turn of the twentieth century, the apple—the "great American fruit" that symbolized the interconnected Anglo-American ideals of modern science and industry, Jeffersonian virtue, and racial and cultural superiority—both transformed the physical and cultural landscape of the territory and was itself transformed. It enticed white settlers to New Mexico with dreams of industrial apples in a horticultural Eden. Settlers arrived, however, to a harsh climate, where moths had their own visions of paradise, and where the deep-rooted culture and history of the place forced them to adjust their vision. Percy Hagerman's lament about a Pecos Valley that had failed to become a "white man's country" hardly resembled Elizabeth Garrett's celebration of fiery-hearted Montezumas amid the "scent of apple blossoms." Garrett's song, full of the condescending imperialist nostalgia that sentimental journalists continued to assign to the Manzano orchard's "marvelous stand against time," nonetheless indicated a mixing of the local non-Anglo and nonmodern context of her horticultural paradise.

A Bright Future

The history of early commercial apples in New Mexico shows us how paying attention to the particularities of crops helps us understand human history. It matters that the *apple* arrived, not just "industrial agriculture," to late nineteenth-century New Mexico. The physical requirements and cultural meanings of the apple shaped the cultural and environmental landscape of the place. The apple enticed white settlers with specific notions of Anglo national identity; Jeffersonian virtue, morality, and health; and the promise of a lucrative export that other crops such as alfalfa—which in reality brought in more revenue—could not. It also brought a virulent pest that required neighborly cooperation that led to coercive laws and cultural critiques that left little room for alternative approaches to horticulture. In short the modern apple ushered a degree of cultural change far beyond what a simple glance at census data would suggest.

For many the apple represented hope for a more Anglo, more modern, and industrialized New Mexico. "As the territory becomes more thickly settled, fruit growing is going to develop faster, and with the influx of settlers into New Mexico this industry awaits a bright future," Fabián García wrote in 1905.[86] The territory's elite researchers, growers, and politicians thus gave the apple a starring role in New Mexico's broader history of immigration and emigration, modernity, and nation-building in the decades surrounding the turn of the century. The apple, due to its physical and cultural characteristics, was simply the easiest way for land developers to transform raw resources—sun, water, and soil—into exportable wealth. Irrigation projects would have been useless to early developers if there were not an enticing crop the water could grow; railroads would have been less profitable without a constant, shippable product. The apple made the dream of prosperous horticultural irrigation districts possible.

By the 1920s, however, the dream was beginning to lose its luster in southern New Mexico, where orchards were being transitioned to cotton fields in large numbers. Farmington became the epicenter of the land of the big red apple, but even there, as the following chapter demonstrates, the industry could not compete against ever-growing competition from apple growers elsewhere and the growing oil industry at home. Two decades after García proclaimed a "bright future" for apples, he offered a more nuanced take on the future of the New Mexico fruit industry. "I am inclined to believe that the old idea of planting large plantations is a thing of the past in this country," García wrote in 1922, "as it takes too much time and money to manage them. I feel that the future fruit business in New Mexico will develop along small, but more numerous, plantations, so that the individual growers can take care of them, instead of having to hire everything done as has often been the case in past years."[87] García's statement, as the following chapter will explain, proved prescient. As New Mexico's apple industry moved north, it also moved away from the predominately Anglo irrigation districts at opposite corners of the state and toward the Hispano homeland of northern New Mexico,[88] where growers gave new meaning to the big red apple and invested heavily in smaller scale, cooperative apple production.

2

Patent Lies and the "People's Business"

The Modern Core of Northern New Mexico Agriculture, 1940–80

Every autumn for decades, until 2011, New Mexicans would wait in miles of traffic along a remote clay road in northern New Mexico for a chance to buy a bag or two of the celebrated Dixon's Champagne apples, which supposedly grew nowhere else in the world. Local news channels hired extra staff members to handle the phones for the deluge of inquiries about when the orchard would open. The annual autumnal pilgrimage to the orchard became a family tradition for many who cherished the apples as a unique and distinctly New Mexican food, the fruity version of the Hatch chile. Sadly the Las Conchas wildfire in 2011 devastated the orchard and put an end to the seventy-five-year-old business. To add to the sad news, despite the often-repeated claims that Fred Dixon found the original wild tree growing in a nearby canyon and later patented it as the Champagne apple, the historical record—and patent office records—make clear that the supposedly rare apple was actually a common Golden Delicious. A beloved icon of New Mexican agriculture was built on a patent lie.

Growing an orchard—complex, scientific, and laborious as it may be—remains a simpler task than growing a legend to go with it. The myth, even more than the apples, accounted for the orchard's success. But a far more pervasive and harmful myth, the romantic figure of the yeoman farmer, preceded Dixon's specious claims of genetic exceptionality. The founder of the Dixon orchard, an advertising executive named James Webb Young, drew on that myth to create for himself the persona of "Old Jim Young," the living embodiment of the Jeffersonian yeoman farmer whose age-old agricultural pursuits represented a nostalgic retreat from modernity. The ad man Young used this nostalgic image—ripe with connotations of agrarian virtue, independence, civic-minded democracy, sweat-driven meritocracy, and white entitlement—to sell an apple he named "Champagne." Young's back-road orchard, and his innovative advertising and marketing strategies, reveal how modernity can originate and spread from places on the periphery. This story also shows us how agricultural producers, as storytellers, become cultural producers and intermediaries who invariably influence the cultural identity of the places they inhabit.

Young sold apples alongside rosy yeoman imagery excised of labor, land, and race struggles, even as other growers throughout northern New Mexico turned to the apple as a potential solution to the region-wide poverty linked to these very struggles. Commercial apple growing, which began to decline elsewhere in the state, rose sharply in the predominantly Hispanic and Native villages of northern New Mexico in the three decades following World War II.[1] As a result of this increase, as well as from the land-grant activism that eventually culminated in the Courthouse Raid in Tierra Amarilla in 1967, local growers teamed up with government agencies to form an apple cooperative in Chimayó, New Mexico. The cooperative represented a key part of the War on Poverty programs in New Mexico that addressed land-based unrest through intensive, export-based agriculture. Proponents of an apple cooperative for northern New Mexico hoped farmers might succeed through agricultural modernization that would allow them to create jobs and compete with growers on a national scale. Opponents derided state-funded initiatives such as the cooperative as ill-conceived, top-down boondoggles that would perpetuate northern New Mexico's ongoing colonial relationship to the rest of the nation. During the short ten years of its life, the cooperative made the apple a centerpiece of larger debates on the economic and cultural direction of the region, and poignantly pointed to the limitations of the very yeoman ideal so successfully sold by nearby Old Jim Young.

Northern New Mexico has a rich history of small- and medium-scale, modern agriculture. Together, the histories of the Champagne apples and the Chimayó apple cooperative offer a fuller portrait of this history—with its successes and failures—than either does alone. Their complementary stories illustrate how the lines between industrial and nonindustrial agriculture blurred in mid-twentieth-century New Mexico. Apple orchards remained complex sites where competing visions of the cultural identity of the state, its relationship to modernity and colonialism, and its relationship to the rest of the nation continued to converge late into the twentieth century.

How to Catch a Fish with an Apple

"Madison Avenue is many places," Norman Strouse, president and CEO of J. Walter Thompson (JWT), wrote in 1961, it "symbolically runs through every part of the country where advertising originates."[2] State Road 22, the long dirt road that leads to an apple orchard in the remote La Cañada de Cochiti at the base of the Jemez Mountains, roughly fifty miles from both Santa Fe and Albuquerque, proves no exception. The orchard and its original owner, Strouse's JWT colleague James Webb Young, both embodied the avenue's long reach and its two-way direction. While the orchard employed industrial technology in the forms of pesticides, smudge burners, irrigation systems, and refrigerated storage, James Webb Young developed even more cutting-edge methods of cultural production. As an executive at one of the nation's top advertising firms throughout the first half of the century, Young led the development of a "scientific yet magical formula"—a blend of market-based research, psychology, and artful appeals to the romance and fantasy rooted in American "folkways"—to spur consumption for the benefit of "modern American Civilization."[3] Young produced and exported both stories and apples to shape consumers' perceptions of the region. Through successfully producing and selling the stories behind his New Mexico products, Young served as a cultural intermediary between New Mexico and the rest of the nation, between ranch and metropolis, and between agricultural production and consumption.

James Webb Young was born in 1886 in Kentucky to a Yankee father and a Southern belle "unreconstructed Rebel" mother. He graduated fifth grade and decided he was done with formal education. Inspired by Horatio Alger tales, he set out to make his fortune and, unlike most, succeeded. He received his first big break as a Bible salesman, despite a lack of personal religious conviction. On the job one day in 1907, he saw an advertisement for a course on *How to Use Words to Make People Do Things* that cost only ten dollars with a dollar down. He later claimed the dollar he sent in the mail that day was the best investment of his life.[4]

Young became one of the most influential advertising men of the twentieth century. He worked his way up to the vice-presidency of J. Walter Thompson, the nation's oldest advertising firm (the firm that would go on to produce Richard Nixon's successful 1968 campaign for the presidency, under the direction of a young Roger Ailes). At JWT, Young helped initiate the use of scientific research in advertising, led the first major effort to export American advertising overseas, led wartime propaganda efforts during both world wars, and was instrumental in the creation of the Ad Council in the 1940s. In his early career, he invented the Legend of Aunt Jemima, arguably the most iconic figure in American advertising history, which, along with his work with Old South imagery in his Maxwell House coffee campaign, ranked among the first advertising campaigns to incorporate Americana. Beyond his work with

JWT, he served as director of the Bureau of Domestic and Foreign Commerce under Commerce Secretary Coolidge; he helped draft the plan for the Bureau of Indian Arts and Crafts; worked closely with the Rockefeller Foundation; and taught at the business school at the University of Chicago. He wrote fifteen books, including the highly influential *A Technique for Producing Ideas*. Not too shabby for a man with a fifth-grade education.[5]

Perhaps one of the most remarkable, if little known, features of his life is his decision in 1927, at age forty-two, to give up his apartment in the prestigious Marguery Hotel on Park Avenue for an adobe house on a remote ranch fifty miles from Santa Fe. He bought the roughly ten-thousand-acre Cañada de Cochiti land grant after one of his sons had expressed interest in dude ranching. The dude-ranching venture failed, but Young and his wife fell in love with the land and decided to stay. He noticed apples on the property, planted long before by Hispanic inhabitants of the land grant, and learned from locals that they seemed to bear consistently every year. Young planted the first trees of the new orchard shortly thereafter and, within only a few years, began selling his apples, at a "neat" 9 percent profit on annual investments, to local grocers, regional truckers, mail-order buyers from around the country, and local customers making day trips to his ranch.[6]

The ideas James Webb Young produced, even more than the apples themselves, led to his orchard's success. Young developed innovative business and advertising strategies that set his apples apart from others grown in the region. He was among the first apple producers in the country to advertise directly to mail-order customers in national magazines; he even managed to sell blemished, small, and wormy fruit when others couldn't or wouldn't.[7] One particularly creative sales strategy, involving a hailstorm that pockmarked his apple crop in 1963, became nearly legendary in advertising circles. After considering whether or not to sell the blemished crop, and risk having his mail-order customers demand refunds on his dime, Young crafted a card that appeared in every customer's box of apples:

> Note the hail marks that appear as minor skin blemishes on some of these apples. These are proof of their growth at a high mountain altitude, where the sudden chills from mountain hail storms which these apples receive while growing help firm their flesh and develop the fruit sugars which give them their fine flavor.

Not only did Young receive no requests for refunds that year, for years to come he actually received requests for pockmarked apples.[8] He had successfully transformed blemishes into badges of quality and had even reinforced his central marketing message that the specific environmental conditions of the ranch made his apples unique and superior. Never mind that hail damage reduces long-term storability, or that hailstorms affect apple growers throughout the country. He was the only man clever, audacious, and perhaps disingenuous enough to claim hail provides "sudden chills" that actually *improve* flavor. This creative spin of a potential problem into a marketable advantage exemplifies Young's advertising acumen, which often teetered on the line between suggestive conceit and actual deceit.

The branding of Young's apples, especially the transformation of his Golden Delicious apples into Champagne apples (and, to a somewhat lesser extent, his Red Delicious into Sparkling Burgundy apples), proved to be one of Young's most successful long-term marketing endeavors. Using language that anticipated contemporary discussions of "terroir," he argued that unique environmental conditions—high altitude, mountain water, volcanic soil— converged to transform a Golden Delicious apple, one of the most widely grown apples in the country, into a truly unique apple that he would eventually trademark as Champagne. The transformation began with a 1947 advertisement in the *Albuquerque Journal* headlined "The Champagne of Apples," which, fittingly, began with an origin story. Young opened the ad by introducing the original Golden Delicious tree, which grew on a hillside in Clay County, West Virginia, and which Paul Stark of the Stark Brothers nursery famously bought in 1914 for $5,000 before promptly enclosing the tree in a padlocked steel cage, wired with a burglar alarm. Young writes:

THE CHAMPAGNE OF APPLES: OLD JIM YOUNG'S GOLDEN DELICIOUS

On a middle-western hillside there is an apple tree growing in a cage—the most valuable apple tree in the world. Through some unknown trick of Nature this tree bore apples such as had never been seen before—apples with a rich golden color in skin and flesh like rare champagne. From this parent tree came the trees on which I grow the same wonderful Golden Delicious Apples in my little Jemez Mountains Valley. There our New Mexico sunshine and cold nights bring them to such perfection that every bite crackles and the juice runs down your lips. People all over America send me for these apples—even from the big apple-growing states of Washington and Oregon. You can get these prize apples by simply asking your Safeway Store for Old Jim Young's Golden Delicious Apples.[9]

The advertisement makes clear that the champagne of apples were Golden Delicious and, although the New Mexico sunshine and cold nights "bring them to perfection," even the original Golden Delicious has "flesh like rare champagne." Over the next fifteen years Young slowly crafted an entirely new "Champagne Apple" by discarding the origin story of the Golden Delicious altogether from his advertisements and instead insisting that New Mexico's environment made *these* Golden Delicious unique. Throughout the following decade, however, Young sold the apples clearly as Golden Delicious. A writer for *New Mexico Magazine* visited Old Jim Young's ranch in 1950 and reported that he bit into "one of those Golden Delicious apples and, by gosh . . . It truly tasted like champagne"; in 1955, an advertisement to truckers mentioned Golden Delicious but not Champagne apples; and even in 1960 an advertisement sold Golden Delicious without mention of champagne.[10] But by 1961 Young refers simply to his "famous 'Champagne' apples"; he ran ads in 1962 that sold Old Jim Young's apples as just "Champagne." By 1963 a trademark symbol accompanies the Champagne apples.[11]

Significantly, Young claimed the uniqueness of the Champagne apples derived not from genetic uniqueness, as the Dixons would later claim, but from the uniqueness of the environment in which it grew. By the late 1950s Young argued that the unique environmental conditions of his New Mexico ranch set apart his apples from the rest. In 1958 he wrote "every bite crackles and juice runs down your lips . . . because I grow them in a beautiful little valley, 6000 ft. up in the Jemez Mountains. Here the volcanic ash soil, the pure, cold mountain water, and the cool summer nights give apples a crispness and flavor no low country can have." For Young, emphasizing "mountain grown" was paramount; he switched his brand name from simply "Old Jim Young's" in the forties and early fifties to "Old Jim Young's Mountain Grown" by the late fifties. By emphasizing environmental terroir rather than genetic difference, Young once again crafted persuasive suggestions without resorting to blatant deception.

On a more basic and less literal level, however, Young's apple advertisements hardly avoided deceit. By creating and taking on the persona of Old Jim Young, Young crafted into his apples one of the nation's most foundational myths: the American yeoman. Variously depicted in popular American imagery as an independent, industrious, virtuous, morally centered, civic-minded, modest, and, importantly though often tacitly, white man who owned his land fee simple, the mythic yeoman had, for much of the nation's history, provided the bedrock to U.S. democracy, justified U.S. claims to expansion and exceptionalism, and served as a key part, in Henry Nash Smith's words, of the "poetic idea . . . that defined the promise of American life."[12] James Webb Young built his career by embracing such poetic ideas; he understood as well as anyone both their power and fallacy.

Young carefully crafted this yeomanly character for the sake of selling apples, not because the image bore any resemblance to his actual life. "There must be a personality shining through all the talk about the product," Young wrote in *How to Become an Advertising Man*. "I have overwhelming evidence that one of the reasons why people buy my Mountain Grown Apples is because they take to a character called Old Jim Young, who chats with them in the advertising." Paul G. Hoffman, Studebaker president and director of the Marshall Plan, would later explain that Young sold his apples by taking off, "at least for a few minutes, the Brooks Brothers flannels and put on overalls. He had his picture taken astride a fence with a corncob pipe and became Old Jim Young, the apple man."[13] Throughout his apple advertisements, Young assumed a folksy, humble voice that regularly addressed women (he made his target audience clear in his writings and often published his ads on the "Woman's Page") to bring the "small fry" along to visit his "little" orchard. At times he took on a God-fearing voice (asking his customers, for example, to "now come see the valley of glory" where his orchard dwells) and he voiced concern for the customers' well-being (and directly appealed to women's sense of maternal responsibility) with advertising messages such as "I want children to have more apples." Such homespun language, often infused with appeals to morality and civic concern, bears little resemblance to the cunning and cynical voice that characterized Young's diaries and professional writings.

No one expects advertising characters to be exact mirrors of reality. But this particular fiction perpetuated the myth of virtue in agriculture by erasing the exploitation of agricultural labor that drove commercial agricultural ventures throughout the country. Inequalities built on differences of race and class created a cheap labor force that allowed Young's business to turn its "neat 9 percent" profit. Young himself did little of the physical work of growing apples; he did not even manage the orchard. Fred Dixon, a white, working-class farmer from southwestern Colorado, took on that job in 1944, including hiring workers, most of whom were Hispanic and Pueblo Indian from neighboring towns, to perform the labor necessary to maintain the ranch and produce the apples. Young paid little for this labor. In 1944 seven men from Cochiti Pueblo did that work, which included tasks such as digging an irrigation ditch by hand. According to Dixon, Young paid the men "a dollar a day," a paltry amount considering a worker making the federal minimum wage at the time would have made well over twice that amount for an eight-hour day. A rare reference to his hired labor reveals Young's ever-present cunning and affinity for psychology; he mused in 1943 that he had been "busy all day in the warm October glow, getting my Golden Delicious apples off the trees. Made every picker wear white cotton gloves, and found the psychological effect of these greatly reduced the number of culls due to carelessness in handling."[14] Such managerial work largely fell to Dixon after he arrived. As orchard manager, Dixon frequently "battled with labor," and eventually shifted from hiring mostly local Indian and Hispanic labor to hiring mostly Mexican migrant laborers, who were paid "piecework."[15]

Young even erased the indispensable and more authentically agrarian Fred Dixon. Dixon, who once explained he "was born and raised in a log cabin" and who gained the nickname "Old Oso" on the ranch after fighting a bear, experienced a full life of farm labor. Yet Young never wrote Dixon into the orchard's advertisements, and in fact never mentioned him in any of his published writings. Young paid Dixon a hundred dollars a month; Dixon later recalled that "we knew what it was to go to bed hungry . . . there were times that hundred dollars didn't go too far."[16] Dixon was well aware of the fallacy of Young's yeoman imagery. "Mr. Young spent two or three months out of the year here," Fred Dixon later recalled. "But he didn't like it. In his writings he'd say he liked it. He'd say a lot of things that weren't true in his writings."[17]

Young, for his part, certainly understood the deception he per-petrated. He told the graduating class at the University of Chi-cago in 1955: "Your lifelong study in the Art of Advertising will be to discover what the Public wants. This creates an Ethical Problem, as it must be clear to you by now that human nature is fundamentally bad and what it wants is always wrong." With a cynical humor and clear disdain for the masses, Young declared that the public represented fish to be caught and that the Latin name for their species of fish was "*suckers economicus.*" To catch these fish—to sell them things they don't actually need and that don't actually serve their best interests—understanding the "quaint folkways" of the public "will be your stock in trade," Young con-cluded. "But if you use [these quaint folkways] to bait your hooks (as you must) there is only one consolation which can be offered you. You will recall the ancient maxim: 'Be Good and you'll be Happy—but you won't have much Fun.' As an Advertising Man you will never be Good, and seldom Happy. But you'll have a lot of Fun."[18]

When James Webb Young died in 1973, so did Old Jim Young. Manager-turned-owner Fred Dixon had learned a thing or two from the ad man, marketing his apples with a decidedly new myth based on specious claims about apple genetics. Dixon claimed that, in the late forties, he had discovered a wild seedling of what would become the Champagne apple, growing in a nearby can-yon. He eventually claimed to patent this tree and steadfastly refused to sell or give a single scion to any other grower.[19] Dixon's myth, tapping into the growing popular understanding of genet-ics in the seventies, perhaps lacked Young's artful suggestiveness but nonetheless continued to illustrate the power of storytelling in New Mexico's agricultural successes.

The U.S. patent office holds no patents for Champagne (or Sparkling Burgundy) apples, and Young's earlier advertisements made clear that the Champagne apple had its genetic origins on a hillside in West Virginia, not New Mexico. Still, customers ate up both the apples and the stories. By the early eighties newspapers reported that the Champagne and Sparkling Burgundy apples were, according to Dixon, "only grown in this canyon."[20] "Mr. Dixon, who is 68 years old and has tended his land for 48 years, recently began the harvest that will last until the end of this month," a *New York Times* travel piece began in 1988. "He and his 80 pickers will bring in Red Delicious and Rome apples as well as two varieties—Champagne and Sparkling Burgundy—for which Mr. Dixon holds the patent and which he said are grown nowhere else in the United States."[21] Dixon would tell an oral historian fifteen years later, "I would say most of the people in this part of New Mexico know what Champagne and [Sparkling] Burgundy [are]. . . . That's the only place in the world they're raised and we own the patents on them and, as I've stated over and over, it's nice to have . . . something that nobody else has and it's good for the state of New Mexico to have something that no other state has."[22] Even as late as 2011, the year the Las Conchas fire devastated the orchard and ended more than seventy years of business in La Cañada de Cochiti, *An Apple Lovers Cookbook* explained that "what really attracts the crowds [to Dixon's] are their signature varieties, which the farm's founder, Fred Dixon, named Champagne and Sparkling Burgundy, after he discovered the two chance seedlings in the late 1940s."[23]

The history of the apples growing on the former Cañon de Cochiti land grant bears several lessons. Agriculturalists might take away the practical lesson that storytelling is an important facet of agricultural success, and advertising often pays dividends. Such advertising allowed Young, and later Dixon, to primarily (and eventually exclusively) focus on local sales and mail-order buyers willing to pay retail prices. Less successful apple operations elsewhere in the region lacked such a focus on advertising. Stories also play a role in shaping the cultural identity of those producing and eating apples. James Young and Fred Dixon sold a notion of uniqueness—built on notions of terroir and eventually also genetics—that tapped into New Mexicans' place-based pride. Yet it also served to whitewash perceptions of New Mexico agriculture by erasing labor and agricultural exploitation through well-worn associations with yeomanly independence, morality, and whiteness. The story of small apple producers elsewhere in northern New Mexico reveals the extent of the whitewashing, and provides an important lesson about the cultural impact of apple-growing on the region.

Tanks in the Mountains and War on Poverty in the Orchards

In 1967 nineteen men, led by the charismatic Pentecostal preacher named Reies Tijerina from a Texas sharecropping family, stormed the Tierra Amarilla Courthouse in northern New Mexico's Rio Arriba County to make a citizen's arrest on the attorney general and free several recently arrested fellow land-grant rights activists. The so-called Courthouse Raid left two police officers injured, made national news, and led to a massive manhunt for Tijerina that included National Guard tanks combing the dirt roads in surrounding mountains. The raid "thrust New Mexico's colonial . . . property disputes into the national consciousness," David Correia argues, and laid bare how the poverty of land-grant heirs throughout the region "was a monument to colonial greed."[24] Yet despite ample scholarly attention given to Tijerina, the Courthouse Raid, and the broader land- and property-rights struggle of the period, scholars have yet to fully examine the regional agricultural context prior to and directly after the raid. Given agriculture's central position in the varied and contested land-use visions for the region, and given the size of the agricultural cooperatives that formed throughout the region in response to the unrest that centered around the Courthouse Raid, such an examination is overdue. A particularly good place to start is the apple orchards that blanketed the irrigated valleys of the region.

By the late sixties apples had become a significant facet of the region's agricultural economy, playing a central role in the broader debate over the economic and cultural direction of the region. Half of all apples produced in the state came from trees growing in small acreages in northern New Mexico, mostly owned by Native and Hispano growers. Many of these commercial apple growers increasingly embraced the basic tenets of modern export agriculture, employing at least some modern technologies—orchard heaters, wind machines, pesticides, mechanical graders, and improved rootstocks—to compete with growers throughout the country. As growers, planners, researchers, and politicians considered the future of the emergent industry, they developed plans for a cooperative that once again placed the apple squarely within broader contestations over modernity and the overall direction of the region.

The cooperative emerged from both unrest and unprecedented optimism. On a warm February day in 1970, a group of politicians, state and national government officials, newspaper reporters, and about 150 apple growers and Española Valley residents gathered in Chimayó to eat apple pie, drink apple cider, and listen to largely hopeful and congratulatory speeches on the newly approved $259,700 federal loan to build a thirty-three-thousand-square-foot apple packing and storage facility in the small town. The new cooperative, officially called the Northern New Mexico Farmer's Cooperative, like nearly all the government-funded, producer-run cooperatives in northern New Mexico at the time, aimed to help producers modernize their operations for increased bulk and out-of-state sales. The co-op would soon provide fertilizer, pesticides, advice on pruning and harvesting techniques; build an automated processing plant to press cider and grade, polish, and pack apples; and provide refrigerated storage for up to twenty-five thousand bushels of apples.[25] Governor David Cargo called the loan "extremely significant," cooperative president John Trujillo suggested it would bring prosperity to the region and "the whole state," and state senator and Chimayó apple cooperative member Arturo Jaramillo went as far as declaring that it could possibly impart the "strongest influence on the economy we've had in the history of the state."[26] Within a year the small, predominantly Hispano town in northern New Mexico would lay claim to an apple shed that was the largest in the state and "the most modern in the Southwest."[27]

The construction of the politically popular facility came after decades of growth in the region's apple industry and several attempts to create lasting cooperatives. Beginning in the mid-1930s, improved roads and the advent of selling directly to truckers (itinerant, often out-of-state, wholesale buyers) increased the profitability of commercial apple growing in the Española area and led to "evidence of renewed interest in apple production" among area growers.[28] This new marketing strategy, along with high prices during World War II, spurred the initial surge in plantings. By the midfifties, roughly a third of all apples grown statewide came out of northern New Mexico, leading the Española Valley Experiment Station to start a test orchard for commercial production in 1953.[29] As the industry grew, so too did the need for growers to organize.

Early ventures at forming cooperatives in the valley, which dated as far back as a fruit exchange spearheaded by L. Bradford Prince in the first decade of the twentieth century, had never achieved lasting success. Cooperatives had failed due to "poor planning, excessive risk sharing, and short supplies resulting from unfavorable weather conditions," leaving a memory of failure that made growers hesitant to try again.[30] The most recent cooperative prior to the Chimayó co-op had been the Truchas Peak Apple Cooperative, a small packing and marketing shed that formed in Española in 1957 but had failed by 1964.[31] Despite its short tenure, the initial success of the Truchas Peak Apple Cooperative encouraged growers to plant more trees and illustrated the need for an expanded shed with refrigerated storage.[32] Additionally, reclamation projects such as Abiquiu Dam in Rio Arriba County in the early sixties led to a 40 percent increase in irrigated land downstream, much of which landowners planted in apples.[33] The region produced fully half of the entire state's apple crop by the late sixties, and growers sought greater capacity for storage, marketing, and horticultural expertise.

Growers needed to organize. New Mexico, due to its high elevation and southern latitude, could produce a ripe crop on average two weeks before the major apple-producing regions in the Pacific Northwest. This environmental advantage created a brief window of high prices that accounted for the bulk of growers' profits. However, because the market window was small and all growers had apples at the same time, growers needed to sell large quantities quickly to wholesale brokers, truckers, or other large buyers. Creating a cooperative would allow growers to sell as a larger unit, increase their marketing leverage, and prevent growers from undercutting each other. Furthermore a cooperative would allow growers to pool resources to increase efficiencies and, most importantly, to expand their storage capacity. Refrigeration would increase growers' sales window for wholesalers, as well as their ability to sell smaller amounts over a prolonged period at higher prices to local markets.[34] Yet by the midsixties the few refrigerated facilities in the state existed almost entirely on larger, well-funded operations such as James Webb Young's orchard; as a result, by the midsixties only about 1 percent of the total crop in New Mexico was sold after the first of November.[35]

The first rumblings of an apple cooperative in Chimayó came from the growers themselves, encouraged by a bumper crop in 1967 and a large joint sale of culls to a processing plant in Colorado in 1968. Seizing the swell of enthusiasm, Arturo Jaramillo, a prominent grower and restaurant owner in Chimayó, helped lead roughly 110 separate growers, mostly with small orchards along the Santa Cruz River and many falling below the national poverty line, to organize. "If this momentum could not now be captured it may be lost for another generation," Arturo Jaramillo remarked, "since the history of promises, attempts and failures in the area is too prominent to forget." Such sentiment echoed a USDA report that had concluded five years prior that "the attitude of growers does not appear conducive for establishing a successful cooperative . . . in part [because of the] unfavorable cooperative history in this area."[36] The newfound momentum among growers to organize derived not only from a few good harvests and their successful sale to the Colorado processor but also from the unprecedented availability of government funding.

When Lyndon B. Johnson declared a "War on Poverty" with the Economic Opportunity Act of 1964, he set the course to significantly fund small, community-led economic ventures throughout the country. By the end of the decade a host of new, government-backed cooperatives proliferated in northern New Mexico. The Home Education Livelihood Program (HELP), founded in 1965 by the New Mexico Council of Churches through War on Poverty funding, especially embraced the establishment of producer-run cooperatives throughout the state and particularly in northern New Mexico. "Many of the underlying causes of poverty can be eradicated by developing a self-sustaining economic base in the rural community," a HELP spokesman declared in 1968, and developing such a base requires "more creative methods for freeing persons from their social bondage."[37] By 1968 these "creative methods" included funding projects ranging from hand-carved furniture co-ops, weaving shops, construction shops, and craftsman co-ops to livestock management programs. The group helped form produce cooperatives in the Mora Valley, the Peñasco Valley, and in the Ruidoso-Hondo Valley of southern New Mexico. In the cases of the Mora and Peñasco cooperatives, which produced crops such as cabbage, onions, carrots, chile, corn, garlic, pinto beans, peas, cucumbers, turnips, and oats on a combined 520 acres, HELP helped growers with equipment and fertilizer costs, business management, and market development.[38]

The Chimayó apple growers reached out to several state agencies and programs funded through the War on Poverty. They initially approached the State Economic Opportunity Office (SEOO), which independently of the Chimayó apple growers' organizing efforts had begun "preparations of a program for a long range, comprehensive apple development operation in this area," as well as the newly formed joint state-federal Four Corners Regional Commission. The state extension service, which had also been leading a development survey of commercial apple growing, soon became involved, as well.[39] Shortly thereafter HELP also joined the effort. The apple cooperative had become a politically popular project that attracted the involvement of many agencies.

Nearly from the outset, however, financial woes plagued the cooperative.[40] Some experts blamed low yields on insufficient pollinator trees; poor cultivation, soil-building, and pruning practices; and inadequate pesticide spraying and spring frost protection infrastructure.[41] Others held that "the small size of the orchards prohibits the use of modern equipment for pruning or topping except through joint ownership." A 1970 New Mexico State University (NMSU) extension service report concluded that "many of these small orchards suffer from . . . lack of frost protection systems, due to the high costs, and failure to control insects cause fluctuations in both production and quality from year to year."[42] A group of planners similarly concluded in 1971 that "the main problem with the hundreds of small orchards from an agricultural standpoint is that those persons merely owning apple or other fruit trees for shade and esthetic purposes do not spray them for diseases injurious to fruit, and therefore, the unsprayed trees become a host to insects and fungi which can then rapidly spread back and infect sprayed trees following a heavy rain."[43]

Yet beyond agricultural issues, organizational and "extreme marketing difficulties"[44] significantly hampered the cooperative. In its first year of operation the cooperative lost $32,000 "due to operational problems and the fact that growers were too eager to sell their product immediately for cash rather than wait to receive higher prices later after processing and sale by the Coop."[45] Arturo Jaramillo articulated this concern succinctly in 1970: "The cooperative is probably the biggest business to come to Northern New Mexico and it is the people's business . . . if [growers] sell to a trucker then they are competing with themselves." In the first years of its existence the cooperative sold mostly to local grocery stores and schools, as well as to brokers as far afield as Los Angeles, east Texas, and Shreveport, Louisiana.[46] Independent truckers were mostly out-of-state buyers that directly competed with the brokers the cooperative sold to; growers' rogue sales to these truckers significantly undercut the cooperative's marketing leverage.

Rogue sales to truckers also contributed to already-existing marketing problems surrounding New Mexico's poor reputation among large apple buyers region-wide. Wholesalers surveyed in 1960 overwhelmingly considered New Mexico apples to be below average quality compared to apples from elsewhere in the United States, describing them as "wormy"; "more perishable"; having "poor color"; not dependably graded, sized, or packed; and generally "over-priced in relation to quality."[47] Throughout the decade researchers and marketing experts continually voiced concerns over poor grading and general low quality in New Mexico apples, and viewed the Chimayó cooperative as a large part of the solution. Yet the cooperative's modern grading facilities solved the issue only as long as individual growers did not make ungraded bulk sales—often in the form of "orchard run" sales—to truckers. A few shipments of low-quality apples were enough to tarnish the region's reputation and indirectly hurt the cooperative. Yet, as the example of James Webb Young's apples clearly illustrates, effective advertising and branding can overcome a certain degree of quality issues; while the lack of sufficient grading and quality control undoubtedly hurt the industry, so too did a lack of effective storytelling.

With significant state funding already invested and with a potentially large amount of political credit to be gained, New Mexico's state agencies, up to the level of direct involvement by the state's governors, stepped in to help with both finding buyers and enhancing the image of the state's apple crop. As early as 1969 Governor David Cargo touted cooperatives as a means to overcome the lack of locally grown produce consumed in state, and pledged to meet with chain-store buyers to "discuss marketing of locally grown products."[48] In 1970 he proposed an "apple tax" to spur local sales,[49] and he even helped facilitate a sale of 22,200 boxes of apples to the Defense Department for soldiers in Vietnam.[50] By 1973 the cooperative still struggled to sell its crop, particularly to local buyers. Cooperative secretary Pamela Mabry Tate wrote to Governor Bruce King in 1973 that, despite significant sales of the region's bumper crop to buyers in Texas, "we wonder why it is taking so long for New Mexico buyers to come to the same conclusion."[51] She appealed to the governor to help them sell their crop. Governor King responded by personally appealing to various state institutions to buy New Mexico apples and by instituting an official "Apple Week" across the state.[52]

No amount of governors' phone calls, agricultural improvements, or improved organizational cooperation, however, could have prevented the cooperative from suffering its most serious setback. In January 1971 temperatures hovering around minus forty degrees Fahrenheit shattered previous records (the region is classified as USDA 6b, which means the average annual extreme low temperature is between zero and minus five Fahrenheit). The record freeze—dubbed "the Big Freeze" in local papers—killed 80 percent of the season's crop.[53] Much more devastatingly, it killed an estimated sixty-five thousand fruit trees in the area.[54] Unlike more typical spring freezes that kill blossoms, these air temperatures sank low enough to kill the trees themselves. The freeze hit northern New Mexico harder than any other part of the state and, more than any other single factor, led to the apple industry's downturn in the seventies. Subsequent spring freezes, along with another extreme winter freeze in 1974, significantly hurt yields at a time when growers most needed strong harvests to repay the loan on the cooperative shed. After the Big Freeze the cooperative "established a loan fund to assist members in securing new trees, removing old trees, financing the application of recommended cultural practices and encouraging installation of frost equipment," but the loss of entire orchards was too severe for many growers to overcome.[55] Alex Mercure, who ran HELP at the time and who then became the assistant secretary of agriculture, reflected in 1978 that "had it not been for freezes and related events, the original co-op probably would have survived."[56]

The slew of setbacks facing the roughly five hundred small-scale apple growers who supplied the cooperative ultimately led to the cooperative's dissolution. Despite an increasing membership role and, in Arturo Jaramillo's words, "tremendous improvement" in orchard management, the growers could not overcome the combined setbacks of bad weather, poor yields, marketing difficulties, and organizational problems within the cooperative. The co-op had repaid only about $25,000 of its original $299,000 loan from the Small Business Administration by February 1978 when it finally shut its doors.[57] Northern New Mexico acreage in apples began to decline; despite renewed efforts to form subsequent cooperatives, enthusiasm for the apple industry at both the grower level and the institutional level never again approached the heights of the late sixties.

Despite being short-lived, the Chimayó apple shed played an important role in broader debates at the time concerning the cultural and economic direction of the region. These debates among scholars, activists, writers, and politicians, which invariably centered on land and property rights issues brought to the fore by Tijerina and La Alianza Federal de Mercedes (a group Tijerina had formed in 1963 that was dedicated to reclaiming Spanish and Mexican land grants in New Mexico), often addressed War on Poverty programs and the proper role of the state in shaping agricultural land use. Some of the most vocal critiques of the War on Poverty in northern New Mexico came from the Española-based newspaper, *El Grito del Norte*. The paper routinely lambasted

HELP's programs as "pacification programs" meant to appease land-grant tensions by appointing leaders that did not truly represent the masses in northern New Mexico. The paper specifically derided its director, Alex Mercure, as a one-man "empire builder" and "New Mexico's #1 vendido [sellout]." Carlos Cansino explained to readers: "Another vendido Chicano was given prominence by the establishment whose name is Alex Mercure. This was done on June 8, 1967 in order to offset the fame that Tijerina was getting among the Chicanos."[58] To the editors and writers of *El Grito del Norte*, HELP's programs represented a government- and corporate-backed effort to quell the revolutionary sentiments sparked by Tijerina surrounding land-grant rights in northern New Mexico. War on Poverty programs—the Chimayó apple cooperative included—did not represent the values of the majority of the region's residents, they argued, investing in economic initiatives that would only perpetuate northern New Mexico's colonial status with the rest of the nation.

As an alternative to War on Poverty programs, *El Grito del Norte* held up the example of a small and ultimately short-lived cooperative farm in Tierra Amarilla called the Cooperativa Agrícola del Pueblo de Tierra Amarilla. The Cooperativa Agrícola focused on barter economies, invoking imagery from the era's hippie commune culture along with nostalgic notions of New Mexico's agricultural past. Its leaders explained in 1969 that "our people in Tierra Amarilla are going to . . . revive the old traditions of working together to feed our people . . . because this is the revolution also. What good is it to fight this long fight for the land, when our children grow up without food? Without a culture?" Implicitly the "culture" of the place derives from a noncommercial, barter-based form of agriculture. Without directly referencing the apple cooperatives, the article further explained, "Last summer, the people in Velarde [in northern New Mexico] lost a lot of apples in the apple sheds and on the trees because of the market not giving them reasonable prices. The market wants to make money, not feed people. So in making a cooperative in Tierra Amarilla, we give the people of Velarde a chance to put their fruit to use [through offering barter] instead of losing it."[59] To its members and supporters the Cooperativa Agrícola served as a significant alternative, economically and culturally, to commercial cooperatives such as the Chimayó apple cooperative.

Academics, activists, students, and public intellectuals added similar criticisms of the War on Poverty in northern New Mexico. Peter Van Dresser, a public intellectual based in El Rito, for example, argued in his 1972 *A Landscape for Humans* that planners and bureaucrats should focus on "intensive and diversified cultivation of high vitamin and protein crops and the raising, fattening, and processing of livestock *primarily for local and regional consumption*," to avoid perpetuating "the second-class 'colonial' status of the regional economy."[60] Clark S. Knowlton, a sociology professor at Highlands University in Las Vegas, New Mexico, argued that, despite some successes, War on Poverty programs in northern New Mexico had generally failed because government officials remained insensitive to the cultural values of the region's residents, and their programs did not directly address "the fundamental causes of poverty such as discrimination, segregation, alienation of land and water resources and denial of due process and civil rights."[61] In addition Knowlton insisted that the land issue must be "thoroughly ventilated" before any significant improvement would be possible.

In response to the onslaught of criticisms, HELP director Alex Mercure emerged as the programs' chief spokesman. Born in rural northern New Mexico and eventually serving as assistant secretary of agriculture under Jimmy Carter, Mercure responded with an appeal to practicality. "We have no argument with attempting to pursue the question of land fraud," Mercure told a journalist in 1969, "but in the meantime, we may not have any heirs left—they might have all starved to death. The whole thing becomes academic in that solution." Mercure pointed to the "various kinds

of economic enterprises," such as the Chimayó apple cooperative, that were particularly worth focusing on in lieu of a "miracle" wherein the land grants were returned to heirs. In direct
response to the Cooperativa Agrícola, he argued that farmers
needed to farm not only for sustenance but for monetary income.
He added that farmers should embrace the idea of the "corporate
entity" and its notion of limited liability, which he considered
"one of the great concepts of middle-class Anglo culture." Implicitly, Mercure argued, a focus on intensive commercial agriculture
represented a reasonable, though hardly ideal, partial response to
the loss of lands. "If some lands should be recovered, fine," Mercure concluded, "but I think we also have to look at what exists
today—and build from there."[62]

This debate reveals an important agricultural context to the
state's political history in the mid-twentieth century. Histories of
this era that have focused solely on land grants and their forest
lands have overlooked an important and complementary story in
the valley lands. The significant number of modern, commercial,
and government-supported apple operations in the region's irrigated valleys helps break down familiar dichotomies that pit the
government against the people, or traditional agriculture against
commercial agriculture. Just as James Webb Young's apple advertisements and marketing strategies illustrate an often overlooked
degree of modernity in the region's agricultural past, the history
of Española Valley's small-scale, modern, commercial growers
debunks notions of timeless tradition. Agricultural systems in
northern New Mexico have been fluid; they have woven modernity with tradition in myriad ways.

The agricultural history of New Mexico helps explain the state's
political history. As land-rights pressure built in the mountains, an
apple industry expanded in the valleys. The growers who helped
build this industry ranged from the many small-acre apple producers who eventually helped form the Chimayó cooperative to
a Madison Avenue executive and his farm manager from Colo-

rado. Together the history of the Young-Dixon orchard alongside that of the apple cooperative in Chimayó reveals the modern core of northern New Mexico agriculture in the mid-twentieth century. These small- and medium-scale orchards blended traditional methods with cutting-edge technologies to build an industry that served the greater Southwest and beyond.

TWO

Cotton

3

The Shifting Subjects of a Southwest King

Cotton, Agricultural Industrialization, and Migrations in the Interwar New Mexico Borderlands

A fake dawn broke upon the staged cotton fields in El Paso in 1926, where a large reveling crowd from throughout southern New Mexico and western Texas gathered to watch a "flock of pickanannies" pick white gold. One of Mexico City's finest *típica* bands provided the soundtrack with their performance of southern plantation songs. The renowned band had nearly missed the show; they were detained at the U.S. border and granted entry only after each member played his instrument to the satisfaction of the border agents.[1] The festivities involved crowning a king and queen, the son and daughter of local elite cotton growers, who sat on their newly built "one-thousand-dollar throne" and presided over a long list of "courtiers," "princesses," "duchesses," and "ladies in waiting." At the cotton palace at Liberty Hall in downtown El Paso, the Old South had met the Old Mexico in the New West.

The real king, of course, was not the young bachelor on stage. King Cotton brought dreams of wealth to irrigated valleys of the region; spurred new migrations of people and seeds; and instigated cultural convergences like the El Paso cotton festival, a display of racist, fetishized Old South aristocratic imagery in the nation's western borderlands. As cotton spread rapidly throughout the irrigated valleys of far western Texas, southern New Mexico, and far eastern Arizona (a region variously termed by contemporary analysts as the "El Paso market region" or the "New Mexico Region"), farmers quickly shifted away from raising a diverse mix of vegetables, alfalfa, and horticultural crops such as apples—which continued to suffer from pests and disease, late frosts, distance to markets, and lack of region-wide cooperation—to the cash crop that seemed much better suited to the region's realities of isolation, aridity, southern latitudes, and western irrigation.

Following its adoption in the region as a commercial crop in the late 1910s, cotton reshaped the cultural and agricultural landscape of the New Mexico borderlands. Cotton's arrival spurred new migrations among farmers and farmworkers, led to new and stronger regional alliances among growers, and strengthened ties between the land-grant college and growers throughout the borderlands. The new cotton economy focused on sourcing genetic material from around the continent, refining it through scientific research and cooperation among growers, and shipping the finished product, as fiber and as seed, to markets throughout the continent and world. As cotton attracted migrations of diverse people and genetic material into the region, it paradoxically led to increased homogenization in the fields themselves. Farmers across the entire region organized to plant a single variety of cotton, often in large, monocropped fields that left little room for soil-building, rotational crops. Yet the history of New Mexico's many early cotton farms, themselves ever-evolving composites of diverse growing systems, reveals this increased homogenization was neither immediate nor complete. One-crop farming belied the early logics of industrialism and often relied, both directly and indirectly, on more diverse farms of all sizes. The industrialization of agriculture, as the history of cotton in the isolated borderlands valleys of New Mexico illustrates, was a contingent process.

Cotton growers in the U.S. South, the antebellum center of global cotton production built on enslaved labor, had by the early twentieth century lost their dominance in global cotton markets. Throughout the world, new cotton-growing regions emerged to successfully compete with southern growers, who struggled with a host of cotton production issues including depleted soils, the spread of the Mexican boll weevil, the inefficiencies of the tenant-sharecropper system, and genetic erosion of cotton varieties. By the first decades of the twentieth century, a major source of increased competition emerged from their compatriots to the west.

Growers had successfully raised cotton in California as far back as the early 1870s, but a cotton industry in the U.S. West had to wait for the arrival of the railroad, an increased availability of labor, the formation of state and USDA experiment stations, and reclamation projects that drastically improved irrigation systems in the early twentieth century.[2] In the valleys of southern New Mexico and far western Texas, cotton production sputtered before surging in the interwar period. The first experiments with cotton began in the Mesilla Valley as early as 1890[3] and about a decade later in the Pecos Valley, but the first sizable commercial acreage in the region emerged only in the Pecos Valley in the early 1910s[4] and toward the end of the decade in the Mesilla and El Paso Valleys.[5] Elsewhere in smaller districts throughout the region, cotton growers followed suit.[6] Both the more common upland varieties and long-staple Egyptian cottons proved well adapted to the region's irrigated valleys.

Cotton grew well in the arid, irrigated West. Western growers' previous environmental disadvantages, such as isolation and aridity, suddenly became advantages. Aridity accounted for the absence of the notorious boll weevil and other pests, while isolation helped prevent cross-pollination among varieties and thus made the crucial task of seed improvement easier.

The long taproot of the cotton plant proved well adapted to periodic flood irrigation between long dry periods. The growing season of southern New Mexico was just long enough to ensure consistent yields, while cotton's salt tolerance made the alkaline soils that plagued much of the West less of a hindrance. Because cotton was nonperishable, long distances to market no longer posed a major problem.

Yet environmental factors alone hardly account for the rise of the New Mexico region as a fiber- and seed-producing hub. Federal expenditures in reclamation, transportation, and seed exploration, and university-funded research and breeding, all made efficient, large-scale commercial agriculture possible. In particular federal reclamation projects such as Elephant Butte Dam and the Carlsbad Project provided ample irrigation that made large-scale cotton growing more controllable and more reliable based on the best agronomic research available. In the years immediately following World War I and the construction of Elephant Butte Dam, commercial cotton in New Mexico and far western Texas became "an exceptionally profitable crop" and quickly transformed the crop regimes of farmers throughout the valleys.[7] The construction of Elephant Butte Dam created roughly 107,000 acres of irrigable land, most of which—along with the existing land planted principally in wheat, alfalfa, corn, beans, vegetables, and fruit—went into cotton.[8] Within only a few years cotton acreage more than tripled in the new federal reclamation areas of Arizona and New Mexico and accounted for over a quarter of the entire gross value of all crops grown in those areas.[9] By 1930 farmers throughout the Elephant Butte district had in some years devoted a full 75 percent of all irrigable land to cotton. Nearly all irrigated farms in the region grew some cotton; cotton provided the lion's share of most farmers' incomes.[10] Cotton production peaked in 1929, but remained a steady and significant source of income for farmers up to and during World War II. Dust Bowl–era Agricultural Adjustment and government quotas in cotton acreage generally led to a retirement of the least productive acreage and therefore did not drastically reduce total production despite reducing acreage.[11]

Shifting Subjects

Cotton production set in motion demographic shifts that transformed the agricultural and cultural landscapes of the region. With the inflow of newly dammed irrigation water and the promise of profits in cotton came "an influx of new settlers" to the valleys of southern New Mexico and far west Texas. Settlers came from throughout the country and from many backgrounds, including a small number of Japanese farmers in the Mesilla Valley and African Americans in the Pecos Valley who grew cotton at the town of Blackdom and, later, El Vado. Yet the vast majority of these new settlers were white farmers "from cotton-growing portions of Texas and other States."[12] In the Pecos Valley, where population shifts were most dramatic, some rural communities resembled small boomtowns. By 1925 a local journalist could report that "as a result of the introduction of cotton here there has been more money in the community than in many years and also an increase in population. It is impossible to supply the demand for houses."[13]

The new populations of white southerners embraced cotton both in and out of the field. Harvest festivals centered around the new crop. Roswell hosted its first "cotton carnival" in 1923, which within a few years attracted thousands of visitors from as far as El Paso and Amarillo, Las Cruces, Santa Fe, and Albuquerque.[14] Formerly the home of the Alfalfa Palace and elaborate apple centerpieces, the annual harvest fair in the Pecos Valley changed its name and image to realign with the new realities of cotton.[15] "Sponsored by the Roswell Merchants' association and endorsed by the entire citizenship," the carnival was "designed in honor of cotton" and featured the crop prominently in agricultural displays.[16] Yet the carnival celebrated much more than cotton; it celebrated a new, cotton-centered teleology of western expansion and served as a moment of collective cultural storytelling. "More than cotton, and . . . more than a carnival," the *Roswell Daily Record* explained in 1924, the event was about "education," "visiting," and the "wonderful possibilities of the soil of the fertile Pecos valley." The carnival featured an Old Timers Parade with "western pioneers" (Elizabeth Garrett among them), "cowboy dances," and a "mammoth historical pageant" that involved hundreds of participants and traced "the development from the early days of the Indians on down to the present."[17] Cotton, as an economic force but also as a powerful cultural symbol, brought people together to craft new stories about their past, present, and future. Cotton in the Pecos Valley, one enthusiastic carnival booster proclaimed in 1927, "will undoubtedly produce . . . the means of livelihood of thousands of people for generations to come. So we enter the carnival to honor the king, Cotton. Let us show due respect to that king."[18]

Cotton festivals throughout the region continued for decades. Eventually Las Cruces and Tularosa developed their own festivals. People throughout the region eventually participated not only in these cotton carnivals but also in the Maid of Cotton pageants put on by the Cotton, Inc.[19] Even across the U.S.-Mexico border, in Ciudad Juárez, where farmers likewise switched to large acreages of cotton following the construction of Elephant Butte Dam, a cotton festival emerged by the 1930s.[20] The embrace of cotton by communities throughout the region reveals that cotton was more than simply a source of income for a few well-off farmers; it affected the entire economy of the region. Cotton-growing communities throughout the New Mexico region viewed the crop as an important element of their cultural stories that, as the historical pageants of the early Roswell cotton carnivals and the 1926 El Paso event illustrate, folded the new commodity from the South into familiar frontier narratives of the U.S. West.

The commingling of South and West extended beyond cultural narratives and into the cotton fields themselves. Irrigated cotton production in the New Mexico region, firmly built on the same tenets of efficient, organized, and scientifically managed irrigated agriculture that defined cotton regions throughout the U.S. West, nonetheless retained elements of southern-style cotton growing not widely seen further west. New Mexico lacked the extremely large cotton farms of California, Arizona, and southern Texas; its large farms that did exist were often individually rather than corporately owned, with paternalistic labor structures.[21] New Mexico also had smaller farms—averaging just over thirty acres—and, principally due to a large landowning Hispanic population in the Rio Grande Valley, a much higher number of owner-operators than elsewhere in the cotton-growing West in the interwar years.[22] The region nonetheless witnessed changes in landownership patterns and a sharp rise in tenancy and sharecropping consistent with cotton growing throughout the country. White newcomers tended to supplant, but by no means entirely displace, older Hispanic farmers, and a new class of mostly Hispanic New Mexican and Mexican tenant and sharecropper cotton farmers emerged.

The region's earliest and most prominent large-scale cotton growers brought experiences of cotton production from both the U.S. West and the U.S. South that, along with the labor and expertise of a mostly Mexican workforce, reveal a conglomerate of approaches to industrial agriculture within the region. The case of Louis J. Ivey, an enormously influential cotton farmer who spearheaded cotton production throughout the Elephant Butte Irrigation District, provides an illustration of the close connections in early cotton production among New Mexico, Arizona, and California. Ivey had spent his youth in the cotton belt of central Texas and, still in his twenties, had "planted the first [cotton] crop at Calexico in the Imperial Valley."[23] "As is generally known," Ivey recalled decades later, "I planted the first commercial crop [in the Elephant Butte District] in 1918, bringing seed from my farm in California. I supplied this seed to all who wished to plant." Ivey provided not only seed but also, for seven years, purchased 75 percent of all local cotton, as well as cotton from parts of southern Arizona.

"After coming to El Paso and until 1925," Ivey explained, "I handled from sixty to seventy-five thousand bales per annum. My shipments and sales were made to domestic mills and mills in England, France, Germany, Spain, Japan, China, and Canada."[24] Ivey built his own gin. He eventually built twenty-one gins in El Paso and Doña Ana counties, as well as a cottonseed oil mill in Mesa, Arizona. Ivey's vertically integrated, global cotton business model mirrored that of large cotton firms in California, Arizona, and south Texas.

Other large farms in the region provided more paternalistic models of large-scale cotton production that focused on a large, highly trained workforce rather than on contracted tenant farmers. Deane Stahmann, for example, planted nine hundred acres of cotton near Ivey's farms in Fabens, Texas, and in 1925 bought the three-thousand-acre former Santo Tomás land grant in the Mesilla Valley with plans to devote up to $100,000 and three thousand acres toward cotton production. Within a few years his large farm, which would eventually span multiple generations and hemispheres to become the self-proclaimed "largest Pecan farm in the world," contained eleven separate "colonias" and a full commissary to house, feed, clothe, and otherwise supply his large workforce of mostly Mexican laborers and their families. While within a few decades pecans eventually reigned on Stahmann's farm, cotton was by far the biggest crop on the farm in its initial decades.[25] Stahmann's farm eventually even bred its own cotton varieties, some of which proved significant in later commercial and university breeding efforts.[26] Missourian William Henry Harroun provided a similar example of a paternalistic, large-scale cotton farm in the Pecos Valley. Harroun first planted cotton in 1917 and by 1940 had 2,570 acres of cotton, making it one of the largest cotton operations in the state. Thirty families lived year-round on the ranch, which had its own store and state-maintained school. The ranch employed and housed fifty year-round farmhands and its own tractor mechanics, store clerks, carpenters, truck drivers, and teachers; during the harvest it hired up to one hundred more itinerant workers—"Okies" from farther east and Mexicans. The sheer size, high degree of vertical integration, and paternalistic nature of cotton farms such as Harroun's and Stahmann's in the region led some observers to note their resemblance to the antebellum southern plantation model. "Here is a plantation," wrote John Collier Jr. (son of the BIA director) about William Henry Harroun's cotton farm in 1940, "complete as the cotton kingdoms of the old South."[27]

The Tyranny of Homogeneity

In New Mexico, as well as throughout west and south Texas, Southern-style paternalism often aligned with emerging doctrines of scientific management and ideals of industrial efficiency. This "industrial ideal," espoused by government officials and college-trained researchers and prevalent on large farms throughout the West, emphasized highly rationalized and organized factory-like farm systems that maximized efficiencies to successfully compete in national and global markets.[28] With the government's stake greatly increased by federal investments in the West, government officials and researchers encouraged growers to organize around cash crops that could not be grown more efficiently elsewhere in the country. Many adherents of this ideal nonetheless viewed crop diversification as an efficient, integral part of agricultural industrialism; they did not initially see agricultural industrialism as necessarily at odds with yeomanly ideals of self-sufficiency. By the Second World War, however, a sense of inevitable monoculture, adjoined with stratified labor models, pervaded the ideal.

The widespread adoption of cotton in New Mexico led some contemporary observers to worry that a largely unrealized industrial ideal had descended into an industrial problem as many growers sacrificed the health of their soil, their laborers, and their local institutions to cash in on high cotton prices and maximize short-term profits. Many growers in the twenties devoted "their entire holdings, including their traditional family gardens," to cotton; while prices were high, they "frequently planted [cotton] right up to the dwellings on farms, for it was more profitable to grow cotton and purchase staple foods than to maintain a vegetable garden." The percentage of alfalfa grown in irrigated lands in the Mesilla Valley dropped 40 percent by the late twenties, and most commercial fruit orchards disappeared altogether.[29] Voices of caution mounted in government reports, extension bulletins, and local newspapers as the landscape rapidly transitioned from a relative patchwork of orchards and fields of alfalfa and vegetables to a more uniform sea of irrigated cotton. "So important has cotton become in the last few years, and so rapid has been the increase in the number of acres planted," one geographer reported in 1931, "that some uneasiness is being felt by the more conservative farmers of the region for fear that it will become a one-crop area."[30] In fact, "some uneasiness" may have been an understatement. "Cotton is king and it looks very much as if he had added the Mesilla Valley to his dominions, but farmers need to watch his reign," the *Rio Grande Farmer* warned in 1923. "Cotton may become a tyrant, a soil robber and finally spell the ruin of the fertile valley."

Many contemporary observers understood soil health to be foundational to the long-term economic and social health of their communities. "No system of agriculture can be permanent and consistently prosperous that does not provide for maintenance of soil fertility," the *Rio Grande Farmer* admonished. "This means crop rotation and the use of livestock on the farm." Yet by the midtwenties, despite significant signs of soil depletion due to unrotated cotton plantings, many farmers, especially the smaller-scale and less capitalized farmers, continued to plant the cash crop with diminishing returns.[31] Throughout the decade, irrigation districts, which had a stake in the long-term soil health of the region in part because they needed farmers to be able to pay off dam construction debt, became accustomed to hearing a lot of "criticism of our farmers for having adopted a one crop system." In various reports and newsletters, officials urged farmers to grow cotton in a "systematic and well planned crop rotation" that dedicated 50 percent of available land to soil-building crops and avoided planting the crop "on the same ground more than once in three years." In one newsletter they offered, from the climatically similar Turkestan, a time-tested crop rotation, which involved seven crops over the course of eight years.[32] Various commentators also warned against creating more alkaline soils through overirrigation and increasing pest pressure by forgoing rotations. The state college, for its part, continually advocated for crop rotations in cotton culture, and even released a bulletin advising farmers to interplant cotton with corn or cowpeas as a "trap crop" for bollworms.[33]

The many calls for diversification were not meant to curb the trend of industrialization in agriculture, but rather to encourage it with longer-term economic benefits and efficiencies. The industrial ideal of the interwar period, in other words, was not synonymous with large-scale, undiversified monocropping. Indeed, despite the propensity of most growers to forgo crop rotations or diversification to cash in on high cotton prices, several of the largest farms—the ones that could afford it—invested acreage and money into soil health through diversified livestock, cover crops, and interplantings. As I examine in depth in the following chapter, no farm better illustrates the role of diversification within the interwar industrial ideal than the three-thousand-acre Stahmann Farms outside of Las Cruces.

Yet even smaller farms in the region grew cotton within a diversified system. The *Reclamation Record* and the *Rio Grande Farmer* often highlighted smaller farms that had profitably diversified their cotton operations. The *Record*, for example, described Tom Watson, a cotton farmer in the Texas side of the Elephant Butte Irrigation District, who grew seventy acres in cotton and twenty-five in alfalfa in 1923. "Farmers in the El Paso Valleys can not afford to confine their operations exclusively to cotton, because no one is in position to say exactly what buyers will pay for lint," Watson argued in the *Record*. "I believe a farmer should have an abundant supply of milk on the farm, about 100 good laying hens, a few hogs, a home garden, and a family orchard." The *Rio Grande Farmer*, eager to highlight a successful and diversified farm, reported on the success of J. J. Hoskins's farm near Anthony. Hoskins interplanted twenty acres of cotton and cabbage, netting $600 per acre; he heavily manured his fields and devoted significant additional acreage to cantaloupes, melons, lettuce, sugar beets, and green beans.[34] Farm Bureau president James Quesenberry similarly emphasized that while he had success with growing cotton principally on his farm, he also grew cantaloupes and cabbage to avoid "putting all his eggs in one basket."[35]

The call for crop diversification had as much to do with labor and social concerns as it did with concerns of soil health. Cotton is labor-intensive, but only during a few times of the year and especially during the harvest. As farmers tore up orchards to make room for cotton, they not only lost potential supplemental income streams to hedge their agricultural bets, they also lost a use for laborers at slow times of the year in the cotton-growing cycle, particularly in the winter, when orchard-pruning would otherwise have helped keep a permanent labor supply in the area. Commentators made the case that crop diversity increased the health of the community as it increased the health of the soil precisely because it spread out labor demands and obviated the need for large numbers of hired laborers and, worse, itinerant laborers. Crop diversification meant staggered work schedules that would help maintain a less stratified, more yeomanly society of self-sufficient farmers. "No agricultural community that depended upon a single crop system of agriculture was ever consistently prosperous," the *Rio Grande Farmer* declared. The paper continued its economic argument for crop diversification with a yeomanly appeal:

> No system of agriculture that requires a large amount of hired labor and cash outlay for labor at one season of the year and a large amount

of idle time on the farmer's hands at other times can result in a prosperous community. Diversification of crops, supplemented by livestock, means continuous employment for the farmer, less necessity for high priced hired labor at any one time and a source of income, because of the variety. . . .

No community dependent on agriculture as the original source of its wealth can be consistently prosperous unless that agriculture is so organized as to provide a continuous income to the farmer. That means a variety of crops and livestock products, some of which go on the market at all seasons of the year.

No agricultural community can be consistently prosperous unless the farmers produce all the food and other products consumed on the farm than can produced on that farm cheaper than they can purchased on the market. . . .

Plan your farm business about one or two major farm enterprises and select other enterprises which can be coordinated with these. Dairying, truck driving, cotton and alfalfa, etc. But do not become a one crop farmer, rob your soil, be idle a large part of the year and hire expensive labor during the rush season.

Class and race concerns undergirded appeals for self-sufficiency. As the supposed "agricultural ladder" became ever more illusory and even farcical, the presence of permanent, dispossessed farm laborers contradicted mythic ideals of yeomanly self-sufficiency. Throughout the cotton-growing West in the first decades of the twentieth century, racial tensions closely interwove with labor concerns.[36] In New Mexico, a Chaves County Department of Public Welfare official alluded to race and class concerns with a succinct response to a 1940 government questionnaire on a possible migrant camp. A migrant camp is a bad idea, he argued; it would only "encourage more of the undesirable class of people to come to the [Pecos] valley."[37]

Despite the success of several diversified cotton farms, most growers planted cotton, and only cotton. A proliferation of large-

and medium-scale, undiversified cotton farms created new labor demands that the local population could not meet. The more homogenous cotton landscape created a more diverse and economically stratified population demographic, as farmworkers moved into and through the region. Mexicans, fleeing the turmoil of the Revolution, provided the bulk of the workforce. "Labor is abundant," remarked state senator J. E. Reinburg in 1923 in regard to cotton. "All that is necessary is to go to the international bridge and haul your pickers to the ranch in car or truck."[38] Yet, as the new U.S. border patrol and increased immigration restrictions took hold, growers began to seek labor elsewhere. By the end of the decade, as dryland agriculture failed in the southern Plains, a pattern of migratory labor, largely fueled by cotton-picking demands, connected the greater Southwest, from Oklahoma to California. "Only in areas near the large towns is the bulk of the cotton picked by Spanish-American or Mexican labor," a government report concluded in 1940. "Negroes from the Deep South come in to pick from time to time, but only in comparatively small numbers . . . for the most part, the migratory farm workers who pick cotton in southern New Mexico are Anglo-Americans from the States east of New Mexico, mostly Oklahoma and Texas."[39]

By the end of the 1920s and throughout the 1930s, many farms, especially in the Pecos Valley, depended on migrant labor. By 1940, 40 percent of the total cotton crop was picked by migrant labor; government officials concluded that migrants were "required" for a successful harvest. Widespread calls for diversification among officials had largely dissipated, only to be replaced with discussions of creating migrant labor camps. In southern New Mexico "the need for migratory labor to assist cotton picking reflected, to some degree at least," one report concluded with a tone of accepting the inevitable, "the development of large-scale farming."[40] Indeed Carey McWilliams, reflecting in 1942 on how "once prosperous small-farming communities have become desert sweat-shops" across the cotton-growing West, concluded that "occupational stratification is an inevitable concomitant of industrial agriculture."[41] As the war began, agricultural industrialization no longer shared common ground with earnest calls for yeomanly self-sufficiency and diversification among many scientific researchers, government officials, and social critics; industrialized agriculture had become largely synonymous with one-crop farming and a migrant workforce.

The shift to undiversified agriculture and its consummate reliance on cheap, temporary labor further eroded the *salus populi* ideals previously associated with agricultural industrialization. As I discussed in the first chapter, turn-of-the-century horticultural boards throughout New Mexico had mandated pesticide spraying in the name of public welfare, explicitly equating disease in commercial orchards to disease in human bodies. Concerns for *salus populi* had extended to agricultural management. Yet the living conditions and public health problems associated with migrant workers undercut this logic. "In general, the conditions under which these people live and work while picking cotton in Southern New Mexico are unhealthy and unpleasant," a 1940 government survey on migratory labor succinctly concluded. The plight of migrants, highlighted by contemporaries such as Carey McWilliams, Paul Taylor, and John Steinbeck, as well as scores of scholars since, is generally well known.[42] In southern New Mexico, migrant cotton pickers frequently camped under cottonwoods with only ditch water to drink. They commonly experienced dysentery and sometimes more serious disease outbreaks such as typhoid, received minimal or no medical services, and most often had to send their children to help in fields instead of to school.[43] The deplorable living conditions in migrant cotton camps show us how the requirements of an undiversified cotton industry redefined public welfare beyond the human body to the health of plants, excluding some humans' bodies altogether. Large cotton monocultures that relied on disease-prone migrant camps to succeed became antithetical to the *salus populi*.

Migrant labor reoriented both the human geography and the geography of resource extraction in the Southwest. The cotton crop in New Mexico and Arizona provided a winter "migrant way station" for westbound migrants headed to the fields of California. "New Mexico serves as a passageway for migratory labor moving westward from Oklahoma and Texas [that provides a] considerable portion of the seasonal labor harvesting the cotton crop in New Mexico," a government report explained. "Southern New Mexico may be regarded as a corridor between the Southern Great Plains and southern Arizona and California."[44] Cotton, being winter-harvested, provided the necessary conduit crop for many westbound workers to pay their way to spring work in California. As commercial cotton farmers increasingly relied on importing migrant labor to export large amounts of cotton, the geography of resource extraction shifted. For western cotton growers to extract resources—water, sun, soil nutrients—and export them in the form of cotton products, they had to *import* resources in the form of laborers. Except for the few months of harvest, those laborers relied on water, food, and social services provided by far-off watersheds and communities. The new cotton landscape effectively outsourced the resources needed to support the people who grew and harvested the crop.

The Acala Borderlands

Cotton industrialized the agricultural landscape of the Southwest Borderlands and spurred broader and more comprehensive regional cooperation among growers than had any other crop in the region.[45] Agricultural industrialization in the 1920s did not mean that suddenly tractors replaced mules; it did mean, though, that nearly all farmers soon planted the same seed.[46] New Mexico's cotton industry homogenized the landscape not by simply increasing monocultures of one crop, but of one variety of that crop. Such a controlled landscape required far more involvement from the state and more cooperation and uniform growing methods among farmers than previously existed in the region. The highly organized collaborative effort among growers and the state college to build a local economy around a single improved cotton variety transformed the Mesilla Valley into a research hub that in turn reoriented its relationship to the surrounding regional cotton landscape. The emergence of one-variety communities in New Mexico—a phenomenon that originated in California, spread throughout the West and eventually the South, and that has been described by Alan Olmstead and Paul Rhode as one of "the largest and most successful cooperative movements in American agricultural history"—required that every cotton grower plant the same single variety in a given district.[47] The case of Acala cotton—the variety most widely grown in one-variety communities in New Mexico and elsewhere in the West—particularly illustrates the new degrees of organization, regional alliances, and transnational orientation that defined industrial cotton growing in New Mexico.

Acala cotton—developed in southern Mexico, further bred by researchers and farmers throughout the U.S. West, and eventually distributed back to Mexico—bound New Mexico to the greater Southwest and Mexico in new ways. In 1906 and 1907 USDA seed explorer Orator Fuller Cook traveled throughout Guatemala and southern Mexico searching for local cotton varieties that showed early maturation, boll weevil resistance, and long and strong fibers. The most promising variety, whose progeny would eventually shape cotton-growing communities throughout the Southwest, came from "a small patch of cotton" on the outskirts of the town of Acala, Chiapas. The diversified, interplanted, small-scale farm where this Acala seed originated provides an example of how early agricultural industrialization fundamentally relied on nonindustrial, diversified agricultural systems. Cook obtained seed from the owner of a nearby "primitive cotton gin" and returned to the United States, where USDA researchers in Oklahoma and Texas soon developed those seeds into the earliest strains of U.S. Acala cotton.[48] Acala appeared especially to thrive in arid conditions, encouraging researchers in both California and New Mexico to focus on developing an Acala strain suited for the arid West. By the mid-1920s, consensus among many Western cotton-growing communities held Acala superior.[49]

In 1923 Cook traveled to New Mexico to personally make the case for forming one-variety districts.[50] The Mesilla Valley Cotton Growers' Association, however, needed little prodding. The association had formed in 1920 initially to help secure labor and ginning facilities but soon focused on organizing farmers in the valley to grow only a single variety of cotton. In 1922 it bought a carload of Acala seed from the Coachella Valley of California; in January 1923 it officially adopted Acala as the only seed its members would grow. The following year several growers splintered off to form the Mesilla Valley Acala Cotton Growers' Association, the first organization in the state specifically organized around the exclusive planting of a single variety.[51] The group formally agreed to work closely with the state college and its USDA cotton field station. The establishment of the field station in 1926 marked the beginning of a prolific and regionally significant era of seed breeding that included the release of Acala 1517 in 1940, an especially important strain not only to regional growers but to seed breeding programs throughout the country.[52] By 1928 this grower-college collaboration expanded into the New Mexico Crop Improvement Association (NMCIA). Fittingly the group first organized in the state college's cotton field.

The collaboration among growers, the USDA, and the land-grant college proved crucial to the early and lasting success of commercial cotton in the region. The founding of the NMCIA followed a college-led effort throughout the decade to get farmers to more methodically and carefully select the seed of all crops. The NMCIA took on various roles, including inspecting cotton fields and gins, organizing seed roguing workshops, and publishing quarterly newsletters.[53] By the end of the decade twelve local, "regularly organized improvement associations" existed in the state, supplying the NMCIA with "certified beans, potatoes, alfalfa, grain sorghums, corn, wheat, oats, barley, and cotton, and several other crops of lesser importance." Most of this seed remained in New Mexico, but even in 1929 "demands from adjoining states are increasing and some orders have been received from Mexico."[54]

Within a few years the association had helped New Mexico growers develop a regional market for more modern, commercially oriented, certified germ plasm. As El Paso became the market hub for cotton, Las Cruces became the research and germ plasm hub for cotton and other major regional crops.

The rise of southern New Mexico as a borderlands seed hub owed to strong state support, widespread grower cooperation, and climatic advantages. By the onset of the Second World War, state college–bred Acala cotton largely defined the cotton-growing region of New Mexico and far west Texas. "I combine West Texas and New Mexico irrigated cotton," Louis Ivey explained to lawmakers in 1945, because "both use identical cotton variety [acala], depend upon the same source for planting seed and use the same seed breeders, which are directed by the A&M college of Las Cruces, New Mexico . . . [both] have identical soils and water, practically the same elevation and climatic conditions."[55] These climatic conditions—particularly high elevation—resembled those at Acala, Chiapas, which not only helped account for Acala's acclimation to and exceptional performance in southwestern cotton fields, it also made climatically similar cotton districts throughout Mexico potential markets for the improved strains.[56] Further, the shared isolation of these one-variety districts from other cotton districts allowed growers to avoid unwanted cross-pollination and maintain seed purity. "Our farmers believe in the one variety crop principle and adhere to it more closely than do the farmers in any other area in the United States," Ivey further explained. "Our area being isolated its cotton does not become mixed through pollinization [sic] as does cotton in the rain-grown area where hundreds of different varieties are planted in close proximity."[57] O. F. Cook in part corroborated this boast. Soon after the USDA introduced Acala to growers throughout the United States, "the usual mixing with other varieties took place, and seed stocks were allowed to deteriorate," Cook explained in 1932. "At that stage the variety might have been discarded completely if it had not been adopted in some of the irrigated districts of the Southwestern States. One-variety communities for Acala cotton . . . made it possible for the seed to be kept pure. With supplies of pure seed available . . . nearly 900,000 acres of cotton were planted in the irrigated valleys in 1929, and a large proportion of this was Acala."[58]

As Las Cruces established itself as a research hub and "seed center," Acala cotton made its way back to Mexico. While cotton fiber seldom crossed the border due to tariff restrictions, cottonseed both for planting and for oil did.[59] The homogenized cotton landscape extended across the border into Mexico and, increasingly, Juárez Valley growers sought the well-adapted Acala seed for their fields. Juárez growers first produced commercial cotton in the early 1920s. Water scarcity defined agricultural choices for Juárez growers throughout this period, particularly in the 1930s when drought and disputes with the United States regarding flows from Elephant Butte intensified.[60] "We were forced to grow cotton because of lack of water," one Juárez Valley farmer explained in 1954. "Before Elephant Butte and Caballo Lakes were constructed on the American side, there was enough water and [we] were able to grow corn, wheat, beans and alfalfa as well as cotton."[61] Nonetheless, by 1939, the Juárez Valley was among the leading cotton-supplying districts in northern Mexico, with twenty thousand acres of land that produced, according to one economist, the "best quality cotton in Mexico." Officials with the Mexican National Department of Agriculture urged Juárez Valley farmers to fight insects and drought by planting only "fumigated, certified" Acala seed in their fields, which the NMCIA was more than willing to provide.[62] In 1947 the NMCIA sold 280 tons of cotton planting seed to "various interests in Mexico including the Department of Mexico," who, according to NMCIA treasurer J. T. Stovall, were "extremely anxious to plant our New Mexico acala 1517 cotton."[63] Demand is high, Stovall explained, because "Mexico's climatic soil and cultural conditions are so nearly the same [as New Mexico] that our cotton is particularly suited for the production of cotton from New Mexico Acala cotton."[64]

Between the world wars the global empire of industrial cotton spread into the newly irrigated lands of southern New Mexico and far west Texas and reshaped regional cultural, socioeconomic, and environmental connections. Recent transplants from further east, enticed by the glint of white gold, settled in the region and bought up newly reclaimed lands and older farmlands alike. With the new tide of cotton-driven migration, the agricultural labor systems and cultural associations of the Old South arrived as well. As cotton acreage grew, so too did regional grower cooperation and a reliance on migrant labor; cotton bound not only the region's growers but also the laborers—from Mexico and, later, from the U.S. South—that followed the cotton harvest. Cotton shared climatic preferences with the arid Southwest and Mexico that also bound those regions in new ways. The cotton culture of New Mexico, enmeshed in a regional cotton culture that extended from Oklahoma and Texas to California to points throughout Mexico, became a highly organized but never fully homogenized cotton-growing region unique to its position in the borderlands.

The new cotton landscape of interwar New Mexico reveals changing ideals of industrial agriculture. Made possible by major reclamation projects, cotton played a significant role in the agricultural industrialization of southern New Mexico. Growers organized around single varieties, collaborating with USDA and state college experiment stations to develop, maintain, and disseminate highly productive and profitable strains of cotton. Although these efforts encouraged a radical new level of crop homogeneity within the emerging ideals of industrial efficiency, early calls for such highly managed cotton culture also made room for crop diversification, small-scale yeomanly self-sufficiency, and varied approaches to managing labor. The process of industrialization in New Mexico's cotton fields followed a winding and contingent path.

Diversification, Paternalism, and the Transnational Threads of Cotton in Southern New Mexico

The Industrial Ideal at Work at Stahmann Farms, 1926–70

"If the farmers back home in Vermillion County could see what I've seen today," the Pulitzer Prize–winning reporter Ernie Pyle wrote enthusiastically in 1939, "they'd swear the age of miracles was here." Pyle had just visited Stahmann Farms, a four-thousand-acre farm twenty-five miles north of the Mexican border in New Mexico's Mesilla Valley. To contemporary observers such as Pyle, the farm defied easy categorization: it was at once a cutting-edge and trendsetting modern wonder of technological innovation but also a nostalgic throwback to a diversified, nonmortgaged family farm. It was immense but noncorporate, farsighted but profitable, diversified but efficient. It was a place where a blond-haired farm owner sang Mexican songs in Spanish, where the workers earned pensions, and where large profits came from products as familiar as cotton and as strange as goose feathers, chicken manure, and an obscure nut that most Americans were not sure how to pronounce. Despite all its oddities, the formula seemed to work. Deane Stahmann, Pyle concluded, "makes money like Henry Ford, and he does it by the same formula—mass production and brains. . . . He's looking forward farther than any man I've ever written about." All added together, Pyle declared, Deane Stahmann "is probably the outstanding farmer in the Southwest."[1]

Over the course of roughly four decades, from the founding of the farm in 1926 to the farm's last cotton crop in the early seventies, Stahmann Farms gained success by embracing a diversified crop regime and paternalistic labor structure that upended simple narratives depicting agricultural industrialization as a linear path toward monoculture and ever more exploitative labor practices. Cotton, perhaps the quintessential symbol of monoculture, became a somewhat unlikely linchpin for the success of the borderlands farm. Even as the farm diversified, it continued to grow vast acreages of the fiber crop and developed a far-reaching cotton-breeding program. Following Deane Stahmann's death in 1970 and the maturation of large numbers of pecan trees, the farm phased cotton out of its rotation—and an era of paternalism and diversified industrial agriculture passed.

Stahmann Farms succeeded not only because of its efficient, multicrop designs but also through its ability to effectively navigate geopolitical and cultural borders. The borderlands farm benefitted from its proximity to Mexico by gaining access to a reliable workforce and a market for products; in turn, a thread of *mexicanidad* wove through the fields and culture of the farm. The farm was not simply a space worked upon remotely by power brokers in distant cities. Rather it was a site of homespun, intricate, interwoven connections—at once transnational and local—that facilitated the cotton economy in southern New Mexico and shaped the borderlands in ways that no distant financier or politician could have anticipated. These relationships not only illuminate the greater economic and cultural fabric of the borderlands, they also demonstrate the important but often overlooked roles of nonindustrial traditions in modern agricultural industrialism. Like many large twentieth-century farms that sought a more modern, efficient, profitable business, Stahmann Farms succeeded only through cultural negotiations and adaptations by farmer and farmworker alike. Its embrace of an industrial ideal that imagined perfect efficiency compelled Stahmann Farms to adopt and rely on agricultural traditions born far from the imaginings of industry.

Midcentury Diversification and the Modern Goose

No farm in the Southwest embraced the interwar industrial ideal of crop diversification more, and no farm carried that ideal farther into the postwar twentieth century than did the four-thousand-acre Stahmann Farms. Deane Stahmann and his father, W. J. Stahmann, a Wisconsin buggy maker with over a decade of success raising cotton, tomatoes, and honeybees near Fabens, Texas, bought the Santo Tomás Land Grant in 1926 and founded Stahmann Farms. The farm instantly became one of the largest cotton farms in the entire region.[2] A decade later the farm purchased the 1,100 neighboring acres known as Snow Farm, perhaps an apt name for a landscape that would soon see flurries of snowy white cotton residue in its late autumn breezes.

Like elsewhere throughout the southern reaches of the irrigated Southwest in the 1920s and early 1930s, cotton, in the beginning, was king. The farm built its own gin and press and regularly planted over 1,500 acres in cotton.[3] Yet, over the course of four decades, King Cotton bowed to a plurality of other crops on the farm as it became one of several key parts in an innovative, diversified system that successfully blended modern industrial and retooled preindustrial methods. From the early thirties through the late sixties, the farm shifted its crop regimes, at times growing sugar beets, cantaloupe, alfalfa, and sorghum, and raising livestock such as sheep, Hereford cattle, and chickens. The crops that worked best with each other and that proved most profitable were cotton and cottonseed, alfalfa, geese, and pecans.[4]

In addition to growing large acreages of cotton, the farm diversified its income stream by developing a highly intensive cotton-breeding program. The initiative began around 1937, when Stahmann became frustrated with the research at the New Mexico College of Agriculture and Mechanic Arts (later the New Mexico State University), which he felt prioritized selecting for disease or insect resistance or for glandless varieties, rather than for qualities such as uniformity, length, or fiber strength, which mill owners desired.[5] By 1941 Stahmann was selling a thousand tons of cottonseed to cotton farms throughout the region.[6] Using Acala 1450 cotton bred at the state college, Stahmann developed two lines of cotton, Mesa Acala and Mesilla Valley Acala, the latter of which he subsequently developed into Del Cerro, a strain grown throughout the irrigated West for much of the twentieth century.[7]

Cotton breeding requires patience and long-term vision. The breeder must wait a full growing season to see how each plant performs before selecting seed. To partly overcome this hurdle, Stahmann employed a few of the most modern technologies available —greenhouses and airplanes—to develop strategies for obtaining two cotton-growing seasons per year instead of one. He began in 1941 by constructing, according to one report, "probably the first cotton greenhouse on a southwestern farm," hoping it would double the number of grow-outs per year.[8] When this effort proved insufficient, Stahmann decided to expand his experiments into warmer countries where he could grow out a generation of cotton during the winter. In addition to maintaining an experimental plot on his farm and eventually developing a 384-acre isolation plot west of Hatch, New Mexico,[9] Stahmann opened a research farm for cotton breeding in southern Mexico in 1949 and later bought 435 acres of farmland in Jamaica to breed cotton.[10] Stahmann built an airstrip on the farm and eventually converted a B-26 bomber for interfarm transport. Heavy rains (and fears that Fidel Castro would shoot down his planes), however, led him to abandon his breeding project in Jamaica and instead grow bananas, coconut, cacao, and sugar cane. By 1965, still committed to breeding a better cotton variety, Stahmann had shifted his breeding efforts to farms in Peru and Ecuador.[11]

Stahmann's cotton-breeding efforts in southern Mexico represented a homecoming of sorts for the Acala cotton with which he experimented. Four decades after USDA seed explorer Orator Fuller Cook's first expedition to the village of Acala in Chiapas, Stahmann decided to further breed the progeny of that seed, which had been manipulated for forty seed generations by USDA and state college researchers, in the region in which it had evolved. A year after he began his operations in Mexico, Stahmann explained his breeding efforts as a way of combating "foreign varieties."[12] Such explanation came with no shortage of irony, given that this effort against "foreign varieties" involved breeding Acala strains, originally from Mexico, in foreign countries (including Mexico).

As much as cotton and cotton breeding were central to Stahmann Farms, cotton hardly became a monocultural tyrant there. Even as early as 1932, as cotton prices sharply fluctuated and the government officials discussed (and soon passed) measures such as quotas on cotton acreage and price stabilization, Stahmann became nervous about relying on a single commodity. He searched for a long-term solution; his gaze fell on a little-known nut tree that state horticulturalist Dr. Fabián García had recently reported with cautious optimism might do well for growers in southern New Mexico. Although scattered seedling varieties of pecans had grown in southern New Mexico for several decades, García had published the results from the first state college experiments with commercial pecan varieties in 1924. In line with the interwar industrial ideal that viewed diversification as concomitant to modernity and agricultural progress, García viewed the pecan as a potentially valuable addition to diversified farms: "Naturally, as the agriculture of the State becomes more highly developed and farming operations more extensive, the more diversification in agricultural activities will have to take place." In a major underestimation of the tree's future success, García concluded, "It is quite likely that the pecan will never become as important a crop in New Mexico as in its native states, but there is no reason why trees of the better adapted varieties should not be more widely planted."[13]

Stahmann took an even more optimistic view. Stahmann purchased the farm's first pecan trees in 1932, interplanted them among the cotton, and immediately became the first large-scale commercial pecan grower in the region. Stahmann's interest in pecans lay not simply in recently successful experiments in New Mexico but also in their perennial nature. In Stahmann's words, it "looked like the country was going socialistic"; he feared the U.S. government might break up large farms and adopt land policies similar to those of post-Revolution Mexico. Hoping the principle of Mexican agrarian law that forbade subdivision of land planted in fruit or nut trees would similarly catch on in the United States, Stahmann decided to "get out of the cotton raising business and begin raising pecans."[14] Stahmann's pecan trees, rooted in the turbulent political atmosphere of the Dust Bowl thirties and the aftermath of post-Revolution Mexico, thus stand as quiet reminders of Mexico's often surprising influence on the New Mexico landscape.

Similar to cotton breeding, pecans required long-term vision. While they begin to fruit after seven years, the trees reach their production peak only after fifty years. Thus the decision to grow pecans involved a plan to continue growing annual crops such as cotton, between the young trees, for decades. Stahmann's bet on pecans also required a long-term marketing plan to persuade American palates to include the previously fringe nut. Stahmann understood that aggressive marketing and advertising were crucial to a modern farm's success. Unfazed by the pecan's lack of popularity, Stahmann planned—as Ernie Pyle wryly reported in 1939—to "advertise, propagandize, beat the drums, and turn us into a nation of pecan eaters whether we like it or not."[15]

By the late 1940s, however, Stahmann had some persistent problems on the farm that even advertising could not fix. One was soil fertility. He was purchasing the entire manure stockpile from nearby Fort Bliss, Texas, for an annual bill of thirty thousand dollars.[16] Horse manure often contained weed seed and rocks that clogged machinery, and was relatively low on key nutrients such as phosphorus and nitrogen, thus representing an expensive investment on a merely adequate product.[17] Another problem was labor. Despite its diversification the farm still had seasonal fluctuations in labor demand that, much to Stahmann's chagrin, made hiring temporary laborers necessary. He searched for ways to create work during the off-season to maintain a permanent labor supply that could handle all the farm's work and obviate the need for additional workers during seasonal rushes. For both problems, Stahmann found a surprising solution in a millennia-old technology: the Chinese weeder goose. Stahmann's addition of this heirloom goose to the farm in 1948 drastically reduced fertilizer costs and labor expenses involved in weeding, while creating year-round work for both men and women that proved essential to maintaining a year-round workforce of families.

Chinese weeder geese love to eat most young tender plants. One of the few exceptions is cotton, which they avoid as they chomp the surrounding herbage. To take advantage of these dietary preferences, workers at the farm would round up the geese at one side of a field, while placing large tanks of water on the opposite end of the field. Attracted to the water, the geese made their way across the fields, weeding and fertilizing as they went, until they reached their mobile watering holes. Working with the ornery geese was few workers' favorite task, but it took only a few people instead of scores to weed acres of cotton. By some estimates two geese could easily weed an acre, replacing the work of twelve laborers. The geese became so popular throughout the cotton-growing South over the course of the following two decades that one Louisiana cotton grower and goose breeder estimated that over a million geese were put to work in the fields in 1963. That same year the University of Tennessee published a report concluding that using geese to weed saved a cotton farmer $21 per acre compared to using herbicides and $26 per acre compared to weeding by hoe. As one former bracero remarked, "It's a sad thing to be replaced by a machine, but to be replaced by a goose is even worse."[18]

To Stahmann the value of the birds went beyond their work in the fields. By the end of the decade Stahmann had become the largest goose-meat processor in the country. Although national goose sales had been falling, Stahmann developed a strategy to market the fowl as "junior geese," which proved popular with "food editors and housewives."[19] Reviving an old tradition of a "Christmas goose," Stahmann again fused older, nostalgic notions of American agriculture with modern, industrial methods. He advertised his geese throughout the nation. "The goose will hang high this holiday season," read one article in the special Christmas edition of an Illinois newspaper, "if a New Mexico farmer can convince American housewives." Assuring readers that Stahmann's geese were not the "overfat bird of yesteryear," the article explained that Stahmann was employing modern techniques—including the modern, balanced diet full of vitamins and giving them an "airconditioned hotel"—in his effort "to stage a comeback for a one-time favorite table treat."[20] The effort proved successful: by 1954 the farm was annually selling nearly two hundred thousand birds nationwide.[21]

In addition to meat, geese provided other income streams. Stahmann built hatcheries and a processing plant capable of dressing and freezing two thousand geese a day. To keep this processing plant running at maximum capacity, he developed another income stream. He sold and "rented" geese to farmers both within the region and throughout the U.S. South. He sold goslings to nearby farmers, who fattened them up on their weeds, then sold them back to Stahmann ten to twelve weeks later. In addition to the meat, Stahmann sold goose down to pillow factories; quills to pen factories; and, according to some accounts, the "honk" to Walt Disney.[22] The goose business became so successful that, according to a *Life* article in 1954, Stahmann began to consider planting only weeds on his four thousand acres. "We hope he doesn't," concluded the *Life* editorialists. "Even if he could make more money that way, business's gain would be art's loss."[23]

Geese were not the only animals on the farm. During the 1940s the farm raised Herefords and sheep; it raised chickens for eggs and fertilizer from 1955 to 1977. By 1965 the farm was gathering and selling 124,000 eggs daily, which it sold to local markets and, via his aircraft, to distant buyers. To feed both geese and chickens Stahmann built a feed mill and manufactured fourteen types of poultry feed based on "formulas set by computers."[24] Although he continued to raise chickens, Stahmann quit the geese business in the late 1960s, around the same time the farm shifted away from growing cotton.[25] Stahmann's use of modern technology to efficiently make use of chicken manure (in lieu of synthetic fertilizer) and weeder geese (bred over several millennia by Chinese peasants) again illustrates a diversified farming model rooted firmly in both modern scientific and in nonindustrial methods.

"Futuristic" Paternalism

Stahmann diversified in part to solve the "labor problem" that plagued cotton growers throughout the country. Stahmann's geese, chicken, and pecan operations helped spread out labor demands and provide year-round jobs for the farm's permanent workforce, both men and women. Men worked in the fields at farm-related tasks, such as machining, blacksmithing, plumbing, and carpentry; women worked in the plants that processed the pecans, geese, and chickens.[26] Fewer men were needed to weed in the summer; more women were required to process the geese throughout the year. The result was a more gender-balanced workforce that allowed Stahmann to hire entire families, who were much more likely to stay than single workers. "Deane Stahmann . . . intended to keep his workers busy all the time," former farm manager Luis Sánchez later explained, "so he had to use his system of diversifying his farm into crops that rotated. They were year round, for the purpose of keeping his people busy. . . . He tried to keep his people and keep his people's people employed all the time."[27]

While diversifying crops spread out labor requirements year-round, Stahmann still had the large task of attracting families to the rural, isolated farm and then retaining their labor year after year. Over the course of Deane Stahmann's life, he tried many strategies to secure labor. One year in Tornillo, Stahmann attempted sharecropping, a system he came to adamantly deplore. He later relied on and advocated for government subsidies for labor during the thirties; employed POWs in the forties; hired braceros in the forties and fifties; and vociferously supported looser border policies for Mexican workers.[28] Reliance on itinerant labor, however, proved costly and inefficient for Stahmann.[29]

Stahmann sought to circumvent the need for itinerant labor by developing a paternalistic company town that provided housing; a pension plan for all workers; and a range of services that included a church, a school, a power plant, a health clinic, a commissary, and blacksmith and machine shops. The paternalistic model largely achieved the desired result. Many workers stayed at the farm year after year; even workers' children sometimes eventually made careers for themselves on the farm. Adapted over the years the paternalistic model lasted only as long as crop diversification on the farm. Stahmann's paternalism contained echoes of southern plantation-era paternalism, as well as Mexican patronage systems, yet neither can adequately explain the emergence of his brand of paternalism in the mid-twentieth century. This model was an outcrop of the modern industrial ideal—built on diversification and vertical integration—that emerged in the twentieth century. It was driven by modern industry, yet incorporated elements of a nonindustrial past. As Douglas Flamming argued about southern mill-village paternalism in the twentieth century, this type of paternalism was a response to early twentieth-century labor trends; it "was not a throwback to the past but a manifestation of regional modernization."[30]

Workers welcomed many of the farm town's features, which were essential to making habitable an area with poor roads and few nearby services. Stahmann began building homes, which he provided rent-free to workers, in the 1930s; he continually improved the plans over the years. Initial homes were simple two-room adobes with electricity but without bathrooms; subsequent homes had three rooms, a bathroom, a sink, and gas stoves. Although the farm encouraged a family-based workforce, single men also worked there. Housing for single men provided much less space; braceros typically shared a room with up to four other workers. The farm also built a commissary, a schoolhouse, and medical clinic. When the polio vaccine came out in the early 1950s, a mobile vaccination truck drove to each farm colonia.[31] Like company towns throughout the nation, the farm had its own baseball team.[32]

While providing workers with housing and services such as a commissary were not unique to Stahmann's farm among large cotton growers in the region, the scale of the town and its breadth of services certainly were. Yet most unique to the farm were not the brick-and-mortar services but rather Stahmann's development of a pension plan for workers beginning in 1945. "In 1945, whoever would have thought of a hired hand doing menial laborer type work of chopping cotton being involved in something like that [pension program]?" recalled former farm manager Luis Sánchez. "It was unheard of. [In] organized labor, perhaps. But in a farming operation . . . it just wasn't done." In fact it came thirty-four years before the United Farm Workers developed the Juan de la Cruz pension plan, which has been incorrectly labeled the "first and only functioning pension program for farm workers in the United States."[33]

Under the Stahmann plan, workers initially agreed to contribute to a retirement fund that would provide workers over sixty-five with $45 a month. This plan then developed into a system in which workers invested in the farm with any amount they could afford and received their payments back plus interest, which increased to 10 percent after four years and up to 30 percent after several more years, whenever they decided to leave. A few years later Stahmann developed a cash-bonus system based on the farm's yearly profits. To workers such as Luis Sánchez, such a system represented a forward-thinking approach to labor. "Deane Stahmann . . . [was] extremely ahead of his times," explained Sánchez. "He was a man who saw a pension plan in 1945. That's very futuristic. For back in those days. Even today."[34]

Stahmann's workplace incentives constituted an innovative, farsighted, and progressive approach to agricultural employment that led many workers to describe their experiences on the farm in a positive light. But the paternalistic model remained at its core nonegalitarian, with a racialized hierarchy that left workers at times suspicious, resistant, and even defiant. Despite a workforce that was nearly entirely Mexican or Mexican American, non-Hispanic white men comprised the farm's "upper management."[35] In the management hierarchy directly below Deane Stahmann—himself a blond-haired man with northern European ancestry—and his family, were four non-Hispanic white men who served as overall farm supervisors to the largely Mexican workforce of managers and workers. In addition non-Hispanic white men also occupied other key positions on the farm, such as commissary manager and payroll manager. Suspicion of upper management among farmworkers was exacerbated by a lack of financial transparency at times. For example workers received certain benefits only if they left "under honorable conditions," which were determined by the controller. As one worker explained, "It was hard to know exactly what was taking place because John Chandley was the controller and he handled all this. . . . If John Chandley didn't think it was a good idea, it wouldn't be done."[36]

Stahmann's paternalism ultimately derived not from charity but pragmatism; he strove to cultivate and control his workforce with the same attention toward efficiency that he applied to his cropped fields. The workers, however, found ways to negotiate the terms, mold their town to their liking, and at times offer subtle resistance to some of the farm's most tightly managed features. A significant degree of this agency came from workers' strong sense of community. The Stahmann community, as other historians have noted, became not just a company town but also an ethnic community. Nearly all the workers were Mexican or Mexican American, speaking Spanish exclusively, and ties to communities in Mexico were strong. Workers described feeling at certain times as though "we were living like we were living in a small town in Mexico."[37] A closer look at the diet and fiestas of farmworkers helps illustrate the significance of this shared sense of community and how cultural negotiations and subtle threads of resistance wove through the borderlands farm.

Food, Fiestas, and Transnational Threads

The Stahmann Farms' commissary, far from the stereotypical predatory "company store" of Ernie Ford fame, provided staple foods and goods with little markup and offered a lenient "revolving credit deal" to workers. "This was not a boutique," recalls Sánchez of the store, but it provided rice, beans, chile, and corn—essential fuels for a hardworking labor force. Though useful, a diet consisting of only commissary goods did not satisfy all workers. While scant sources exist, a few oral histories suggest that workers augmented their diet in ways that subtly defied the farm's efforts at controlling its cultural landscape. Whether to avoid the commissary on the larger cotton farms or simply to augment their diet with foods their paychecks alone could not afford, farmworkers procured their own food in the wild and in their gardens. One of the best sources comes from Consuelo Márquez, a Stahmann employee and farmworker's daughter, who offers a small glimpse into the diets and dietary changes that midcentury New Mexico farmworkers experienced.

Originally from Chihuahua, Consuelo Márquez's parents lived in Arizona before settling in the Mesilla Valley in the years following the construction of Elephant Butte Dam. When her father first arrived in New Mexico, orchards and vegetable farms still predominated, and he managed to work on farms in exchange for the right to grow and sell food from a small plot on the farm. Márquez explained how, in addition to the food her father grew and raised, their family ate many wild foods. "My father . . . put it in his feet . . . [and] put a string in his way," Márquez explained about the river turtles (*ecotejas*, as she called them) her father would catch. "When [the turtle] came out with his neck to see who was there, my daddy caught the neck." Her father then roasted the turtle in the oven, shell and all, and scooped out the flesh for his family. It was "good meat," Márquez remembered, "a little sweet and a little vinegar." Her father also caught and roasted mesquite worms that burrowed by the roots. "They had beautiful meat, too," Márquez recalls. Her father dug "wild potatoes" that were "very tasty." "And fish," Márquez remembered, "all the time." She remembers making fish stews, often with the fish heads to increase flavor. When her father caught elvers, or *anguias*, their name for eels, he roasted them in the oven and cut them into small chunks. Those who fished for eels, Márquez explains, benefited from the irrigation needs of agriculture. "Every time they stop the water from the rivers, there are those eels." Trapping the eels via dam meant a short-term gain for anglers and, of course, the long-term doom of the eels.[38] "So you see how people lived long ago," Márquez concluded, emphasizing the healthiness of what they ate: "[the food] was clean of everything."[39]

The meals of Márquez's childhood reveal a rich cultural diversity within farm fields in 1920s southern New Mexico and an intimate knowledge of the landscape. Foods such as American eels, mesquite worms, turtles, and wild potatoes—hardly traditional mainstays of the dominant cultures of the region—reveal an importation of food knowledge that derived from diverse cultural backgrounds. Traditionally mesquite worms are a delicacy little known outside Mexico, whereas the tradition of eating elvers is more firmly a European one, with particularly deep roots in places such as the Basque Country in Iberia.[40] The Márquez family diet suggests the development of a new, place-based diet that was influenced by diverse cultural traditions yet wholly unique to the local landscape.

The meals also reveal an ability to carve out independence amid the industrializing landscape of southern New Mexico, which changed over the course of Márquez's childhood and early adulthood with the widespread adoption of cotton. As Márquez raised her own family at Stahmann Farms, she lived more firmly in the wage economy of industry and less in the barter economy her father had raised her in. She found that Stahmann discouraged workers from procuring their food independently; workers could not raise livestock larger than chickens and, except for victory gardens during World War II, did not have access to garden space. Occasionally one of the farm's supervisors raised a dairy cow, offering workers milk for a "nickel a quart."[41] Otherwise the farm provided food only through the commissary. "Stahmann Farms gave us a loan and we couldn't buy anything [not from] his store," Consuelo Márquez explained. "We had to [buy at] the commissary. [Stahmann] didn't like for us to go outside of his town and get what we wanted. . . . He got mad with us."[42]

Despite such discouragement Márquez explains that workers nonetheless managed to procure their own food and shared knowledge that allowed them to circumvent the commissary. "When I was living at Stahmann farms, the people that came with Stahmann from Mexico . . . taught me many things . . . so we really didn't need many stores," Márquez explained. "We could live by the land. Everything."[43] Márquez's account reveals a thread of resistance to the controlled landscape of the farm. These acts of resistance, even as subtle as pooling community knowledge to "live by the land," reveal how even the industrial farm retained critical spaces of nonindustrial agriculture. In this case the food that literally fueled the farmworkers—themselves essential fuel for the industrial project—derived from local, unregulated spaces rooted in nonindustrial traditions.

While diet represented a daily form of cultural negotiation, agricultural fiestas marked the calendar with days that provided workers the time and space to celebrate their work and lives in ways largely independent of Stahmann's project. At Stahmann Farms in the mid-twentieth century, worker celebrations of San Isidro, as well as the annual harvest fiesta, Christmas, and Mexican and U.S. independence days, exposed the limits of Stahmann's paternalistic efforts at workforce control and the subtle merging of nonindustrial traditions into the life of the industrial farm.

The largest festival days were for San Isidro (May 15), harvest, and Christmas. The honoring of San Isidro, the patron saint of farmworkers who represented an alternative to the mythic yeoman of Anglo-American tradition, illustrates how farmworkers celebrated their work on their own terms. A priest came for San Isidro, and festivals in the early years of the farm centered on the performance of the *matachines*, facilitated by the colonia's *mayordomos* and performed by a group dressed in costumes that traveled to each colonia. The dancers were all farm laborers, asking for a good crop and a "good time." "It wasn't really a fiesta like we have now," Sánchez recalled. "There wasn't a meeting of all these people eating food and everything else. They called them *matachines*. . . . It was an event that was as much Catholic as it might have been Native American. . . . A festival in the form of a dance, much like they do in Tortugas. But this was asking for a good crop."[44] Although early fiestas featured mostly *matachines*, later ones became more complex celebrations with food and invited guests. They expanded to include celebrations of September 16 (Mexican Independence Day) and the Fourth of July.[45] Farmworkers recall occasional visits by movie stars from Juárez during fiestas.

The festivals grew out of farmworker culture but nonetheless required Stahmann's participation. Stahmann often "organized" them, sometimes hosted them, and always tried to dictate the terms.

"Mr. Stahmann didn't like parties at his farm," one former farm-worker recalled. "When he made some type of party, he would make it for us, but he didn't like for us to make some for ourselves. He had everything in his store except beer or any other type of liquor."[46] Luis Sánchez explained further: "The parties that Mr. Stahmann would allow on the premises were not parties that would be rowdy. Not parties that would be extra loud. Not parties that were involving and possibly creating problems because we all had to work together."[47] In Sánchez's view, Stahmann "allowed" the fiestas not because he "liked parties" but because the celebrations were effectively a right of the worker. "[Stahmann] let those people exercise their rights or their desires to do so in this very small way," Sánchez explains. "And it was a small way. It wasn't big. It wasn't what they call *fandango*, which we call in Mexican, a big to-do. . . . It was just something that was tradition."[48]

fandango

The Contingent Ideal

By the midsixties, despite the general postwar national trend away from diversification, Stahmann's vertically integrated, closed-loop system of diversified farming remained efficient and profitable. As the farm continued to use chickens to fertilize and geese to weed the cotton growing among the pecan trees, it had grown into the state's largest chicken farm and the world's largest goose farm and pecan producer. The pecan grove yielded up to eight million pounds of nuts a year; annual cotton production, though reduced, still averaged five hundred acres; and the farm's breeding efforts had expanded to Peru and Ecuador. Nearly five hundred employees continued to live permanently at the farm; each year several workers cashed out comfortable pensions. All the while the farm had become a "target of nationwide interest in its unusual diversified agriculture" and begun to attract over a thousand visitors annually for those who, as one newspaper put it, wanted to witness "one of the prime examples of successful diversified farming in the country."[49] Yet change was in the air.

The sixties marked a turbulent moment for both nation and farm in the former Santo Tomás Land Grant. Building on his father's outspoken contempt for leftist politics, Deane Stahmann Jr. vowed to leave the country if Lyndon B. Johnson, whom he considered too far left, became president. When the moment came, he moved to New South Wales, Australia, to build a pecan empire down under; Stahmann Farms now spanned two hemispheres. Meanwhile life was changing on the New Mexican farm as the pecan trees began to reach full maturity and Deane Stahmann's health began to fail. He died in 1970; shortly thereafter a new generation of managers sought to cease cotton production, phase out the seed-breeding and nursery business, and sell the poultry flocks to focus more on the lucrative nut.[50] The end of diversification coincided with the dissolution of many of the farm's worker services and its pension plan, and with the gradual end of organized agricultural fiestas.[51] Paternalism gave way to a wage system for workers largely living off the farm; the change signaled the end of a strong farm-based community.

The history of Stahmann's cotton era helps underscore the fluidity and contingency of the industrial ideal of mid-twentieth-century agriculture. Seemingly incongruous ingredients—diversification, paternalism, and industrialism—fit into a successful formula for one of the region's largest and most innovative farms of the twentieth century. From the outset the farm's embrace of diversification and paternalism echoed the interwar industrial ideal as it strove to create a more modern agricultural business. The farm became a marvel of modernity—its fleet of aircraft for dusting crops and transporting goods, its air-conditioned chicken houses and carefully designed feed formulas, its multinational cotton-breeding greenhouses—that continually embraced the latest scientific and technological advances in the name of profit, control, and rational efficiency. "His success can be largely attributed to having everything under control," Ernie Pyle remarked after his 1939 visit. "He controls the moisture, the fertility of the soil, all diseases. Everything is right under his thumb. Practically nothing is left to the whims of nature."[52]

Yet, as this chapter has shown, modern methods alone do not fully explain the success of the industrial farm. Even deploying the latest and most expensive technologies, Stahmann's efforts at regulating both land and labor faced limitations. Stahmann's industrial dream required negotiations with the workforce and natural landscape that often produced solutions rooted in nonindustrial agricultural methods. Whether it was the army of weed-eating geese, the huge flocks of soil-building chickens, the seed originally bred in southern Mexico, or the *matachines* dancing for San Isidro, the modern farm relied on elements of nonindustrial agricultural tradition that, though seemingly antithetical to the industrial project, found new life at the farm.

THREE

Chile

5

Crossing Chiles, Crossing Borders

Dr. Fabián García, the New Mexican Chile Pepper, and Modernity in the Early Twentieth-Century U.S.-Mexico Borderlands

New Mexico's official state question—"Red or green?"—inquires tongue-in-cheek about chile preference to celebrate one of the state's leading crops and economic engines. Implicitly the question also signals pride for New Mexico's Hispanic and Native cultural heritage. This official display of pride came roughly a century after New Mexican politicians and other territorial elites debated, in explicitly racist terms, whether New Mexico was modern and white enough to become fully incorporated into the union.[1] As these elites sought to distance New Mexico's population from its indigenous heritage and its neighbors to the south, a Mexican-born horticulturalist at New Mexico's land-grant college, Dr. Fabián García, bred a new chile variety that embodied an alternative vision of modernity for New Mexico. The new chile pepper encouraged a more industrialized, more culturally inclusive borderlands and set the course for an industry that would eventually define the state's cultural identity.

García held an important position as a cultural and agricultural intermediary that shaped his work with the iconic chile. As horticulturalist at the New Mexico College of Agriculture and Mechanic Arts (NMAM), later New Mexico State University

121

(NMSU), in Las Cruces, New Mexico—positioned more squarely in the borderlands than any other land-grant college in the United States—García helped disseminate cultural and agricultural change in all directions in early twentieth-century New Mexico. The number 9 chile, as García called the new variety, was more than simply the first scientific and industrial chile pepper; it embodied a pan-Hispanic and nationally inclusive vision for New Mexico that encouraged cultural transformations both within and beyond the borderlands. García's efforts transformed more than the chile's genetics; his efforts represented the first major step in producing a modern crop that the nation as a whole could more readily consume. Perhaps better than any other single crop variety, the number 9 chile reveals the intersections among modernity, race, and nation within the wider economic and cultural network of the early twentieth-century U.S.-Mexico borderlands.

García was "born of humble parents" in 1871 in Chihuahua, Chihuahua. Two years after his parents died, his grandmother brought him to the mountains of southern New Mexico, where as a boy he recalled being terrified by encounters with Apaches. His grandmother eventually landed a job in Las Cruces with the prominent Casad family, who treated him "as a member of the family, in all respects," sending him to grade school and then NMAM, which they had helped found. García became a naturalized U.S. citizen in 1889, graduated from NMAM's inaugural class of 1894, and shortly thereafter joined the faculty as a horticultural assistant. He worked on a wide range of projects at the college (particularly with fruit trees), spent a year doing graduate work at Cornell University in 1899–1900, and in 1907 married Julieta Amador, whose family had deep-rooted business and social connections with Mexico. His disparate experiences and connections from an early age cut across cultural, class, and geopolitical lines.[2]

When he began his seed trials in 1907 as the college's newly appointed horticulturalist, García sought to transform the chile pepper from a regionally significant crop into a national one. Already the most culturally and commercially significant crop for many Hispanic farmers throughout the state, the chile pepper, García believed, could be improved. He bred for a more consistent, narrower, fleshier, and more peelable chile for canning purposes. He also sought a milder pepper to appeal to people elsewhere in the country that might be unaccustomed to pungent flavors.[3] Such transformations in the chile would require hard work on his part, but would also require a transformation on the part of the farmers who grew the crop and the consumers who bought it. Farmers needed to be more diligent seed savers and to embrace a scientific approach to agriculture, he argued. He believed people outside the Southwest had to "educate" themselves about traditionally Hispanic foods of Mexico and the U.S. Southwest in order to embrace the chile. Cultural changes, within and outside the Southwest, came part and parcel with agricultural ones.

Hispanic farmers throughout New Mexico grew the chile pepper more than any other nongrain crop, and regarded it as a symbol of their heritage. In 1848 topographical engineer William Emory described the chile pepper as "the glory of New Mexico," and a food that "the Mexicans considered the chef-d'oeuvre of the cuisine, and seem really to revel in it."[4] Forty years later, an 1884 *Rio Grande Republican* article reaffirmed *chile colorado* as the "national dish" of the "native" population in Las Cruces. Several generations later, further north, Fabiola Cabeza de Baca reflected, "When we think of New Mexican foods, naturally the chile dishes come first." The chile pepper—growing in the field, drying by the house, and simmering in the pot—provided a defining mark on the cultural landscape of New Mexico and a source of collective pride. "Unless one has watched the farm families as they weave and string the chile pods," Cabeza de Baca explained, "one has missed a delightful work of art and skill."[5]

Throughout much of New Mexico during the late nineteenth and early twentieth centuries, chile peppers were just as important commercially as they were culturally. The *Rio Abajo* (*Albuquerque*) *Press* reported on February 2, 1863, that Congress took "fifty thousand dollars out of the pockets of the people of the United States to make us good roads for intercommunication and the transportation of chile colorado to market." Several decades later the rail connection between Santa Fe and Colorado had gained the nickname "Chili Line," by many accounts because of the loads of chile peppers it carried out of the state. While chile production had peaked in some northern New Mexico counties by the turn of the century, chile production in other northern areas was still increasing as late as 1924. In that same year García estimated that growers exported 75 percent of the crop grown in Santa Fe County out of state.[6]

In the southern part of the state at the turn of the century, commercial production was more limited. García mentions chiles neither in his lengthy 1903 summation of horticulture in the state nor in an updated report to the National Irrigation Congress in 1908. Only in 1910 did his revised report include the chile, describing it as principally a crop grown by "Mexican farmers."[7]

Nonetheless García explains in his 1908 *Chile Culture* that "the use of chile in the United States is increasing every year; the American people are beginning to cultivate a taste for it, and thus a greater demand is being created for this vegetable."[8] The increasing popularity of canned green chile provided the most promising development for the industry. Canneries in both Los Angeles and Las Cruces had begun canning green chile, mainly for local and regional consumption. Theodore Rouault started a canning business in Las Cruces in 1896, growing the majority of the vegetables for it himself. Business thrived. In 1903 he saw no need to ship any canned goods east because he had "a ready market in New Mexico, Texas, and Arizona for the product of my cannery and, indeed, I can not meet the demand, especially for the canned green chili. The greater portion of my goods find a market right here in New Mexico."[9]

García saw great potential in this emergent canning industry and sought to develop a chile specifically suited for it. He later recalled that the success of the canning industry, along with the difficulty of peeling and processing native chile, led to the initial experiments. García explained in 1934: "The old native pods formerly used in the green chile industry were usually quite wrinkled, with a sunken shoulder and a thin flesh. In peeling the pod, if it had a sunken shoulder, the women who used to do the peeling had first to get the skin from inside the stem and as it went over the ridge from the stem end it would break off. Since millions of pods had to be handled in this way, we felt that a variety easier to peel would be an economical development for the industry."[10] By principally breeding for traits that would transform the chile into an efficient, cannable export crop that could be grown and processed on larger scales, García bred the first chile variety to be eaten primarily green and year-round for markets near and far. A chile bred to be canned green not only helped make the future state question possible in any season of the year, it suggests that the question of red or green is also a question of more traditional versus more modern.[11]

García bred the chile by methodically crossing and selecting for desirable traits among fourteen strains over several successive seasons. He planted each strain in small test plots, recorded their performance under a variety of controlled conditions, and within a few years began discarding ones that performed poorly. After several seasons of initial selecting, he sent the seeds of the most promising strains to "collaborators"—farmers throughout New Mexico—who grew them and reported how they performed under a variety of conditions. After roughly a decade of such careful and methodical experiments, strain number 9 emerged as the most desirable for industry purposes. It possessed the smoothness, fleshiness, and sloping shoulders that processors desired. It was also less pungent than landrace chile and, as a side effect of selecting only healthy plants in the trials, was more resistant to chile wilt.[12]

García approached the chile with faith that it could be continually perfected through modern science and the progress of civilization. "Naturally, after the Spaniards came across and found that this vegetable [the chile pepper] was being eaten by natives . . . no doubt because of their higher civilization, they developed more palatable dishes. I believe that the present [chile] recipes . . . have been improved upon by the Spanish conquistadores," he began a historical account of the chile in 1934. "Naturally, with highly developed civilizations and home economics developments, the old native methods of preparing these [chile and frijol] dishes have been materially improved upon." Such improvements include enhancing the enchilada with an "egg that is fried and placed on top of the tortillas after you have put the cheese and the onions on them. It has been stated that the idea of using an egg with the enchilada originated with the [largely Anglo] miners in and around Pinos Altos and Silver City, New Mexico, back in the early 80's." For García, technological change drove this teleology of improvement upon the foodways of the native crop. Chile grinders were a "material improvement," he emphasized, over grinding by hand, while careful, methodical breeding outperformed the ways of early "New Mexico tribes [who,] naturally, had no idea about plant breeding and plant improvement."[13]

A vision of a more inclusive borderlands shaped García's project of modernizing the chile. He believed in a unified Hispanidad that stretched across the U.S.-Mexico border. Many intellectuals and elites in northern New Mexico in the early twentieth century deemphasized historical ties to Mexico, choosing instead to highlight their whiteness through their Spanish roots and perpetuating what John Nieto-Phillips has called the "White Legend."[14] Hispanic elites of southern New Mexico and elsewhere in the U.S.-Mexico borderlands, though at times employing a similar strategy of claiming whiteness, more often promoted a "pan-Hispanic" ideology that emphasized Mexican rather than Spanish symbolism and a binational ethnic solidarity among Mexicans and Mexican Americans on both sides of the border. La Alianza Hispano-Americana, a mutual aid society founded in late nineteenth-century Tucson, helped develop and spread this ideology.[15]

García paid dues to La Alianza for much of his career and, though hardly outspoken about his Mexican heritage, embraced the organization's binational message and his Mexican roots. Alfredo Levy, general attorney of La Alianza in Mexico City, described García in 1930 as a "Mexican" who represented "a pride for our race." In 1943 a federal education inspector in Ciudad Juárez told García that he was "a great friend of the Mexicans because he was born in Mexico [and] is of our race."[16] García freely acknowledged his Mexican roots, keeping a copy of the national anthems of both Mexico and the United States in his desk. While some La Alianza members at times claimed whiteness, García did not. He instead claimed a pan-Hispanic Nuevomexicano identity and proudly declared that the blood of "the native New Mexican runs through my veins."[17] Perhaps the most explicit indication that García did not claim whiteness comes in a letter from Bonney Youngblood, a USDA experiment station official and longtime friend. He wrote to García in 1944: "I recall you are part Yaqui and part Spanish. . . . Perhaps you know that the people of Mexico are much prouder nowadays at least of their Indian than of their Spanish origin, and from the way you have talked with me in the past, I imagine you are of the same opinion. Am I correct?"[18] García's reply, unfortunately, is lost to the historical record.

La Alianza formed in part as a response to pervasive racial discrimination throughout the borderlands. As the country witnessed a rising tide of nativist sentiment during the first decades of the twentieth century, racial tensions in places like Las Cruces only increased. The Ku Klux Klan, while not nearly as prevalent in New Mexico as in neighboring Colorado and Texas, nonetheless had a brief but active presence in southern New Mexico in the 1920s that centered in Las Cruces.[19] García likely gravitated to the organization in part because of the discrimination he felt as the only Mexican American faculty member at the college. One particularly explicit example of direct racism toward García came when he applied for a horticulturalist position at the San Juan, Puerto Rico, experiment station. According to a colleague who supplied a "recommendation letter" for the job, "[García] is a thoroughly honest and conscientious worker and is quite industrious but being a Mexican he shows rather less initiative than would be expected of a white man of equal mental ability."[20]

Racial bias tinged even some of García's closest relationships with white colleagues. His friendship with USDA experiment administrator Bonney Youngblood, for example, speaks both to García's ability to bridge cultural borders and the subtle limitations of those efforts. After various visits from Youngblood to New Mexico, the two men developed a close relationship that lasted García's lifetime. In a particularly inspired letter from Youngblood that opened with "Muy Distinguido Don Fabián Mio" and closed with "your hand is kissed by an humble Texan who prides himself in being your friend," Youngblood expressed clear admiration, respect, and affection for García:

> Having bedded down at night on the deserts in the days of your youth with your ovejas hombres and mujeres (secretos) with no canopy above you but the stars in the heavens; no music to lull you to sleep but the wail of coyotes or the bleats of hungry borregos y borregas; and with nothing between you and the mujeres secretos y senoritas to signify mutual protection and continence, you have imbibed the beauties of the desert landscape. Living in the midst of natural loveliness and grandeur, you have acquired a depth of thought and aspiration which New Mexican society could ill do without.[21]

García, even in such poetic praise from a close friend, can nonetheless not quite escape Youngblood's tendency to *guisar* the chile breeder's story with racialized sexual stereotypes and clichés of the Wild West. Years later, requesting from García a biographical sketch for a USDA publication, Youngblood perhaps revealed his own desires when describing those of the editors: "They want your story to be as pungent . . . as your peppers themselves."[22]

García envisioned not only an inclusive borderlands but also a more scientific and industrial one. He believed that New Mexicans—Hispanic, Native, and otherwise—should embrace science, and that non-Natives and non-Hispanics in New Mexico and throughout the nation should welcome Hispanic culture. In a 1928 speech to the Mesilla School, García relates this attitude in a story about "a friend of mine who was connected with the Department of Agriculture [and] has accepted a very responsible position from the United Fruit Company." García explained that the friend had recently asked if he could "recommend a young man, preferrably [sic] a Latin American, who was properly trained in agriculture and could give instruction in Spanish." If not, his friend asked if he could recommend a "North American who could speak Spanish." Regrettably, García explained, he could not recommend anyone to his friend, and a "wonderful opportunity was lost."[23] More than simply asking Hispanic students to modernize, García expressed a vision for a modern United States that accepted and embraced its Hispanic population and neighbors.

García's work in Mexico also reflected his broader vision for the borderlands. Throughout his career García frequently visited Mexico, informally advised Mexican farmers, occasionally met with high-level Mexican officials throughout the country, and even served as a guest lecturer in Mexico in 1930 for a course on agricultural research and education sponsored by the Department of Agriculture.[24] His particular influence on Mexican agriculture was apparent as early as 1906. In that year the newly founded Juárez experiment station's inaugural report listed various fruit trees that experiment stations in Arizona, Texas, New Mexico, the Juárez station, and "catalogs," had recommended. While the report used the abbreviations "Ariz.," "Tex.," and "E." for Arizona, Texas, and Juárez, respectively, the abbreviation for New Mexico was simply "G.," which "represents that this variety has been recommended by el Sr. D. Fabián García, expert arboriculturist and member of the New Mexico Agricultural Experiment Station."[25] By 1910 García's work in Mexico had extended to high levels of development. In that year García visited with the Mexican minister of foreign relations (and former governor of Chihuahua), Enrique Creel, in Mexico, "in search of further information in the development of his work." The Mexican Revolution seems to have halted momentum on such "development," though eleven years later the governor of Chihuahua requested García join him on a trip to view "the same farms that will be irrigated by the Conchas, so that [the farmers] will be better able to appreciate your instructions."[26]

García also had a hand in Mexican agriculture through his ongoing relationships with former students either farming or working on agricultural policies in Mexico. For example, Arnulfo Landaverde, a former NMSU student who had recently accepted a post in the Mexican Department of Agriculture, wrote to thank García for sending him copies of the college catalog and to ask García whether he would look over the statement he was to read to the Department of Agriculture regarding Rambouillet sheep. He expressed his "high affection and gratitude for the different ways in which [the college] deigned to help me during my stay in this State [California] and outside it, deeds that are already well known by the leadership of agriculture [Dirección de Agricultura] of my country."[27]

García's influence more often came through casual advice to Mexican farmers. Reynaldo Talavera, a former student of García's living in Chihuahua, Mexico, wrote to García seeking copies of university bulletins on the "tomatoe, potatoe, onions and especially beets for feeding cows or what we call here 'remolacha forrajera'" In García's reply, in which he stated that he would "be glad to discuss all the problems that you have on your mind on the growing of onions, tomatoes, chile, beets and potatoes," he also mentioned that "the last time I saw you was on the trip to Chihuahua to discuss the building of the highway between El Paso and Chihuahua."[28] Here García reveals not only his influence over farmers in Chihuahua but also hints at larger connections such as a highway project that would significantly open up agricultural markets throughout the borderlands.

Mexican government officials and farmers were not the only ones to approach García about Mexican agriculture. In 1920 William S. Myers, who had telegraphed him nine years earlier as a representative of the Texas-based Mexican Land & Colonization Co., wrote to him, in light of the Mexican Revolution, that "recent changes in Mexico suggest the possibility of our opening an office in that country." Specifically Myers inquired whether he, or someone he could recommend, would be willing and able to "[carry on] experiments and demonstrations, and generally [be] diplomatic and able to conduct a Propaganda Office" in Mexico. Myers sought an agricultural expert to report on "the big money crops of Mexico, and [give] us some intelligent idea as to whether the growing of these crops is going to expand and whether it would be free from political interference in the future. In other words, is Agriculture going to progress and develop in Mexico, or not?"[29] García served as a mediator, both formally and informally, between U.S. agriculture and Mexican agriculture on several levels: he informed Mexican officials and educators, farmers on both sides of the border, and perhaps even U.S. investors.

His chile-breeding work represents yet another level of mediation. The number 9 had genetic roots throughout the borderlands. García wrote in his *Chile Culture*, "The common strain of Mexican chile that has been grown in this section for a number of years . . . is being replaced in the Mesilla Valley by other better varieties that have been introduced in late years." He used those varieties—the *negro* and *colorado* chiles, along with twelve strains of the *pasilla* chile (then quite popular in Chihuahua)—to develop the number 9. His Chihuahuan *chile pasilla* seeds were brought to him by Carlos Romero, an agricultural student from

Chihuahua who later returned to farm in Chihuahua. The *chile negro* seed he used was from an undisclosed location in Mexico, brought to him by New Mexican farmer Francisco Rivera. The *chile colorado* seed came from California, secured by local businessman Theodore Rouault, though it also may have had recent New Mexican origins.[30] Emilio Ortega, who founded a cannery in Los Angeles in 1896 and is responsible for the term *Anaheim pepper*, apparently visited New Mexico sometime in 1890 and brought back seed. As the travel log of these chiles suggests, the number 9 drew its genetic base from throughout the U.S. Southwest and Mexican North.[31]

The strains used for the experiments were themselves shaped over many generations by farmers and gardeners throughout the Southwest, working under a variety of environmental conditions and agricultural systems. These years of labor are embedded, so to speak, in the genes of the chile. The number 9, derived from these experiments, was thus a consolidation of geographical areas across the borderlands. Considering this consolidation of past and distant labor in the genome helps illustrate how the land-grant school facilitated a region-wide interchange of knowledge and material resources.

Professional and university breeders, García included, commonly sourced seeds locally, regionally, and globally to breed modern industrial varieties.[32] Simultaneously a strictly regional and a transnational crop, the number 9 chile differed from most university breeding projects in its reliance on local connections on both sides of the international border. Common intermediaries such as seed catalogs, professional plant hunters, or the USDA seed introduction program were simply not useful. This was a local crop that needed a local border-crosser to successfully transform it into a more industry friendly, nationally digestible crop.

It needed, too, an intermediary to encourage changes in both farmer and consumer. García understood the new variety would be a valuable resource only if farmers collaborated in the process by taking on a more diligent and systematic approach to seed selection. "There are always some plants in the field which tend to revert back," García wrote in his bulletin on the pepper in 1921, "consequently, it is very necessary to select seed in the field."[33] This ongoing process required a transformation within the farmers themselves. "As a matter of fact," he wrote in his 1908 *Chile Culture*, "our New Mexico chile growers do not pay any attention to the selection of the seed, and as a result of this we are producing a very variable product."[34] Indeed throughout his tenure García appealed to farmers to share his strong faith in science. In a lecture based on an 1898 U.S. government publication on hybrids, García repeated the authors' claim that "scientific investigations have shown clearly that the possibilities in the improvement of our useful plants are almost unlimited," but added in his own words that farmers and gardeners frequently miss the opportunity for such improvements because "selection is not made very systematically, perhaps on account of a lack of knowledge on the subject on the part of the operator."[35] The modern, scientifically derived chile, García believed, came part and parcel with more modernized and scientific farmers.

García joined other experiment station scientists and extension specialists on various trips throughout the state to spread the gospel of science. His audience received him with both enthusiasm and, occasionally, disdain. In 1923 Bonney Youngblood and García traveled up the Rio Grande together, stopping at various pueblos. One pueblo, however, tried to "run [them] off the reservation."[36] Years later he wrote Youngblood, "I wish I could repeat [that] trip that you and I made," recalling how "we got into the Indian dance and feared for our scalps."[37] In a letter to García eleven years later, relating to a possible project in Navajo country, Youngblood remarks, "I'll not ask you for a letter of introduction to the Navajos, since I already know from experience what at least one group of Pueblo Indians think of you!"[38] A year later Taos pueblo elders objected to a county extension garden project, on the grounds that "anything that had been recommended by the Government had usually been an expensive habit, and that they had found themselves poorer after trying out these things than they had originally." Despite the complaints the elders were eventually persuaded; García sent up seed from Las Cruces.[39] Whether García sent up his newly released number 9 or not, it is clear that he, as with the extension agents throughout the state, experienced a mixed reception depending on the audience and the context.

García's vision for the chile pepper required not only a transformation among those that grew it but also those that ate it. Though he bred primarily for traits that would allow for more efficient canning, García also selected for mildness—presumably to appeal to Anglo consumers throughout the country—understanding that non-Hispanic consumers in the Southwest and beyond needed to develop a taste for the pungent fruit if the industry were to take off. While a less pungent chile would certainly help the pepper's marketability, so too would a change of taste among consumers. "Some of our New Mexico people are becoming quite interested in the use of some of these native products [tortillas, frijoles, and chile]," he wrote to Bonney Youngblood in 1934, "and I only wish it were possible for a national educational campaign to be started to get people to eat these products more than they are doing."[40] In the context of prevalent anti-immigration sentiment in the United States during García's trials and the first decades of the number 9's introduction, García's wish for a "national education program" reflects the subtle challenge of normative U.S. tastes inherent to his work with the chile.

The number 9 never became a fully dominant variety among New Mexican chile growers. While it became quite popular in the southern and central parts of the state, many farmers in the north, where landrace varieties proved hardier, did not grow the variety. In 1924 García reported that production had recently increased 300 percent in Santa Fe County, but growers there were planting landrace varieties, not the number 9, because it was too hot (this indicates that while García may have bred for mildness, the final result missed the mark). Further south it gained wide popularity but never entirely replaced other varieties. A Las Cruces grower remarked in 1921 that while the number 9 performed well in the field, "we find that the small native chile sells the best. . . . We wish the No. 9 was of the smaller size, as the native people prefer the small hot chile to the mild large variety."[41] Later, in 1934, García wrote that the number 9 was widely used in New Mexico, but because it ripened late, was especially "an excellent variety for the warmer sections."

Despite its limitations many New Mexicans throughout the state embraced the project of improving the chile pepper. Fabiola Cabeza de Baca, the famed champion of northern New Mexico foodways, exemplifies this cultural acceptance. In an undated speech (likely from the forties), she explains, "The chile grown, even 50 years ago, in the northern counties, was a small pepper and very hot. Horticulturalists, from our College of Agriculture, conducted experiments in crossing the early varieties with less pungent, better size and quality chile, which resulted in the improvement of the product."[42] Her approval of the scientifically "improved," and more easily canned, number 9 chile points to an acceptance of new technologies we see in other facets of her work, such as her Spanish-language bulletins that advocate home canning.[43] In this sense such an openness toward the reworked culturally iconic crop confirms how Cabeza de Baca, in the words of historian Virginia Scharff, "worked to venerate and preserve a more mixed and dynamic New Mexico heritage [and] reworked the world in which she moved, with an eye on both the past and the future."[44]

The creation and popularity of the number 9 chile helps illuminate how the greater borderlands shaped this "more mixed and dynamic New Mexico heritage." Cabeza de Baca and García, who knew each other well and developed a deep mutual respect after traveling on a farm demonstration train together throughout northern New Mexico in 1930, wrote extensive, often affectionate letters to each other until García's death. "There isn't a person in this country who I admire more . . . than you," Cabeza de Baca wrote him in 1943. She continued, "I believe that every *hispano* should feel honored that we have one of our own blood who was able to lift himself to such an elevated position."[45] Cabeza de Baca certainly drew lines to emphasize the distinctness of Nuevomexicano culture in her writing: she insisted that "one must use New Mexican products" to get a "genuine" New Mexico taste; she used cookbooks to distinguish "New Mexican" from both "Mexican" and "American" foodways.[46] Yet her relationship to García and her support of the number 9 suggest she understood such lines to be more blurred than strictly defined. More broadly her relationship with García and the number 9 offers an important window into how influences from southern New Mexico and the larger borderlands region informed the intellectual, agricultural, and cultural identity of northern New Mexico.

The number 9 represents an important chapter in the history of chile pepper industry in New Mexico and of New Mexico's relationship to modernity and nationhood. The number 9 served as one of the genetic strains for the Sandia variety, which was developed in the 1950s and remains an important variety for the New Mexican chile industry. Its significance, however, stretches far beyond its genetic legacy; the development of the number 9 represented a fundamental shift in the idea of the chile. No longer bred primarily for local and seasonal consumption, the scientific chile crossed geopolitical, seasonal, and cultural borders. García's work, as Carmella Padilla states in her 1997 *Chile Chronicles*, "laid the groundwork for turning a regional food into a national food [and] above all . . . made chile into a science."[47] Such change reverberated well beyond the agricultural fields of New Mexico. Bred for a more modern and inclusive region and country, this physically and culturally reworked chile forged new paths of agricultural and cultural exchange both within and beyond the borderlands.

6

The Evolution of a Modern Pod

The Industrial Chile and Its Storytellers in New Mexico

"Chile is my legacy," famed Las Cruces writer Denise Chávez
wrote in 1996. "So is the hot pungency of this southern land, the
miles of earth tilled and seeded, yielding crops valuable and cherished." In the five decades between Fabián García's death in 1946
and Chavez's words, chile had grown from a relatively small and
local crop in Chávez's hometown to one of its chief export crops.[1]
Along the way, it had become a powerful cultural symbol throughout the state and, for many, a legacy nearly synonymous with a
people and a landscape.

The chile industry in New Mexico owed its growth to a strong
collaborative public-private effort among chile producers, processors, and the land-grant university that extended from breeding
to branding. One hundred years after the first chile experiments
began at the small land-grant college, the work of researchers at
NMSU extended beyond selectively breeding the pepper to selectively rewriting its story. These efforts helped growers and processors scale up production and compete in national and international
markets. They also helped propel the chile pepper as a symbol of
New Mexico identity that provided a source of pride and unity,
while also exposing cultural divisions and tensions surrounding

modernity. As the industry worked hard to shape the story of the pepper, and as many in New Mexico offered counternarratives, the chile itself continued to evolve with the changing landscape. Within its fiery heart the chile contains a distinctive set of genes and stories that speak to a diversity of cultural identities and values within the state. And the stories, like its genes, keep changing.

The Growth of an Industry

1970's

Beginning in the early seventies, the chile industry began to boom. A crop that had previously been grown by small-scale farmers throughout the state now became the focal point of a major new industry in the Mesilla Valley of southern New Mexico. Many factors contributed to this shift, including access to nearby and relatively cheap labor from Mexico, and a large and growing international demand for peppers that foreign and domestic growers elsewhere struggled to meet.[2] Breeding efforts at NMSU and other universities throughout the Southwest also proved significant to the industry's growth, as Fabián García's successors at NMSU continued to breed chile specifically suited for industrial production.

#6

Breeding developments began in 1950 when NMSU breeder Dr. Roy Harper released the New Mexico number 6, which derived from an "undetermined varietal origin" and was milder, higher yielding, shorter, more uniform in color, and faster maturing than the number 9.[3] This pepper, "particularly well-suited for the processing industry and for producing green chile for the fresh market," helped facilitate the beginning of a significantly scaled-up industry, with its labor-saving qualities such as concurrent maturation and easy destemming. The number 6, bred to be milder and renamed the number 6-4 in 1957, remained an important staple variety for the industry throughout much of the twentieth century. Harper's successor, Dr. Roy Nakayama, later emphasized how much mildness had contributed to the new variety's success. "The big difference, actually, way back then—even prior to 1955—was that about the only variety available here was a real hot chile.

Too doggone hot for most," Nakayama recalled in 1976. "Most of it was native chile, with some New Mexico No. 9. That No. 9 was larger-bodied, but it was too hot. . . . We couldn't sell it outside the state." These new varieties aided the transition from a state-wide to national market, marking a "transition from a cash crop for producers with small acreages to an attractive, high income crop in modern irrigated agriculture."[4]

Subsequent varieties developed at NMSU had less impact on the industry. In 1974 Roy Nakayama released the NuMex Big Jim, which grew nearly a foot long and was by most accounts the largest chile variety known. Crossing a small Peruvian variety with an "Anaheim," native Chimayó and other New Mexican varieties, Nakayama bred for pods that "mature concurrently, making machine picking—and thus greater acreage—possible." Though this chile never became a staple variety among proces- sors, it became "a favorite of home gardeners and chefs for making chile rellenos."[5] Despite the Big Jim's limitations for wide-scale production, the industry had promotional use for the new pep- per and its breeder. Gaining the moniker "Mr. Chile," Nakayama served as the official judge at chile cook-offs and competitions and became a local celebrity as part of a larger campaign to promote the chile. Nakayama became an icon when the industry, increas- ingly becoming nonlocal and faceless, needed a face.[6]

Though locally developed varieties played a significant role in the industry's growth, New Mexico growers also adopted variet- ies of peppers from elsewhere that had never before been com- mercially produced in the state. Pioneers of the chile industry, Emma Jean and Orlando Cervantes, for example, helped build the state's chile industry by growing Tabasco and cayenne pep- pers largely to be processed into Louisiana-style hot sauce. In search of a new crop, Orlando Cervantes began growing cayenne peppers in 1972 for a Cincinnati-based hot sauce company with processing plants in Louisiana. He soon began producing the peppers for other Louisiana hot sauce producers in New Iberia.[7]

In 1973 he began growing Tabasco peppers for the McIlhenny Company in New Iberia, Louisiana.[8] "One day I saw a bottle of Tabasco sauce at the supermarket and thought maybe we could grow them," Orlando Cervantes explained a few years later. He contacted McIlhenny's, who decided the hurricane-free, beetle-free, irrigated desert of New Mexico offered a good opportunity for the company. The company agreed to provide all the seeds, which were propagated in a Texas greenhouse and then shipped to the New Mexico farm to be planted. Within three years the Cervantes were harvesting one hundred acres of the specialty crop, mashing it on site and shipping it back to Louisiana in white oak barrels to finish fermenting (for three years) before being bottled.[9] By the nineties the Cervantes' farm was focusing primarily on cayenne peppers for Louisiana-style hot sauce, and shipping their peppers internationally as far as Saudi Arabia. In addition to New Mexico–grown peppers, the Cervantes' operation expanded into Mexico. In 1987 the farm began growing some of their chile in Mexico (in Jalisco, as well as in Flores Magon, Delicias, Ascensión, and Obregón in Chihuahua); by 1996 Mexican-grown chile comprised half of their operation. From Mexico to New Iberia, from New Mexico back to Mexico, the Tabasco and cayenne peppers' journey highlights the regional ties of agriculture in the Southwest that extended into both Mexico and the U.S. South.[10]

As the example of the Cervantes' farm suggests, new chile varieties developed at NMSU, although instrumental in the industry's rise, did not alone facilitate the chile industry's boom. Seeds developed elsewhere, processors such as the hot sauce companies in Louisiana that Cervantes worked with, and local processors of New Mexico green chile proved essential to the industry's initial success. In 1959, for example, a local cannery bought all the available seed of the newly developed 6-4 variety to distribute to contracted growers; by 1977 there were at least seventeen major processors in the Southwest. The development of more easily peeled varieties, along with the emergence of widespread refrigeration, also gave rise to a wholly new product, frozen green chile, the specialty of processors such as Encanto Foods (later Bueno Foods).[11]

Promotional Stints and a
"New Cuisine for 'Modern Civilization'"

Processors played an important role not only in purchasing chile from farmers but also in promoting the chile. Mountain Pass Cannery (the producer of Old El Paso salsa in Anthony, Texas, from 1918 to 1968) led the effort by underwriting chile research at NMSU during the industry's initial years and sponsoring events such as a "green chile recipe fiesta" and green chile cook-off at NMSU in 1972.[12] These events, along with the creation of the Hatch chile festivals in 1971 and the passing of a bill in the New Mexico legislature in 1965 to make chiles and pinto beans the state's "official vegetables," represented the bulk of early promotional efforts surrounding the chile pepper industry.[13] In 1973, however, NMSU funded its own chile promotional group. Convinced that a "promotional stint involving the chile might be good for the university," university president Gerald Thomas set aside funding to create the International Connoisseurs of Green and Red Chile, which soon became the biggest promotional group for the chile in the state, with a membership of over three thousand by 1977. Mountain Pass, like several processors, helped fund the effort. The university's collaboration with the industry had extended from seed to sales.[14]

The Connoisseurs employed various strategies for chile promotion. They published cookbooks, staged chile cook-offs, sent "care packages" of chile seeds to far corners of the globe, and put on conferences. They even helped escalate a "Great Chile War" in the U.S. Congress in 1974, by providing New Mexican chile products and an NMSU cookbook to seven non–New Mexican congressional members who had reportedly claimed the superiority of *their* state's chile. In addition to the chile products they sent, they also offered to stage a chile cook-off in New Mexico, with none other than Roy Nakayama as presiding judge.[15] Engaging the power of celebrity, in fact, proved a successful and lasting strategy for the group. In addition to boosting membership rolls with obvious candidates such as processors, growers, and restaurateurs, the group worked hard to secure the support of celebrities such as Bob Hope, Vikki Carr, Paul Harvey, and Lawrence Welk.

Following the dissolution of the Connoisseurs in the early eighties, new public-private efforts took hold. Entrepreneur Dave Dewitt, a former radio host from Boston who moved to New Mexico in the seventies, took a prominent lead in chile promotion and worked closely with the university. Dewitt published *The Fiery Cuisines* in 1985 and soon went on to coauthor several works with Dr. Paul Bosland. In 1987 he founded *Chile Pepper Magazine*, and a year later he started a chile-industry trade show, the National Fiery Foods Show. In addition, NMSU, working closely with growers and processors who continued to help fund chile research and promotion, helped start the Chile Pepper Institute in 1992. With an educational and research-based mission that included publishing newsletters and books on peppers, sponsoring an annual conference, conducting pepper research, and serving as a seed bank and as an "international clearinghouse and archives for information related to Capsicums," the institute in part aimed to "solidify the Institute's and NMSU's position as the national leader in Capsicums research and education."[16]

The New Mexico chile industry grew alongside changing national tastes for hot peppers; from the beginning, the industry's chile promotional efforts played off a broader cultural movement surrounding chile peppers. Partly because of breeding efforts by Fabián García and his successors, consumers throughout the nation had become increasingly aware of chile-based foods, most commonly in hot sauce and regional variations of "chili." As popularity for hot foods increased, a subculture of chile "aficionados" emerged around the country that centered on chile cook-off competitions, tongue-in-cheek bravado, and fierce claims, via the hot pepper, to regional superiority. The Chili Appreciation Society International (CASI), formed in 1967 after an infamous chili cook-off, began staging regional chili cook-off competitions throughout the country. Winners convened for an annual national cook-off, which raised money for local charities and offered a fun celebration of local folk cuisine.

The culture of the early CASI events shaped the promotional strategies of the Connoisseurs. The Connoisseurs' name not only matched the tongue-in-cheek rhetoric of the national cook-off culture, it also directly played off the word *international* in CASI. The invocation of internationalism served to recenter Las Cruces as a hub of Capsicums and to move the image of the industry away from solely local or regional markets. The word *connoisseurs* also cast the chile as a high-class vegetable. This tactic of up-classing the chile, complete with global celebrities on their membership rolls, seemed to work. Chile farmer Ray Enriquez, who in 1976 was growing over six hundred acres of chile, attributed the growing chile industry not only to an increased number of processors but also to an expanding taste for New Mexican food beyond the region. Part of this newfound appreciation for the chile, he explained, was in how it was perceived: "When I was a kid this kind of food was considered poor Mexican dishes. People would get together and plant one acre of chile that would take care of four or five families. Now chile dishes are considered gourmet food."[17]

Yet the work of promoting the chile involved more than simply presenting the chile as a classy, more palatable vegetable for the broader U.S. public; it ironically also involved rhetoric, often heavily tinged with machismo and racial stereotypes, that tapped into deeper underlying tensions surrounding elitism and modernity.[18] In "The Great Chili Confrontation," H. Allen Smith recounts the first chili cook-off in 1967. Smith, a northerner who had taunted nearly all Texans with his published declaration that "nobody knows more about chili than me," faced off against a Texan in Terlingua, Texas. Smith wrote in jest to his counterpart prior to the competition: "It must surely be the case that you have strong currents of northern blood coursing through your veins; it seems to me that, even though you might not know it yourself, when you were an infant you were kidnapped somewhere in the Middle West or East and spirited off to Texas, possibly by Kickapoo Indians or Canary Islanders [whom Smith elsewhere claimed had invented chili]. It is simply impossible that you could be an unsullied Texan, else you would not be able to carpenter up such a fine dish of chili."[19]

The macho, race-laden rhetoric revealed deep regional tensions and anxieties surrounding modernity. As historian David Scofield Wilson argues, "the great chili cook-off phenomena of the post-Johnson era has its origins" in an old American populist literary genre—best characterized by Mark Twain—that mocked the stuffy, elitist, "seaboard Brahmin" culture of the upper classes. Additionally these cook-offs, Wilson writes, "are high-spirited affairs, featuring a good deal of light-hearted self-mockery and playful showing off," and typically included a healthy dose of "posturing and bombast [that] radiates a mock-macho air and turns on putting women and children out of the picture." The cook-offs highlighted manly self-sufficiency (winning chili recipes often contained meats such as rattlesnake, raccoon, or porcupine), and the pepper itself was at times used as a symbol of masculinity. Yet behind the self-mockery lay a more serious criticism of modernity. "Hot peppers mark a new cuisine for 'modern civilization,'" Wilson argues, "but a 'civilization' not too 'sissy' or childish; in short, a 'natural, manly' civilization." To Wilson the cook-offs "flaunt chili or chiles as signs of their self-conscious distinction from whatever they take to be 'mainstream' American life."[20] And here, with an appropriation of a critique of modernity for the purposes of a modern industry, lies a recurring irony of modern agriculture. The Connoisseurs' cook-offs promoted the chile pepper in an effort to make it more mainstream, in part, by appealing to popular disdain for the mainstream. Just as James

Webb Young had instinctively understood as he donned the Old Jim Young persona, the appeal to the antimodern could itself be a vital part of the modern industry's toolkit. The transformation of the chile pepper from a regional ingredient of "poor Mexican dishes" into a modern food with widespread popularity thus required an inventive promotional strategy that tapped into existing anxieties surrounding modernity. Such a strategy proved successful; by 1997 Dr. Paul Bosland could proudly claim that "chile has transcended an esoteric crop and has become part of mainstream America and the world."[21]

The Evolution of the Modern Pod

The promotional strategies of the industry included subtle ways of crafting a narrative about the national pepper industry that placed New Mexico at its center. One basic strategy was to standardize the spelling of the word nationwide to conform to New Mexico's traditional, Hispanized *chile*. Neither the word *chile*, which derives from the Nahuatl *chilli*, nor *chili*, which is in turn an Anglicized form of *chile*, constitutes an original spelling of the fiery fruit. Yet languages continually evolve and spellings change. For most of the twentieth century the name of the pungent pepper was most often spelled *chile* in New Mexico and *chili* elsewhere in the country. As Dr. Benigno Villalon of Texas A&M University explained to Dave Dewitt in 1987, "The term chili pepper should be avoided completely [and] the word *chile* outside New Mexico has very little meaning." Instead, Dr. Villalon advised, "introduce the word capsicums as a periodic substitute for 'peppers[,]' this is universal."[22]

Even NMSU researchers and writers up until the early seventies at times used the two spellings interchangeably in official publications.[23] For example, in 1973 NMSU published a cookbook on "prize-winning" green chile recipes from the contest the university had hosted in conjunction with Mountain Pass Cannery. The cover of the cookbook reads, "Green Chili Recipe Fiesta," while the introduction spells the title of the cookbook as "Green Chile Recipe Fiesta." Within the cookbook, in fact, the authors explain that, while they prefer the Spanish spelling of *chile* (the apparent typo on the cover notwithstanding), a "chile is a chili is a chilli."[24] Yet as the New Mexico chile industry's branding efforts took off, a chile was no longer a chili. By the late seventies the Connoisseurs made a concerted effort to insist on *chile* as the only proper spelling of the hot pepper; this work was continued by Dave Dewitt and Paul Bosland into the eighties and nineties.[25] As Dave Dewitt later explained, "nomenclature" had become important. "One thing that Paul Bosland and I did [was] to get newspapers to change the spelling," Dewitt explained. "We got the *Dallas Morning News* to change it to an 'e.' We got the *El Paso Times* to change it, we got the *Washington Post* and the *New York Times* to change. . . . We got the AP *Stylebook* to say both were permissible . . . that's what I call a positive thing toward standardizing nomenclature."[26] Standardizing nomenclature was, however, just one small part of a larger effort to solidify New Mexico's place as a central player in the evolving narrative of the chile pepper. Another facet of this effort involved retelling the story of New Mexico's "patron saint of chiles."

The historical record is clear: Fabián García did not become the territory's horticulturalist until 1906 and, as is unmistakably clear from his writings, his "preliminary work" of breeding chile did not begin until the spring of 1907.[27] For over a century these basic facts shaped the story of the chile. Ruth Sneed, as just one of many examples, published a brief history of chile for the Extension Service in 1960 that explained, "It all started back in 1907, when Fabián García selected and planted the seeds of three varieties of chile."[28] In 1988 Bosland, citing García, writes that "Fabián García, the first chile pepper researcher, began in 1907 to investigate ways in which to improve chile pepper production methods and cultivars for New Mexico"; he repeated this assertion in 1993.[29]

A few years later, however, a new narrative emerged. Bosland wrote in 1996, "The New Mexican pod-type was developed in 1894 when Fabián García at New Mexico State University began improving the local chiles grown by the Hispanic gardeners around Las Cruces, New Mexico."[30] This uncited claim, which Bosland has repeated over the course of two decades, not only pushes the date of García's initial experiments up thirteen years, it falsely claims that the peppers used in García's experiments were all local when, in fact, the *chile negro* came from Mexico and the *chile colorado* from California.[31] Meanwhile Bosland's colleague Danise Coon similarly began to tell a new story, claiming García began his experiments in 1888.[32]

Given Bosland's intimacy with García's writings and his previously accurate portrayal of the historical facts, it is difficult to imagine that this new narrative was simply a research error or typo. Regardless, the altered historical dates helped bolster the university's new, industry-friendly claim that the "New Mexico" pod type originated solely in New Mexico. Around the same time that Bosland stopped using the accurate 1907 date for García's initial trials, he also had largely stopped using the term *Anaheim type* in favor of *New Mexico type*.[33] Bosland eventually insisted that "all New Mexican type chile peppers grown today gained their genetic base from cultivars first developed at New Mexico State University"; that "Anaheim is a cultivar within this pod type [and its seed] originated in New Mexico"; and even that "the 'Anaheim' seed originated from 'New Mexico No. 9' grown in New Mexico and was brought to California in 1896."[34] A few correctives to this statement are in order. First, because we know that landrace chile long preceded NMSU cultivars and that germplasm from landrace chile in fact went into developing several NMSU cultivars, it is incorrect to simply give credit to the university and not the many generations of farmers in New Mexico who developed those landrace varieties over centuries of growing seasons in a short-season, arid climate. Second, Ortega's business had begun over a decade before García began his experiments to improve the chile in New Mexico (and, needless to say, the number 9 chile, which was released in 1921, could not have made its way to California by 1896).[35] Yet, if García began his seed trials in 1894, as Bosland's new story goes, then perhaps Emilio Ortega's founding of a chile business in Anaheim in 1896 would not threaten New Mexico's claims to be the sole fountainhead of a new pod type and its industry.

Despite irrefutable evidence in the historical record against a pre-1907 chile trial in New Mexico, this new narrative has caught on and even grown. In a 2014 lecture to the Los Alamos Historical Society titled "Chile—New Mexico's Hottest Harvest," Dr. Stephanie J. Walker of NMSU reiterated the claim. With her own embellishments to the story, she made it clear that New Mexico's claim to chile originality was at stake:

> If anyone ever calls these fruit Anaheim-type, as proud New Mexicans you need to correct this, okay? The only reason we have Anaheim chile is because a gentleman named Mr. Ortega visited Fabián García while he was doing his genetic research. 'Wow this is great stuff you have here, Fabián. I'm going to take some of these seeds back with me to California.' So he did. He started his own selective breeding program there, and developed what we like to say [is] the nice mild, kind of wimpy Anaheim cultivar. So basically the Anaheim-type is an offshoot of New Mexico type. So it's really a New Mexico pod-type or long green chile. Anaheim is just a cultivar that was basically kind of ripped off from New Mexicans.[36]

On the surface the university's constructed narrative of the chile may seem like an oddity that hardly merits much attention. Yet the evolution of a new history of the chile pepper points to several larger trends in the history of industrial agriculture in New Mexico. First, the effort to rewrite certain elements of the crop's history illuminates the extent to which the public university's goals had grown to match those of the industry. Second and more broadly, the new narratives point to a powerful and essential, though too often forgotten, force in modern industrial agriculture: storytelling. In this case the role of breeder extended beyond the physical plant to include the stories it embodies. Dr. Fabián García began the groundwork for the modern chile with his seed trials in 1907; Dr. Paul Bosland, by propagating a new origin myth that set García's trials back to 1894, helped complete the process. Just over a century after García's initial seed trails, the chile pepper, enshrouded in myth and laden with new stories designed to boost sales and serve industry, had become fully modern.

The Fire of Rebellion

Yet as the New Mexico chile industry endeavored to solidify New Mexico's chile superiority in relation to other states and regions in the country, within the state new narratives emerged that challenged the industrial chile developed at NMSU. In 1984 Jeanne Croft reported, "While chile's gastronomic delights are celebrated, it also serves as a catalyst for occasional combat. It's not surprising that any substance capable of commanding such affection also has the power to evoke considerable controversy. From the chile-producing areas in the foothills of the Sangre de Cristo Mountains in the north to the lower reaches of the Hatch/Mesilla Valley in the south, New Mexico chile growers and chile lovers argue over whose chile is best."[37]

Although chile growers in southern New Mexico had long tended to grow different varieties of chile than those in the north, based primarily on differing lengths of growing season, an open disdain for the other's chiles did not emerge until the rise of a large-scale chile industry in the seventies. Only rarely did commentators mention the differences among northern and southern chiles prior to the industry's boom. "It's a commentary on the Anglicized tastes of the southern part of the State that a milder *chile* is more popular," one writer declared in 1958, "while north of Socorro into Albuquerque, Santa Fe, Taos, and small northern villages they like their *chile* as hot as possible. No doubt that's one of the reasons more *chile* of the native variety is grown in the northern areas."[38] Though such writers used ethnic differences to explain the differences in chile varieties grown north and south, little animosity surrounding these differences emerged in the written record until the emergence of a large-scale industry in the south.

As the chile industry began to swell in the south, to many in the north the northern New Mexico chile became a symbol of racial pride, antimodern sentiment, and even rebellion. Historian Fray Angélico Chávez in 1974 illustrated a growing urge to associate the chile pepper not with the science and emerging industry of southern New Mexico, but rather with the valleys of the north, *mestizaje*, and general Nuevomexicano resilience. Invoking the story of Bonnie Prince Charlie, Chávez's rendition of the chile makes it solidly a folk creation bred to serve the villagers of the north, not the industrialists of the south. With no mention of Dr. Fabián García nor of other individual seed breeders, Chávez's story personifies the chile and the landscape that shaped it:

> You might regard me as a Bonnie Prince Chile . . . , even if I'm not a Briton or a Scot. . . . Neither am I a Spaniard, as so many of my dear subjects think when they class me among "Spanish foods." Am I Mexican then? It all depends on breeding and certain attitudes. First of all, I am genuine American by birth and blood—Indian if you will. Actually, an Aztec demi-god originally. I was then called *Chili* or *Axi* in my very first native land. My temper then was so infernally hot that, whether I was dressed in summer green or autumn red, those people worshipped me like a god. So fierce was I that they had to marry me to a mild princess called *Tomatl*, showering us with fragrant flowers and sweet spices in order to withstand my divine anger. . . . But ages ago when I moved up here, to the high narrow valleys of Alcalde and Embudo, of Santa Clara and Cochiti and other

such enchanted places, a great change came over me. I turned from a fierce vengeful god into a jolly mellow prince while keeping my sharp wit. Whereas I once had been adored with some dread for my pugency [sic], I was now loved for my flavor. It was this enchanted land that did it, her short hot summers and crystal sunshine caressing my shoulders while cool mountain waters bathed my feet, and then her nipping but still clear-aired autumns vesting me with handsome vigor. No need of bedding me down with tomatoes or burying me in spices. Here I am loved for myself. In this way I am really Spanish here, pure *castizo*, for being taken purely for what I am. I am Spanish and Pueblo New Mexican, to be more exact, as I keep on warming the cockles of the heart with princely flavor and adorning the home with necklaces of coral.[39]

By the end of the century northerners made a more explicit break from the industrial chile. "Down there in the south, a lot of those chiles are as big as a banana, but they taste like cardboard, no flavor at all," explained El Guique chile farmer Orlando Casados Sr. "This is the best place for growing chile in the whole world." Some writers went even further, directly setting the northern chile in opposition to its intrastate neighbor to the south with a spirit of proud anti-industrialism. "Rebellion is in our blood here in the north where Reies López Tijerina's Courthouse Raid of 1967 was only one in a long series of uprisings against governments, corporations and individuals that attempt to usurp our rights and curtail our proud lifestyle," Jim Segal declared in 1996. "Our northern chile is just that rebellious. Gnarled and twisted, it refuses to lie flat on the grill for roasting. Likewise, it is not as readily 'stuffed' as the Big (and more obedient) Jims."[40]

For many the chile stood as a proud metaphor for the greater culture of northern New Mexico that seemed set on a different course from its southern counterpart. "Northern New Mexico may be one of the few places left in the country where a quasi-indigenous agriculture is still practiced," Stanley Crawford wrote in 1997. "Few other areas of the country have so successfully resisted or deflected or transformed the cultural flood tide of Anglo-European culture. The state forms the center of a culinary bioregion, with chile at its flaming heart." For Crawford, as for Chávez and other writers before him, the northern chile was wholly separate from, and even categorically opposed to, the university-bred industrial chile; it was a proud, racially charged symbol of resistance against the forces of modernity that had shaped the irrigated valleys of the south. Crawford explained that "some crops lure a person, or a people, into projecting their desires and hopes upon them, and gradually they yield to the human imperative to become what is desired. Difficult, stubborn, attractive, fiery, chile is one of those [crops], perhaps best of all."[41]

Yet such a sharp north-south narrative misses much of the nuance surrounding the diversity of opinions in the state and the varying approaches to modernity in all corners of New Mexico. Northern growers, in fact, have continued to grow university varieties, including the "Espanola Improved" and its derivatives, which blended the Sandia (itself a derivative of the number 9) and northern landrace chiles. Meanwhile in southern New Mexico the chile has signified more than the industry-driven narrative. Las Cruces writer Denise Chávez, for example, recalled in 1996 how her freezer full of green chile had felt "un-American" to her as a child. In a recollection of Fabián García, she assigned her own meaning to the man and to the crop that had shaped her valley. "Each land has its patron saints. I remember my mother, Delfina Rede Chávez, talking about Dr. Fabián García. . . . The Father of Chile, she called him." In a testament to the community's respect for García, Chávez continues, "She was someone who knew the value of genius, and to her, he was a man unlike any other. She recalled visiting him at McBride's Hospital in Las Cruces, where he lay on his deathbed, alone, nearly forgotten. 'He was a great man, *pobrecito*,' she lamented, 'only his own hometown didn't know it.'"[42]

A Twenty-First-Century Pepper:
Hatch, Chile Nativo, and the GMO Outcry

"Over the past few years here in California, the Hatch chile craze has been building up to a crescendo," syndicated columnist Gustavo Arellano remarked in 2013. "Every year, El Rey Farms holds a massive Hatch chile roast at La Puente High School [in La Puente, about twenty miles from Los Angeles]. . . . When it comes down to flavor and sense memory, rest assured that transplanted New Mexicans are on guard. They know their Hatch, and they want it to be genuine."[43] Indeed La Puente has not been the only place far from the Land of Enchantment where green chile roasters have recently sprouted up in grocery store parking lots, farmers markets, and celebratory events. Nearly ninety years since Fabián García expressed a wish for a "national education program" on chile-based cuisines, the smell of roasting green chile has wafted its way from coast to coast. As Arellano's statement attests, the recent nationwide enthusiasm for green chile has often centered on a desire for chile grown in the small town of Hatch in southern New Mexico. The town's marketing success has brought awareness of New Mexico's chile industry to a wide swath of the national population and helped bolster New Mexico's brand as the epicenter of chile cuisine. Yet with its successes have come concerns that once again reveal New Mexico's fraught relationship with modernity.

The small town of Hatch at the northern end of the Mesilla Valley, like others around it, had witnessed many crops—apples, cotton, and chile among them—in its fields since its founding in 1851. But it wasn't until the town threw its first chile festival in 1971, when a crowd of 1,500 threw horseshoes, drank beer, crowned the state's first "Chile Queen," and awarded blue ribbons for green chiles, that the identity of the place began to squarely align with the fiery fruit.[44] The town soon thereafter declared itself the "chile capital of the world"; since then, as the popular festivals have continued and as processors such as the Hatch Chile Company have spread the Hatch name, chile eaters far beyond New Mexico state lines have developed strong associations between the small town and New Mexico chile. The associations have become so deep that the term *Hatch chile*, which refers to chile grown in the town of Hatch and not a particular variety of chile, has become nearly synonymous with New Mexico chile in many parts of the country. The town's reputation as the epicenter of chile production and its iconic status as a near synonym with New Mexico chile peppers can largely be attributed to the town's chamber of commerce, but it also more broadly benefited from early efforts by groups such as the Connoisseurs and, later, the work of Paul Bosland and Dave Dewitt, among a host of other writers, to promote the chile pepper and, especially, the New Mexican chile pepper grown industrially in the state's southern irrigated valleys.

With the success of the Hatch name came concerns and criticisms from both within and outside the New Mexico chile industry. One industry concern was that out-of-state and foreign farmers and marketers were labeling chile grown elsewhere as "Hatch chile." Responding to these concerns, in 2011 the state passed the New Mexico Chile Advertising Act, which made it illegal for someone to mislabel a chile as New Mexico–grown. The act also made it illegal to label a chile as coming from a particular town, such as Hatch, unless it had been certified through the state to have been grown there. A separate concern among some within the industry was that the Hatch brand was beginning to subsume the broader New Mexico brand of chile. Dave Dewitt, for example, argued that the marketing tactics of Hatch producers and boosters deceived the public at the expense of the broader New Mexico brand. The "Hatch thing [is] a major con. . . . You're fooling people," Dewitt explained.[45]

What the growers have done is take Hatch and turn it into a trademark . . . they're trying to make Hatch synonymous with New Mexico chile. . . . And so they've got Texans saying Hatch chile, instead of New Mexico chile, and they have now invented a new valley. They've invented the "Hatch Valley," which is only the northern half of the Mesilla Valley. You can't just arbitrarily go around inventing a valley. . . . I talked to the *Sun-News* reporter who was writing about this, and I said, "You can't do that." And he said, "Well, everybody calls it the Hatch Valley." I mean, you can call a dog a cat. It doesn't make it one.[46]

Yet, as the story of the Champagne apple suggests, calling a dog a cat might not make it a cat but, with the right branding strategy, hardly anyone would know the difference.

As the Hatch chile became a household name throughout the country, tensions among New Mexicans over the "genuine" identity of the New Mexico chile came to the fore. The *chile nativo* (native chile), most often associated with the small town of Chimayó in northern New Mexico, became a local foil for the industrial chile. *Chile nativo* refers to landrace chile varieties that have developed in local valleys over the course of centuries without the use of modern agricultural science or breeding methods. These varieties—the same hard-to-peel, variable, and inconsistent peppers Dr. Fabián García and his successors sought to improve—are well adapted to local environments and, as often claimed by their advocates, taste better than industrial-bred chile. While there are many landrace chile varieties, often named after the valleys or towns where they developed—Escondido, Jemez Pueblo, Velarde, and Santa Domingo Pueblo, to name only a few—by far the best known is the variety from Chimayó, often portrayed as a holdover of traditional agriculture resisting death at the hands of industrial agriculture.[47]

Previous divisions surrounding chiles grown in New Mexico have only deepened in recent years. One source of division came with a proposed bill in the state legislature that earmarked money toward developing a genetically engineered (GE; or, alternatively,

GMO, short for genetically modified organism) chile pepper at NMSU. General anti-GE sentiment had already been growing in the state, where in 2006 a group of Pueblo farmers and a group of predominantly Hispano farmers and their advocates codrafted a "declaration on seed sovereignty" emphatically stating that "genetic modification and the potential contamination of our landraces by GE technology [is] a continuation of genocide upon indigenous people and [are] malicious and sacrilegious acts toward our ancestry, culture, and future generations."[48] Learning of the proposed bill in 2008, a small group of citizens and small-scale agriculture advocates swiftly mobilized to fight the plan. The group introduced a Farmers Liability Act that aimed to protect farmers from being sued if patented genes from GE chile cross-contaminated their fields. Though it never passed, the proposed act struck a chord of fear in many small farmers, gardeners, and consumers that the GE chile was not a mere annoyance they could live with, but rather an existential threat to the very soul of the chile pepper and its farmers' livelihoods. The chorus of protest gained in volume through the voices of prominent global activist Vandana Shiva and local intellectuals, such as University of New Mexico folklorist Dr. Enrique Lamadrid.

For Shiva and Lamadrid, the threat went deep. "Vandana Shiva tells us that one of the most cynical strategies of the Second Green Revolutions [sic] is to desensitize people by targeting their most culturally iconic plants, such as Eggplants in India and Chiles in New Mexico," Lamadrid explained. "If people accept the 'genetic engineering' of their signature cultural crops, then they will not notice or complain when the Big Four move in—corn, soybeans, cotton, and canola."[49] Although this analysis presupposes a grand "strategy" in vague terms (and also seemingly ignores the reality that genetically engineered cotton had already been well established in the fields of New Mexico), the statement illustrates how much the industrial chile had become perceived as a corporate evil and an existential threat to the agricultural, cultural, and personal health of New Mexicans.[50] To further develop this point Lamadrid took to an old form of storytelling in collaboration with local historian Juan Estevan Arellano and New Mexican folk musician Cipriano Vigil. The three men composed a creative commentary on the GE chile debate in the form of a traditional *corrido,* or ballad, that pitted the *Chile Chimayoso* (Chimayó chile) against a hypothetical genetically engineered chile they dubbed Chile Número 10. In the corrido, the two chile trade verses, duking it out for chile supremacy in the state. At stake, the authors make clear, is not just the soul of the chile but of the New Mexican people. "The chile and its seeds belong to our state," they exclaim. "If we lose them completely, we'll be sent to hell."

In contrast to the number 9 and the imaginary number 10, the chile nativo in the corrido is delicious and strong, piquant and rooted, divine and heroic. "From my test tube I have come to defeat your people," the newfangled chile sings. The modern chile is soulless, "motherless," sterile, sinister, bland, preferred among "capitalists," and, ultimately, weak. Throughout the corrido the authors mark a clear distinction between the rational science of the industrial chile and the nonmodern religiosity of the native chile, with roots in Catholic and Native religious traditions. Harkening back to the language of Fray Angélico Chávez roughly fifty years earlier, the poets write that the native chile was "born of water and sun and only seek[s] peace from God," and was "born in Teotihuacan . . . of divine origin." "I was reborn in the floating gardens, of the Red Earth Mother, son also of Tlaloc, Lord of water and rain. I am also god son of Lady Chicomecoatl, mother of nourishment." With no mention of breeders, the native chile sings, "God raised me." As the corrido ends, the native chile calls the modern chile a "sickly . . . lazy rubber chile . . . born in a laboratory. I will never, never permit that you injure my people." With that proud and unequivocal rebuke of modernity, the native chile claims a triumphant victory.

The corrido is ripe with sharp dichotomies and simplifications that mask the nuanced history of the chile. The corrido does not, for example, address the limited embrace of Fabián García's number 9 chile among many throughout the north and his continued legacy there. After all, some of the most celebrated farmers in northern New Mexico today grow chiles that derive part of their genetics from the number 9.[51] Yet, although Lamadrid concedes that the number 9 is of "more honorable stock" than the hypothetical Número 10, he firmly places the number 9 in the lineage of modern chiles that stand against the native chile. "The staple of the chile revolution of the twentieth century," Lamadrid writes in his introduction to the corrido, "Chile Number Nine gave birth to all the modern varieties such as Big Jim." (This claim, in fact, is only true if taken figuratively; the Big Jim, like all NMSU varieties except the Sandia and its derivatives, does not contain genes from the number 9 line.) "But," Lamadrid continues, "as connoisseurs can attest, complexity and flavor were sacrificed to achieve size, uniformity, and dependability."

Despite, or perhaps because of, the sharp dichotomies portrayed, such storytelling within the campaign against the GE chile proved effective. Although the industry strategized "to promote GMO as environmentally-friendly agriculture" and develop "GMO market-friendly packaging" as early as 2003, the consumer pushback against the idea of GE chile was substantial; perhaps as a result, no GE chile yet exists in commercial production.[52] Nonetheless, though the rhetorical battle over a proposed GE chile has somewhat subsided in recent years, animosity from northern, small-scale chile growers toward the chile industry has continued. The most recent issue surrounds the NM Chile Advertising Act (2012) and its amendment, "Expanding the Violations of the NM Chile Advertising Act" (2013), which made it illegal for a grower to use the name of a town, river, or any other geographic feature without first registering with the state. This regulation, opponents argued, would hurt small-scale northern New Mexican farmers growing seeds named after their towns or valleys, such as Chimayó. As one chile nativo grower declared, the burdensome regulation "threatens the local autonomy of seed and food sovereignty."[53] With advertising squarely at the fore of the debate, the fight over the chile had firmly become a fight over its story.

The Ever-Evolving Pod

"As any self-respecting chilehead knows," wrote journalist Kent Paterson in 1999, "New Mexico is the center of the U.S. chile universe." Such a statement testifies to nearly three decades of concerted efforts within the industry to promote the state's chile-growing status. In the nearly two decades since Paterson wrote these words, however, the state's chile production has declined and its centrality in the "chile universe" has been challenged by growers elsewhere.[54] The industry has suffered in competition from Mexico, China, India, Peru (all of whom produce far more chile than growers in the Land of Enchantment) and, to a smaller extent (but especially irksome to New Mexicans), Colorado.[55] Despite this competition and the state's decline in actual production, the cultural weight of the New Mexico chile pepper's stories, far more than the sheer weight of its actual harvests, continue to contribute to the state's outsized position in the national and international chile landscape.

The industrial chile has many legacies in New Mexico. From north to south, and encompassing a diversity of opinions throughout, the rise of the industrial chile has brought forth new narratives and counternarratives about the people of New Mexico who, like no other population in the nation, cherish the fiery vegetable. The industrial chile pepper has left a profound mark on the cultural landscape of New Mexico. Like cotton and apples before it, it has brought with it hopes of economic gain, inspired popular festivals, and sparked migrations of people that have in turn influenced the culture of the place. As Kent Paterson writes, "In southern New Mexico, chile . . . helped change the demographic and social makeup of the southern counties, drawing in a new wave of Mexican immigrants."[56] Yet the industrial chile had a unique impact that goes beyond dreams of wealth, celebrations, and demographic shifts, which, as I show elsewhere in this book, had followed previous industrial crops into the region. What the chile did, and previous industrial crops did not, was to bring that industrialization into the heart of the New Mexico cultural identity. For the first time New Mexicans throughout the state associated their very culture with a crop that was industrially produced.

With that change came a level of both pride and conflict. As the industry boomed and New Mexico chile became more prominent nationwide, the pepper became even more laden with rich, and often conflicting, narratives about the people who grow, depend on, and cherish it. The new narratives that emerged for the chile pepper fell in line with a long tradition of "invented traditions" in American agriculture. From grand narratives such as Jefferson's mythic yeoman farmer to small tales such as Old Jim Young's Champagne apple, the agricultural history of the nation is rife with stories that stretch the truth in projecting a more marketable image of American farm life. These stories fall into a broad category of invented traditions that, in the words of Chris Wilson, "rework serviceable fragments from our regional, family, and ethnic traditions, mixed with borrowings from other times and peoples, and leavened by pure invention."[57] Such traditions, Wilson explains, often tap into a growing, popular anxiety over modernity; they are modern tools designed to mask their very modernity.

In the case of New Mexico and its famed chile pepper, inventions ranged from new narratives about the origin of the first scientific chile to new mythologies of a native chile, complete with a divine voice that spoke for a people rejecting many of the tenets of modern agribusiness. On one end of the spectrum, these inventions bolstered New Mexico's claim to a central place in modern agriculture; on the other end, they bolstered its claim as a site of resistance to modern agriculture. In all cases the stories attached to the chile pepper reveal not only the prominence of storytelling in American agriculture but also how New Mexicans celebrated and contested the greater project of modernity in their fields and with their pens.

Conclusion

If you were to take a drive through the agricultural valleys of New Mexico sometime in the early autumn these days, you would likely find the living legacies of the stories that have filled these pages. In the north and in the higher reaches of the state, perhaps you'd come across some old apple trees, with dead branches and roots clinging to a riparian water table, still bearing fruit where not even a building from the old homestead still stands. Perhaps, too, you would see some orchards newly planted with cider varieties for an aspiring craft-cider industry that has emerged in recent years, mixed alongside a scattering of mature orchards dating back roughly half a century, when many throughout northern New Mexico planted apple trees.

In the south of the state, you would likely drive past lots of cotton, inconspicuously hiding in plain sight among the broader groves of pecan orchards and the iconic chile fields that blanket the irrigated acres of the southern parts of the state. Despite the ubiquity of chile peppers in statewide branding and marketing, the number of acres planted in chile statewide has dropped significantly over the past nearly three decades from its peak in 1992; as of 2019 acreage planted in cotton exceeded the acreage planted in chile nearly tenfold.[1] Chile growers often point to international competition, persistent drought, and a lack of inexpensive, seasonal labor as significant factors in the crop's decline. Meanwhile, in the north, farmers in Pueblos and in villages across northern New Mexico continue to grow landrace chiles on a small scale. Several of these landrace varieties are threatened and hard, if not impossible, to find commercially.[2]

The agricultural landscape you'd be driving through reveals more than a contemporary portrait of high-desert agriculture. Look closely and each of these crops bear not only a fruit or boll but also an intangible harvest of stories attached to a long history of shifting visions for the state. As we have seen, the history of a people is intricately entwined with the history of the plants they grow, consume, and, sometimes, celebrate. This history of apples, cotton, and chile in New Mexico brings to light these entwined relationships and helps illustrate how the region's agricultural past fits into the broader social, cultural, and environmental history of the Southwest and the nation. The histories of these crops in twentieth-century New Mexico explain migrations of plants and people; reveal the contingencies of industrialization and the contestations surrounding modernity; and underscore the powerful cultural effects of agriculture.

Migrations have been a continual theme in these stories. Agriculture, though often associated with farmers deeply rooted on a single farm in a single place, is a dynamic process that encourages relocations of many sorts. "I think it's indisputable," syndicated columnist Gustavo Arellano concluded, as he mused on a New Mexico green chile roast at a Los Angeles–area event in 2013, "that genuine New Mexican food finds its roots in relocation and migration."[3] With roots that stretch back through the twentieth century to Fabián García's work as a borderlands intermediary who bridged cultural divides and sourced seeds from throughout the greater Southwest, the New Mexico chile's appearance in Los Angeles represented an ironic homecoming in the long history of agricultural migrations that have defined the agriculture of the region. Whether it has been the growers and workers who all brought diverse cultural customs, or the seeds and plants that came laden with embedded labor, stories, and (sometimes) pests, New Mexican agriculture in the twentieth century has witnessed constant migrations of plants, insects, and people that have had a significant impact on the physical and cultural landscape of the region.

These migrations, which were born out of the desire to industrialize the agriculture of the region, point to a broader history of modernity and agriculture in New Mexico. Each crop has brought with it modern technologies and innovations—from pesticides and spray laws to innovative advertising, from highly organized seed districts to greenhouses, from scientifically bred seeds to carefully crafted stories about those seeds—that have led to new agricultural possibilities and broader cultural change. Yet, as a swell of modernity has unfurled in the region's agricultural landscape, farms became the site of resistance and contestation to modernity, as well. Whether it was a small-scale apple grower protesting spray laws, a group of workers at Stahmann's organizing *matachines* dances, or writers and scholars creating counternarratives to entrenched stories of the modern chile, seemingly small moments in the state's agricultural past have added up to a sustained challenge in rethinking the course of the agricultural industry.

This course of industrial agriculture, we have seen, has been nonlinear, conglomerate, and highly contingent. For all those concerned with the current problems surrounding industrial food production, the contingencies of the industrial past may provide a hopeful reminder that change is possible. This nonlinear history of agriculture also points to the myriad ways industrial agriculture has relied on various "nonindustrial" forms of agriculture. Upon close examination a binary consisting of two wholly separate agricultural systems gives way to a more nuanced portrait of countless agricultural approaches interconnected in many and often surprising ways. Whether it has been industrial seed, such as Acala cotton or Sandia chile, with a genetic legacy shaped by countless generations of farmers developing the seed in small-scale diversified systems, or whether it has been Chinese weeder geese cultivating thousands of acres of cotton, old technologies born far from industry have helped industrial growers succeed. Beyond the physical technologies, modern agriculturalists have also often employed the imagery of nonmodern traditions to help sell their products, such as in the case of boosters using the *manzanas mejicanas* to promote New Mexico's apple industry or James Webb Young employing the yeoman myth to sell apples to New Yorkers. Industrial agriculture is a malleable set of systems that, in many ways, has relied on traditional forms of agriculture.

As this book has focused heavily on the cultural side of agricultural industrialization, we have seen that storytelling is not an afterthought to modern agriculture, but rather is a central component. From the mythical origins of the Manzano apple orchard to James Webb Young's Champagne apples, from the early cotton festivals to Stahmann's "junior geese" and pecans, and from Fabián García's musings over a national education program surrounding chile to recrafted narratives of Fabián García himself, storytelling has been a common thread of efforts to bring success to agricultural industry in the state throughout the twentieth century. Yet, as the example of the chile nativo and the public outcry over a GE chile highlights, stories have also been central to efforts to resist facets of industrialization. The integral nature of storytelling to both agricultural industrialization and its countermovements provides a potential lesson for all those interested in seeing changes in agriculture or agricultural policy: it may be just as useful to take hold of pen as it would a hoe.

Stories of crops, like the seeds of the crops themselves, continually evolve. Similar to seeds that have been bred and manipulated to suit the needs of growers or an industry, stories about crops reflect a people's deeper cultural values. Also like seeds, whose genetics continually adapt to their climate, stories of plants change along with the cultural and social landscape they live in. Just as breeders cannot easily maintain a seed's genetics after it leaves their test plots, storytellers cannot easily claim a final word on the story of any plant. Crops and their stories coevolve, shaping each other in ways that no single person could easily predict. This book, an investigation on the coevolving relationship between crops and their stories, is ultimately itself just another story in the long, ever-evolving, and continually contested history of the agriculture of the region.

Notes

1. For a few examples of exemplary commodity histories, see Evans, *Bound in Twine*; Kurlansky, *Salt*; Mintz, *Sweetness and Power*; Sackman, *Orange Empire*; Bowman, *Blood Oranges*; and Soluri, *Banana Cultures*.

2. Okie, *The Georgia Peach*, 2; Ott, *Pumpkin*, 6. Philip Pauly in *Fruits and Plains* and Jared Farmer in *Trees in Paradise* both present particularly good examples of recent monographs that investigate the cultural meanings of multiple crops introduced to the United States in the nineteenth and early twentieth centuries.

3. Deborah Fitzgerald argues that an "industrial logic" developed after the First World War that drove American agriculture. "Science, technology, and the spirit of rationalism . . . characterized industrial agriculture," Fitzgerald explains, "maintained by a new class of people and institutions [i.e., economists, farm managers, agricultural college researchers, extension agents, rural banks and insurance companies, and agricultural businesses] whose principal purpose was to modernize the whole agricultural enterprise." Fitzgerald, *Every Farm a Factory*, 6. For a seminal work on biological innovations in the history of U.S. agriculture, see Olmstead and Rhode's *Creating Abundance*.

4. Sackman, *Orange Empire*, 86; Wald, *The Nature of California*, 5.

5. Cooper, *Colonialism in Question*, 126.

6. As this book illustrates, rather than follow a simple, triumphalist narrative that completely derides "traditions," modern agrarian stories often celebrate elements of the "traditions" they aim to supplant. In a form of imperialist nostalgia, industrial agriculturalists have at times painted the agricultural legacy of nonindustrialists into a nostalgic past that is at once virtuous but woefully ill equipped to navigate ever-changing complexities of the global marketplace. For more on imperialist nostalgia, see Rosaldo,

"Imperialist Nostalgia." For seminal works on modernity and tradition, see Bendix, "Tradition and Modernity Reconsidered"; and Hobsbawm and Ranger, *The Invention of Tradition*.

7. Fullilove, *The Profit of the Earth*, 220; Kloppenburg, *First the Seed*, 14; and Kingsbury, *Hybrid*, 370.

8. Kerrigan, *Johnny Appleseed and the American Orchard*, 191.

9. Beckert, *Empire of Cotton*.

10. Okie, *The Georgia Peach*, 8.

11. Fullilove, *The Profit of the Earth*, 9.

1. Before Aliens, There Were Apples

1. On Pat Garrett's orchard, see Metz, *Pat Garrett*, 150.

2. Wheat, corn (for feed), sorghum, oats, and alfalfa all brought in more total revenue than apples throughout this period; by 1920 cotton and beans also brought in a more valuable crop than apples in the state. See *United States Census of Agriculture: 1935*, vol. 1, pt. 3, 863, 869.

3. Canaigre, *Rumex hymenosepalus*, is also known as Tanner's dock and is native to the U.S. Southwest. Late nineteenth-century industrialists briefly considered it a potentially important crop to support the region's tanning industry. See Bowcutt, *The Tanoak Tree*, 48.

4. Several historians have illustrated how western horticulturalists embraced science and modernity during this time. For examples in California, see Farmer, *Trees in Paradise*; Sackman, *Orange Empire*; and Sandul, "The Agriburb." For a Pacific Northwest example, Jason Patrick Bennett argues that "the process of establishing fruit farms was only made possible with the tools of modern technology," which led to the production of a "new vision of modernism—a vision that combined promises of fantastic profits and dreams of nature's harmonious bounty." Bennett, "'Nature's Garden and a Possible Utopia,'" 226–27. Elsewhere Bennett explains that the orchard landscape of the early twentieth-century Pacific Northwest represented a rural "alternative modernity" that "valorized a partnership between farmer and nature through the insights of agricultural science." Bennett, "Blossoms and Borders," 27.

5. Folger and Thomson, *The Commercial Apple Industry of North America*. The predominant regions were the Northeast, the Mid-Atlantic, the Midwest, the Ozarks, the Intermountain West, and the Pacific Northwest. Folger and Thomson claim that it wasn't until the 1890s that commercial orchards in the Midwest (Illinois, Arkansas, Missouri) took off and that commercial orchardists nationwide planted apples in large numbers. Prices for apples were high in the late 1880s, stimulating planting throughout the country. In Washington, major commercial plantings did not begin until 1894, with the most extensive plantings happening from 1900 to 1908 in the Yakima Valley, and not until 1903 in the Wenatchee Valley. Hood River was commercially planted in the last years of the nineteenth century. In California, the Pajaro Valley was planted

with commercial orchards earlier, from 1880 to 1900. See also Magness, *Apple Varieties and Important Producing Sections of the United States*.

6. García, "History of Fruit Growing in New Mexico," 84.

7. García, "History of Fruit Growing in New Mexico," 84; "Fruit," *Santa Fe New Mexican*, October 25, 1871, 1; and "Vegetable and Fruit Gardens Wanted," *Santa Fe New Mexican*, July 23, 1875, 1.

8. In addition to the orchards of John Chisum and Chase, the Bull and Casad orchards in the Mesilla Valley serve as preeminent examples of large-scale, successful orchards. See *Report of the Governor of New Mexico to the Secretary of the Interior*, 493. Thomas J. Bull made "large quantities" of apple brandy and wine, and even wowed Santa Feans in 1876 with a mammoth apple that measured thirteen inches in diameter. See the *Santa Fe New Mexican*, August 29, 1876, 1. By 1890 one visitor described Bull's orchard as a "bonanza." See A. W. Small, "A Visitor's Testimony," *Rio Grande Republican* (Las Cruces NM), February 15, 1890, 1.

9. "The Chase Orchard," 20–21. See also, "New Mexico . . . ," *Decatur (IN) Daily Democrat*, December 28, 1907, 3.

10. Fabián García, *Apple Culture under Irrigation*, 3. As García describes, the Rio Grande Valley developed smaller, but locally important, apple districts from Taos to Mesilla, as did the Mimbres Valley. Otero, Lincoln, Colfax, Mora, Grant, and San Miguel counties also developed small but locally significant apple districts in the late nineteenth and early twentieth centuries. For examples of booster literature promoting New Mexico's potential apple-growing greatness, see Women's Auxiliary Committee, World's Columbian Exposition, *San Juan County, New Mexico*; and "A Fruit Belt," *Santa Fe New Mexican Review*, June 28, 1899, 1, which includes the claim "New Mexico is destined to become the leading apple country in the world."

11. Bogener, "Ditches across the Desert," 24–25, 183; For more on Chisum's orchard, see Anderson, *New Mexico*, 2:796.

12. Bogener, "Ditches across the Desert," 135.

13. Bogener, "Ditches across the Desert," 155–56.

14. *The Pecos Valley*, 6.

15. Bogener, "Ditches across the Desert," 161–62.

16. Bogener, "Ditches across the Desert," 163–66. For Hagerman's famous refusal, see William J. Parish, "Sheep Husbandry in New Mexico, 1902–1903," *New Mexico Historical Review*, January 1963, 60–61. See also García, *Proceedings of the Thirty-Eighth Convention of the American Pomological Society*.

17. Boosters never failed to allay prospective horticultural settlers' fears about water supply. Despite the dependable surface and ground water, water estimates throughout the valley were nonetheless routinely placed absurdly high. At one point estimates on how many acres could be irrigated from the Carlsbad Project, for example, ranged from four hundred thousand to seven hundred thousand. In the end, only forty thousand were irrigated. See Bogener, "Ditches across the Desert," 260. As in Roswell, San Juan growers at times considered their water "inexhaustible." "Our water supply

is inexhaustible," wrote one grower, [illegible] to Prince, Junction City [Farmington], N. Mex., August 21, 1894, microfilm, r. 109, sub. ser. 11.19, TANM.

18. Folger and Thomson, *The Commercial Apple Industry of North America*, 62–63.

19. Well into the 1920s Roswell had the advantage in freight costs over any other region in New Mexico—and even over other apple-growing regions like Montrose, Colorado, and Hood River, Oregon—to important markets such as Dallas, Kansas City, Chicago, and New York. For example, the freight charges from the apple district of Hood River, Oregon, were 76 percent higher to Dallas and Kansas City, 62 percent higher to Chicago, and 7 percent higher to New York than from Roswell. For good comparative maps of apple freight charges within and outside New Mexico, see A. L. Walker, "Farmers' Cooperation in New Mexico, 1925–1926," in NMSU LDC.

20. See Folger and Thomson, *The Commercial Apple Industry of North America*, 62.

21. Pendleton, *San Juan County*, 55.

22. William Locke to L. Bradford Prince, September 2, 1890, microcopy, r. 107, sub. ser. 11.19, TANM. See also Crawford, *Under the Apple Tree*, 85.

23. Pendleton, *San Juan County*, 41.

24. Crawford, *Under the Apple Tree*, 6.

25. William Locke to L. Bradford Prince, September 2, 1890, r. 107, sub. ser. 11.19, TANM.

26. William Locke to L. Bradford Prince, r. 104, sub. ser. 11.19, TANM. See also Crawford, *Under the Apple Tree*.

27. Pendleton, *San Juan County*, 41, 49, 51.

28. While documentation of Navajo workers is scarce, some evidence of early participation as laborers exists. See, for example, "Picking Apples at Cunningham Orchard," Farmington Museum, NMDC. For later accounts of Navajo apple workers, see Crawford, *Under the Apple Tree*, 46–47.

29. Griffith et al., "Ecoregions of New Mexico."

30. Pendleton, *San Juan County*, 65.

31. For example, Jasper Hall and Jesse Frazier were two notable nineteenth-century Colorado grafters.

32. The diversity of available apple varieties developed by nurserymen in the mid- to late nineteenth-century United States has led some scholars to dub the period the Golden Age of Apples. See, for example, Burford, "Apples," 79; and Calhoun, *Old Southern Apples*, 8. By the early 1890s, when at least twenty apple varieties were still considered well suited and marketable for the area, agricultural experts had begun to recommend growers select only a few varieties to make bulk sales and joint shipments easier. See F. C. Barker et al., "A Productive Valley," *Rio Grande Republican* (Las Cruces NM), February 17, 1893, 1.

33. New Mexico's land-grant college was founded in 1888 and originally called Las Cruces College. During its first full academic year it became known as the New Mexico College of Agriculture and Mechanic Arts, a name it retained until 1960, when it officially became New Mexico State University. For general histories of experiment

stations at land-grant universities, see Geiger, *To Advance Knowledge*; and Marcus, *Agricultural Science and the Quest for Legitimacy*.

34. Local, young, white women often packed apples and sometimes picked apples, as well. For photographic examples in the Farmington District, see "Hyde Exploration Company Apple Pickers," 1900, and "Hyde Exploration Co. Apple Pickers," 1907, both in Farmington Museum, NMDC. For Roswell District examples, see "Packing Apples B. Cleve Orchard," Elk NM, October 16, 1908, Image no. 01010793, MS 0101, and "Packing Apples at Roswell, New Mexico," Roswell NM, March 24, 1904, Image no. 02231001, MS 0223, Thomas K. Todsen Photographs, both in New Mexico State University Photographic Collections. Some later photographs (c. 1930s) indicate Navajo women also picked apples. See "Picking Apples at Cunningham Orchard," Farmington Museum, NMDC.

35. Mary Hudson Brothers, "Farmington Apple Industry," *Farmington* (NM) *Times Hustler*, August 12, 1938, 2.

36. Judge J. F. Wielandy reports the first sighting of the worm by a "French gentleman named Bouquet" in Pojoaque, New Mexico, who had first noticed the moths in his trees in 1889. See Townsend, *Notices of Importance concerning Fruit Insects*, 6. For an early history of the codling moth's migration, see Simpson and Howard, "The Codling Moth," 13–14.

37. The moth first arrived in the Mesilla Valley in 1892, the Farmington District shortly thereafter, and the Pecos Valley late in the decade.

38. Bureau of Immigration of the Territory of New Mexico, *Eddy County*, 9, 10.

39. "Apples in New Mexico," *Agriculture and Horticulture*, 1898, Bulletin no. 2, Territorial Bureau of Immigration, microcopy, r. 96, fr. 1041, p. 12, NMTBIR.

40. Pendleton, *San Juan County*, 29.

41. "New Mexico," *Decatur* (IN) *Daily Democrat*, December 28, 1907, 3.

42. Quoted in "The Chase Orchard," 20–21.

43. Townsend, *Notices of Importance concerning Fruit Insects*, 7.

44. Townsend, *Notices of Importance concerning Fruit Insects*, 6–7.

45. Townsend, *Insecticides and their Appliances*, 4, 6.

46. Cockerell, *Preliminary Notes on the Codling Moth*, 60.

47. Cockerell, *Preliminary Notes on the Codling Moth*, 57, 60, 68.

48. *Rio Grande Republican* (Las Cruces NM), November 5, 1897, 3. A Mesilla Valley Horticultural Society in November 1897, led by spraying advocate Dr. James H. Bailey, decided on the starvation method. A month or so earlier, the society had met because "[growers] must devise means to fight the codling moth successfully or quit raising apples." See *Rio Grande Republican* (Las Cruces NM), October 1, 1897, 3.

49. García, "Report from the Horticulturalist," in *Eighteenth Annual Report*, 31.

50. García, "Report from the Horticulturalist," in *Nineteenth Annual Report*, 26–27.

51. Townsend, *Insecticides and their Appliances*, 9.

52. Keffer, "Spray the Fruit Trees."

53. García, *Spraying Orchards for the Codling Moth*, 4.

54. Leading this effort were the college and the New Mexico Horticultural Society, which was founded in 1886. Territorial governor L. Bradford Prince led the effort

along with some of the territory's most elite (and mostly Anglo—only three of eighteen original board members had Spanish surnames) orchardists, politicians, and lawyers, whose work to develop the "horticultural industry in New Mexico" came in tandem with broader efforts to modernize the territory that centered on pest control in fruit trees. The group organized expositions to showcase New Mexico fruit throughout the territory and country, and held lectures on pest control in Santa Fe; it also took the lead on developing and enforcing early orchard inspection laws.

55. Townsend, *Notices of Importance concerning Fruit Insects*, 6–7.

56. Nicholl, *Observations of a Ranchwoman in New Mexico*, 64–66.

57. Cockerell, *Entomological Observations of 1894*, 50.

58. Bailey, *Cyclopedia of American Agriculture: 1909*, 530–31.

59. Townsend, *Scale-Insects in New Mexico*, 3.

60. Novak, *The People's Welfare*, 203. Philip Pauly offers a brief history of late nineteenth- and early twentieth-century horticultural board policing, with an emphasis on the interstate and international pest-control policing; see Pauly, *Fruits and Plains*, 131–64.

61. Percy Barker to the Doña Ana County Board of Horticultural Commissioners, July 1, 1892, folder 82, box 3, DACNMR.

62. F. N. Page to Gov. Hagerman, Guadalupe County NM, March 1, 1906, microcopy, r. 159, fr. 646, TANM. Emphasis in original. Resentment among small growers toward spray laws emerged throughout the country at this time. For example, see Okie, *The Georgia Peach*, 115–20. For an example of how growers elsewhere in the country more broadly viewed pest issues as a problem of social control, see Giesen, "'The Truth about the Boll Weevil,'" 683–70.

63. Magness, *Apple Varieties and Important Producing Sections in the United States*, 2.

64. James E. McWilliams describes an "insect paradox," where efforts to control the environment through insecticides have been undermined by those very means of control, in McWilliams, *American Pests*. For codling moth resistance to lead arsenate, see Rebecca Claren, "Farming's Toxic Legacy," *High Country News* (Paonia CO), December 13, 2010, http://www.hcn.org/issues/42.21/farmings-toxic-legacy.

65. Botkin and Hamiel, *Spray Residue on Apples in New Mexico*.

66. "Agricultural Quiz at Rotary Club Yesterday Brought Out Numerous Interesting Facts," *Roswell (NM) Daily Record*, January 19, 1923, 1.

67. Mary Orr, "Manzano—America's Oldest Apple Orchard," *New Mexico Magazine*, July 1935, 47.

68. Florence M. Hawley, "Yes, We Have No Old Apples," *New Mexico Magazine*, August 1936, 17.

69. "The Oldest Bearing Apple Trees in America," *Albuquerque (NM) Journal*, December 2, 1911, 6.

70. A. H. Garnett to Governor Otero, "Manzano Day Picnic, July 24, 1905," July 17, 1905, microcopy, r. 137, fr. 401, TANM; "Manzano Picnic Well Patronized," *Santa Fe New Mexican*, July 23, 1907, 1.

71. "Will Graft Old Apple Tree Scions," *Rio Grande Republican* (Las Cruces NM), January 30, 1912, 4. Silver City also had a "300 year old" apple tree it celebrated. "The old apple trees supposed to be 300 years old planted by seeds brought by priests with Pizarros Expeditiion [*sic*] to the North near Silver City, New Mexico." Palace of the Governors Photo Archives, New Mexico History Museum, Santa Fe, NMDC, http:// econtent.unm.edu/cdm/singleitem/collection/acpa/id/5473/rec/104.

72. "Garden of Eden in New Mexico," *Albuquerque* (NM) *Journal*, October 13, 1911, 8; "The Garden of Eden Is as Fertile as Ever," *Albuquerque* (NM) *Morning Journal*, December 12, 1911, 6; and *Santa Fe New Mexican*, February 10, 1907. It should be noted that nowhere in the Book of Genesis is the forbidden fruit named as an apple. For a discussion on the origins of the forbidden fruit as an apple, see for example Appelbaum, *Aguecheek's Beef*.

73. Nicholl, *Observations of a Ranchwoman*, 59, 64.

74. Nicholl, *Observations of a Ranchwoman*, 59.

75. F. C. Barker et al., "A Productive Valley: The Candid Opinion of a Practical Fruit Raiser on the Products of the Valley Written by Request for the Republican," *Rio Grande Republican* (Las Cruces NM), February 17, 1893.

76. "Garden of Eden in New Mexico," *Albuquerque* (NM) *Journal*, October 13, 1911, 8.

77. *Farmington* (NM) *Enterprise*, March 13, 1908. Associations of the apple with both middle-class whiteness and misconceptions of the apple as native to North America were ubiquitous to the nation. Philip Pauly writes, for example, "Apples, everyone agreed, were model Americans whose naturalization had been effortless and whose ability to improve was remarkable. Horticulturalists had to remind readers that in spite of appearances, the genus *Malus* was not a primordially New World fruit." Pauly, *Fruits and Plains*, 67. For a comparative discussion of boosterism and race in the history of the orange industry in the South Texas borderlands region, see Bowman, *Blood Oranges*, chap. 2.

78. Pendleton, *San Juan County*, 27, 31.

79. "Money in Apples," *Santa Fe New Mexican*, May 7, 1904, 1.

80. Folger, *Commercial Apple Industry of North America*, 129.

81. Starr, *Inventing the Dream*, 128, 134. For explicitly drawn associations between whiteness and horticulture in late nineteenth-century California, see Tyrell, *True Gardens of the Gods*, 118–19.

82. Sandul, "The Agriburb," 201.

83. Farmer, *Trees in Paradise*, 239; M. E. Dane to Prince, November 4, 1889, r. 104, Prince Papers, TANM.

84. Folger and Thomson reflect this sentiment, writing, "Intensive fruit regions are necessarily thickly settled and provide social advantages superior to those in the average rural communities. The desire to live among educated persons and to have the advantages of excellent schools and churches and means of social recreation is strong." Folger and Thomson, *Commercial Apple Industry*, 129.

85. Bogener, "Ditches across the Desert," 307.

86. García, "History of Fruit Growing," 88.

87. *Proceedings of the Thirty-Eighth Convention of the American Pomological Society*, 112.

88. For a definition of the Hispano homeland in northern New Mexico, see Nostrand, *The Hispano Homeland*.

2. Patent Lies and the "People's Business"

1. Using census data from 1940 through 1978, and defining northern New Mexico as San Miguel, Mora, Taos, Sandoval, Santa Fe, and Rio Arriba counties, the percentage of statewide apples grown in northern New Mexico jumped from 14 percent in 1940 to 36 percent in 1945. It remained at roughly that percentage for the following two decades, before again shooting up to 49 percent by 1978. See the *United States Census of Agriculture: 1945*, vol. 1, pt. 42, county table 2, 48–51; *United States Census of Agriculture: 1959*, vol. 1, pt. 42, New Mexico, chapter B, table 11, 158–60; *United States Census of Agriculture: 1964*, vol. 1, pt. 42, New Mexico, county table 13, 284–87; and *United States Census of Agriculture: 1978*, vol. 1, pt. 31, New Mexico, table 32.

2. Norman H. Strouse, "Madison Avenue Is Many Places," in Sandage, *The Promise of Advertising*, 77.

3. Forde, "Celluloid Dreams," 175–89, (188 quoted). In the first decades of the twentieth century, JWT was at the cutting edge of employing market research in advertising (see Cox, *Selling Dixie*, 42), and Young, especially later in his career, emphasized blending market research, statistics, psychology, and an understanding of "folkways" into advertisements. See Manring, *Slave in a Box*, 94.

4. Young, *Ego-Biography*; and Young, *The Itch for Orders*, 2–3. Fred Dixon told an interviewer in 2003 that Young was "the smartest man I ever knew . . . he was an atheist, his first job was selling Baptist bibles." Fred Dixon, interview by Ramona Rand-Caplan, June 15, 2003, transcript, p. 9 [tape 1, side A], OHP-NMFRHM.

5. Manring, *Slave in a Box*, 91–109.

6. Paul Hoffman, "Introduction," in Sandage, *The Promise of Advertising*. On the old trees of La Cañada de Cochiti, see Fred Dixon, June 15, 2003, 31, OHP-NMFRHM. On his profit, see Young, *The Diary of an Ad Man*, 50.

7. Fred Dixon later recalled that, the first time they met, Young told him not to smash a wormy apple because "I'll sell every one of those." Dixon then asked, "You'd sell a wormy apple?" and Young replied, "Yes . . . they'll all sell." Fred Dixon, June 15, 2003, 12, OHP-NMFRHM.

8. Sumner, *How I Learned the Secrets of Success in Advertising*, 201–2. See also "Here's a Blessing in Disguise," advertisement, *Santa Fe New Mexican*, October 1, 1961, 22; and "Young Victim of His Own Salesmanship," *Santa Fe New Mexican*, December 18, 1964, 3.

9. "The Champagne of Apples," advertisement, *Albuquerque (NM) Journal*, October 21, 1947, 8.

10. C. E. Hellbusch, "Old Jim Young's Big Red Apples," *New Mexico Magazine*, January 1950, 35; "Apples," advertisement, *Albuquerque (NM) Journal*, October 18, 1955, 20; "Garden Fresh Fruits and Vegetables," advertisement, *Albuquerque (NM) Journal*, 1960; and *Santa Fe New Mexican*, September 15, 1960.

11. "Here's a Blessing in Disguise," advertisement, *Santa Fe New Mexican*, October 1, 1961, 22; advertisement, *Santa Fe New Mexican*, October 11, 1962, 16; and "Now See the Valley of Glory," advertisement, *Santa Fe New Mexican*, November 3, 1963, 16.

12. Smith, *Virgin Land*, 123.

13. Hoffman, "Introduction," in Sandage, *The Promise of Advertising*.

14. Young, *The Diary of an Ad Man*, 220.

15. Dixon, June 15, 2003, 51–52, OHP-NMFRHM.

16. Dixon, June 15, 2003, 83, OHP-NMFRHM.

17. Dixon, June 15, 2003, 42, OHP-NMFRHM.

18. Young, *The Compleat Angler*.

19. Dixon, June 15, 2003, 27, 32, OHP-NMFRHM.

20. Peter Eichstaedt, "Apples: Dixon's Crop Cut Short; 'Freeze, Hail Made Waste,'" *Santa Fe New Mexican*, October 9, 1983, B1.

21. Catherine C. Robbins, "At the Nation's Table," *New York Times*, October 5, 1988.

22. Dixon, June 15, 2003, 1, 32, OHP-NMFRHM.

23. Traverso, *An Apple Lover's Cookbook*, 120–22.

24. Correia, *Properties of Violence*, 2.

25. Andrea Hughes, "A Good Harvest—At Last," *Santa Fe New Mexican*, September 23, 1973, 49.

26. "Valley Apple Cooperative Gets $333,000 Loan from SBA, EDVC," *Santa Fe New Mexican*, January 27, 1970, 6.

27. Gray and Stucky, *New Mexico Agriculture—1970*, 42.

28. Cockerill and Callaway, *Economics of the Production and Marketing of Apples in New Mexico*, 11, 63–64.

29. "Because of the interest in commercial fruit production in the [Española] valley, a tree fruit variety orchard was established at this station during the springs of 1953 and 1954." Trujillo, Hooks, and Sullivan, *Tree Fruit Variety Trials*, 1.

30. Berberich, *Considerations in Establishing a Fruit Storage and Marketing Facility*.

31. John Curtis, "Fruit Trade Booms in Northern Areas," *Santa Fe New Mexican*, October 13, 1957, 14.

32. "Apple Project Loans Sought," *Santa Fe New Mexican*, May 20, 1962, 11.

33. Burke, Sullivan, and Vastine, *An Economic Base Report*, 2.

34. See Burke, Sullivan, and Vastine, *An Economic Base Report*, 30. The authors state that New Mexico apples not sold within a few weeks after harvest had "little chance of competing with Washington apples at a later date unless rapidly cooled and stored at low temperature." See also Berberich, *Considerations in Establish a Fruit Storage and Marketing Facility*.

35. By the midsixties, the Española Valley was capable of growing eight hundred thousand bushels of apples, yet apple growers across the entire state had the capacity to store only fifty-seven thousand bushels under refrigeration. See Berberich, *Considerations in Establishing a Fruit Storage And Marketing Facility*. On the packing facilities at the Young orchard, see Burke, Sullivan, and Vastine, *An Economic Base Report*, 18.

36. Berberich, *Considerations in Establishing a Fruit Storage and Marketing Facility*, 18. On bumper crop of 1967, see "New Corporation Forms to Take Over Chimayo Apple Co-op," *Santa Fe New Mexican*, February 23, 1978, 43.

37. Max K. Jones, "Social Research Design: Home Education Livelihood Program Research and Demonstration Project," c. 1968, folder 32, box 2, FLQP.

38. "Report to Legislative Council, June 21 1968 from Home Education Livelihood Program," folder 34, box 2, FLQP.

39. "Report for the Governor: Status of the Apple Program; Chimayo/Española," Winter 1969, folder 1096, box 57, serial no. 10066, OEO-HELP Correspondence, collection no. 1969-001, DFCP. As this document points out, the growers selected organizing committees and appealed to state and federal entities for help securing a long-term, deferred payment loan for material costs and a two-year management grant "to provide expert services."

40. "New Corporation Forms to Take Over Chimayo Apple Co-op," *Santa Fe New Mexican*, February 23, 1978, 43.

41. Burke, Sullivan, and Vastine, *An Economic Base Report*, 42–53.

42. Gray and Stucky, *New Mexico Agriculture—1970*, 42.

43. Larson et al., *Comprehensive Plan*, 55.

44. Burke, Sullivan, and Vastine, *An Economic Base Report*, 1.

45. Larson et al., *Comprehensive Plan*, 29.

46. "Valley Apple Co-op Concerned over Quick Sales to Truckers," *Santa Fe New Mexican*, September 10, 1970, 13.

47. Stallings and Boyer, *Wholesale Fruit and Vegetable Markets in El Paso and Albuquerque*, 10–11. This report adds, "When asked about preference for New Mexico produce in comparison to that of the rest of the United States, wholesalers generally thought that New Mexico lettuce, onions, carrots, chile, sweet potatoes, cabbage, and cantaloupes were average or above depending on price, but rated New Mexico tomatoes, apples, and Irish potatoes average or below" (i).

48. Press Release from the Office of the Governor, n.d. [likely 1969], OEO-HELP Correspondence, box 57, serial no. 10066, DCP.

49. "Growers Backed on Tax to Promote NM Apples," *Santa Fe New Mexican*, August 28, 1970, 23.

50. "Shipment of Apples Set Nov. 13," *Santa Fe New Mexican*, November 4, 1970, 47.

51. Pamela Mabry Tate (Secretary of Northern New Mexico Farmers Cooperative) to Gov. Bruce King, October 1973, "Northern NM Farmers Cooperative," folder 1471, box 126, series VII, collection no. 1972-009, BKP-I.

52. Gov. Bruce King to David Best, October 25, 1973; Gov. Bruce King to Elaine Weinshenker [manager of New Mexico Union Food Services], October 25, 1973; and

Col. (ret.) Norman E. Fisher [business manager at the New Mexico Military Institute] to Gov. Bruce King, October 30, 1973; all in folder 1471, box 126, BKP-1.

53. "Chimayo Apple Crop Called 'Good' but Market Slow," *Albuquerque (NM) Journal*, October 10, 1973, B4.

54. "Valley Fruit Growers Plan Workshop Series," *Santa Fe New Mexican*, December 9, 1971, 4.

55. USDA Agricultural Research Service, Farmer Cooperative Service, and Four Corners Regional Commission, *Appraisal of the Apple Industry in the Four Corners Region*, 70.

56. "New Corporation Forms to Take Over Chimayo Apple Co-op," *Santa Fe New Mexican*, February 23, 1978, 43.

57. "New Corporation Forms to Take Over Chimayo Apple Co-op," *Santa Fe New Mexican*, February 23, 1978, 43.

58. Carlos Cansino, "After the 'Courthouse Raid' . . . ," *El Grito del Norte* (Española NM), April 1, 1970, 4.

59. "New T. A. Co-op Revives," *El Grito del Norte* (Española NM), March 10, 1969, 4.

60. Van Dresser, *A Landscape for Humans*, 111.

61. Knowlton, *Some Observations about the Relative Lack of Success*, 96.

62. Alex Mercure, quoted in Frankie McCarty, "North N.M. Poverty, Land Issue Linked," *Albuquerque (NM) Journal*, October 9, 1969, 1.

3. Shifting Subjects of a Southwest King

1. To add injury to insult, after the show the bandleader's priceless violin was stolen. Still in serape and sombrero from the performance, the "impressive and dejected" bandleader explained to a journalist that "the wonderfully sweet tone cannot be matched by violins made nowadays." See "King Cotton to Reign Supreme in Border City," *Albuquerque (NM) Morning Journal*, December 2, 1925, 2; "Mexican Tipica Orchestra Cuts Govt. Red Tape," *Albuquerque (NM) Morning Journal*, January 13, 1926, 3; and "Theft of Fine Old Violin at El Paso," *Roswell (NM) Daily Record*, December 31, 1925, 1.

2. Stamen, "Genetic Dreams," 103, 139.

3. "A Visitor's Testimony," *Rio Grande Republican* (Las Cruces NM), February 15, 1890, 1. The college experiment station first planted cotton in 1891.

4. Stewart, *Cotton Growing*. By 1916 the college began its first cotton variety trials in the Pecos Valley.

5. Overpeck and Conway, *Cotton*, 3. One of the first commercial cotton plantings in New Mexico was likely planted in the first years of the twentieth century by Francis Tracy, a Pecos Valley farmer who claimed to have planted the first commercial crop of Egyptian cotton in 1902 and to have introduced the Durango variety of cotton to the valley.

6. The largest cotton-growing districts in the New Mexico region were in the Pecos Valley, the Mesilla Valley, and the El Paso Valley. Smaller districts included counties north of Elephant Butte Dam and south of Albuquerque; well-irrigated parts of

far western New Mexico and far eastern Arizona. There was a small amount of dry-farmed cotton in far eastern New Mexico, which often was marketed separately from the irrigated cotton of the New Mexico region.

7. B. P. Fleming to L. D. Howell, September 18, 1931, folder 16, box 2, Cotton Products in Mesilla Valley, sub. ser. B, Office Files 1931–1940, series 2, EBIDR.

8. Leding, *Community Production of Acala Cotton in New Mexico*, 3.

9. "Cotton Growing on the Southwestern Projects," *Reclamation Record*, January 1925, p. 7, folder 10, box 206, MSS 394 BC, DCP. The article reports that whereas in 1917 only 40,000 acres of cotton had been grown in Arizona and New Mexico, by 1923 over 135,000 were planted and accounted for over a quarter of the entire gross value of all crops grown in those areas.

10. B. P. Fleming to L. D. Howell, September 18, 1931. In 1929, 75 percent of irrigable land was in cotton. See also Schönfeld La Mar, "Water and Land in the Mesilla Valley," 227.

11. "Migratory Labor in Southern New Mexico," 1940, p. 3, folder 37, box 17, MSS 289, USSCSR-8.

12. Leding, *Community Production of Acala Cotton in New Mexico*, 3.

13. "Cotton Brings New People to Pecos Valley," *Albuquerque (NM) Morning Journal*, January 14, 1925, 1.

14. Cecil Bonney, "Cotton Carnival Nears," *Roswell (NM) Daily Record*, September 6, 1930, 15.

15. Weigle and White, *The Lore of New Mexico*, 386.

16. H. S. Hunter, "Old Settlers' Parade Today Features Roswell's Carnival," *El Paso (TX) Herald*, October 5, 1928, 1. Despite the focus on cotton, the article noted that "the apple orchards also are the pride of the county."

17. "Chaves County Cotton Carnival to Be Held Here on Oct. 9–10–11," *Roswell (NM) Daily Record*, September 29, 1924, 1.

18. "Cotton Prospects Better Now Than Ever Before, Survey of Situation in Valley Now Shows," *Roswell (NM) Daily Record*, September 30, 1927, 25, 31

19. The Roswell cotton carnival became the eastern New Mexico state fair. Cotton, Inc. is the trade organization of the cotton industry in the United States.

20. Although bull fights, rather than World Series broadcasts or rodeos, provided some of the entertainment, the Juárez event similarly revolved around the process of crowning a cotton queen from local, most often elite, girls. (When a "rural girl" who "picks cotton" won in 1951, it made headlines in the local paper.) The fair continued for decades, often hosting Mexican movie stars, prizes for the most "industrial exhibits," and military displays. The festival corresponded with Mexico's independence celebrations of September 16 and had a nationalist feel. See "Juarez Princess Is Selected," *El Paso (TX) Post-Herald*, September 2, 1936, 6; "Chico in Bullfight in Juarez Oct. 11," *El Paso (TX) Post-Herald*, October 10, 1936, 7; "Governor Will Crown Queen of Juarez Fair," *El Paso (TX) Post-Herald*, September 5, 1947, 12; "Railroad Reduces Fares for Fiesta," *El Paso (TX) Post-Herald*, September 10, 1947, 8; "Queen of Juarez Fair Plows,

Picks Cotton," *El Paso* (TX) *Post-Herald*, September 5, 1951, 1; "Offer Prize for First Juarez Cotton Bale," *El Paso* (TX) *Post-Herald*, July 15, 1952, 21; and "Juarez Stages Largest Independence Day Parade," *El Paso* (TX) *Post-Herald*, September 16, 1960, 1.

21. Paternalistic labor agreements were largely absent elsewhere in the cotton-growing West. Moses Musoke and Alan Olmstead explain that California cotton growing by the 1940s was mostly handled by labor contractors; farmers had little direct contact with their laborers: "The California farm worker was more akin to an agricultural proletarian than to a rural peasant. The proverbial paternalism of southern planters toward their tenants which supposedly delayed modernization had few parallels in California." Musoke and Olmstead, "The Rise of the Cotton Industry in California," 395–96. Another glaring difference between cotton growing in the New Mexico region and California is the presence of worker strikes in the 1930s in California but not in New Mexico. By 1941 the six largest cotton farms in the state ranged from two thousand to three thousand acres. See Johansen, *Migratory-Casual Workers in New Mexico*, 6. In Texas, however, Neil Foley argues that the paternalistic, scientifically managed, corporate "cotton ranches" of south Texas fell in line with the model throughout the irrigated West. In fact, however, New Mexico's paternalistic cotton farms were more often individually owned, smaller, and fewer in number than elsewhere in the West. See Foley, *The White Scourge*, chap. 5.

22. Johansen, *Migratory-Casual Workers in New Mexico*, 6. In the Mesilla and El Paso valleys, typically the newer and younger farmers embraced cotton more readily. In her 1984 dissertation, Schönfeld La Mar interviewed several old cotton farmers who recalled the introduction of cotton. They recounted to her that the "new" farmers first planted cotton, followed by the more established "old" farmers. Schönfeld La Mar, "Water and Land in the Mesilla Valley," 224–27. For details on cotton acreages, see *United States Census of Agriculture: 1950*, vol. 1, pt. 30, "New Mexico Chapter A Statistics for the State," state table 12: Specific Crops Harvested, 14. The average acreage in cotton for farms in New Mexico was: 31.6 acres in 1920, 36.6 acres in 1930, 31.7 acres in 1940, and 82.6 acres in 1950. After the war, the acreage jumped to an average of 82.6. In California, by contrast, the average acreage in farms producing cotton hovered just under 70 during the same period, and jumped to an average over 100 after the war. See *United States Census of Agriculture: 1950*, vol. 1, pt. 33, "California Chapter A Statistics for the State," state table 12: Specific Crops Harvested, 14. The average acreage in cotton for farms in California was: 69.96 acres in 1920, 69.78 acres in 1930, 59.5 acres in 1940, and 103.12 acres in 1950. By the early 1980s the discrepancy had grown to an average acreage of 116 in New Mexico, compared to an average of 437 in California (*United States Census of Agriculture: 1982*, chapter 1, table 40, California and New Mexico). The average acreage per cotton farm in New Mexico, while less than that in California, was nonetheless greater than averages east of the Mississippi, which hovered under 15 during this time. See Musoke and Olmstead, "The Rise of the Cotton Industry in California," 391. Even into the 1950s New Mexico had more owner-operators than in the major growing regions of Texas, the Mississippi Delta, or the southeastern piedmont. See Faught, *The Operations of Local Cotton Marketing Agencies*, 40.

23. "Life of Louis J. Ivey-Cotton Farmer," http://www.lrl.state.tx.us/scanned /members/bios/Ivey_Louis_Joseph_Family.pdf.

24. Louis J. Ivey to Messrs. Thompson, Greggerson, Simons, Squires, Payne, and Brinkman, El Paso, Texas, September 5, 1938, folder 8, box 95, subseries B, series 2, EBIDR. See also "2010: Louis J. Ivey was Father of Area's Cotton Industry," *El Paso* (*TX*) *Times*, June 26, 2010.

25. Luis Sánchez, August 3, 2001, transcript, p. 5 [tape 1, side A], OHP-NMFRHM.

26. Smith and Cothren, *Cotton*, 150–51.

27. John Collier Jr., "Cotton . . . ," *New Mexico Magazine*, July 1940, 19.

28. Fitzgerald, *Every Farm a Factory*, 3, 22.

29. Schönfeld La Mar, "Water and Land in the Mesilla Valley," 226–28.

30. Foscue, "The Mesilla Valley of New Mexico," 16.

31. Schönfeld La Mar, "Water and Land in the Mesilla Valley," 238. Based on oral testimonies, Schönfeld La Mar argues that farmers who had been in the Mesilla Valley longest, who tended to be older and Hispanic, often rotated later and more reluctantly than newer farmers, who often had more capital.

32. "Cotton Growing on the Southwestern Projects," *Reclamation Record*, January 1925, p. 7, in folder 10, box 206, DCP. The rotation plan was: "(1) Cotton, two years; (2) corn, followed by a green manure crop such as cowpeas or tepary beans, one year; (3) barley, followed by a green manure crop, one year; (4) cotton, one year; and (5) alfalfa, three years."

33. Eyer, "Planting Corn as a Trap Crop to Protect Cotton Against the Cotton Bollworm."

34. "Hoskins Farm Report Shows Profitable Yields," *Rio Grande Farmer* (Las Cruces NM), June 21, 1923, 9.

35. "Farmer Realizes More Than $150 an Acre Net," *Rio Grande Farmer* (Las Cruces NM), November 8, 1923, 8.

36. California cotton growers, for example, "associated cotton with slavery and African-Americans." See Stamen, "Genetic Dreams," 145.

37. *Migratory Labor in Southern New Mexico*, Economic Surveys Division, Soil Conservation Service, Southwest Region, Albuquerque, N. Mex., 1940, p. 3, in folder 37, box 17, USSCSR-8.

38. "Valley Cotton Farmers Form Organization," *Rio Grande Farmer* (Las Cruces NM), September 20, 1923, 1.

39. *Migratory Labor in Southern New Mexico*, 10. According to Johansen, 10 percent of migratory laborers in 1941 were African American. The remaining 90 percent were white, mostly from Oklahoma and Texas, and to a lesser degree Kansas and Arkansas. Johansen, *Migratory-Casual Workers in New Mexico*, vii, 4.

40. *Migratory Labor in Southern New Mexico*, 3, 5.

41. McWilliams, *Ill Fares the Land*, 72.

42. See, for example, Steinbeck, *The Grapes of Wrath*; McWilliams, *Factories in the Field*; and Taylor, *Migratory Farm Labor in the United States*.

43. *Migratory Labor in Southern New Mexico*, 11–12.

44. *Migratory Labor in Southern New Mexico*, 3, 4. See also McWilliams, *Ill Fares the Land*, 71.

45. Given that cotton competed on a global market, and not local ones, cooperation came easier with cotton than with regionally marketed crops such as apples. As George Meager, Las Cruces Chamber of Commerce president, argued to farmers in 1923: "You don't need fear competition [with each other]—the amount of cotton we can raise cannot [affect] the world price on the crop." Quoted in "Valley Cotton Farmers Form Organization," *Rio Grande Farmer* (Las Cruces NM), September 20, 1923, 1.

46. See Olmstead and Rhode, *Creating Abundance*.

47. Olmstead and Rhode, *Creating Abundance*, 198.

48. Cook and Doyle, *Acala Cotton*, 9. Throughout his Mesoamerican travels, Cook collected varieties of cotton that could perhaps acclimate to the United States. In Guatemala he noted that locals grew a very early maturing cotton and allowed wild turkeys in the fields to control boll weevils. Farmers removed the early-ripening cotton plants before they competed with interplanted peppers. This practice created a short-season cotton that had potential for shorter-season regions of the U.S. South and West. Again, traits such as early maturation, valuable for industry, often derived from diversified, small-scale agricultural systems. See United States Bureau of Plant Industry, *Seeds and Plants Imported*, 128. The quest for a solution to the problem of the boll weevil, which had arrived in the United States via Mexico, also intricately bound together the cotton regions of Mexico and the United States at this time. See Giesen, *Boll Weevil Blues*, chap. 1.

49. Smith and Cothren, *Cotton*, 141–54.

50. "Grow Only One Variety of Cotton to Improve Your Local District," *Alamogordo* (*NM*) *News*, November 22, 1923, 1. Olmstead and Rhode describe Cook as the "father of the one-variety community movement." Olmstead and Rhode, *Creating Abundance*, 164.

51. Leding, *Community Production of Acala Cotton in New Mexico*, 4, 5.

52. Smith and Cothren, *Cotton*, 149–54.

53. See *New Mexico Crop Improvement News* 1, no. 2 (September 1, 1938), in folder 1, box 20, Ms 246, FGTP.

54. "New Mexico Farmers Produce Good Seed," *Lincoln County* (*NM*) *News*, August 30, 1929, 7.

55. Louis J. Ivey to Hon. Tom Connally, July 2, 1941, p. 2, folder 8, box 28, MNP.

56. Acala, Chiapas, receives considerably more rain than the U.S. Southwest per annum. The ability to irrigate Acala strains in the U.S. Southwest allowed growers to overcome this difference, and allowed Cook to write in 1927 that "little difficulty was encountered in the acclimatization of cotton in the United States," in part because, annual rainfall totals aside, a "similarity of conditions in the Acala districts in Mexico to those of Texas." Cook and Doyle, *Acala Cotton*, 10.

57. "Testimony read, and discussed, into the record by Louis J. Ivey of El Paso Texas as a witness before Senate Sub Committee on Irrigation and Reclamation," April 5 and 6, 1945, Washington DC, folder 1, box 62, sub. ser. B, ser. 2, EBIDR.

58. Cook, *Cotton Improvement through Type Selection*, 6.

59. "Hundreds of bales of Juarez Valley cotton" entered El Paso for eastern U.S. markets briefly in 1950, which was the "first large amount of cotton ever to pass through El Paso from the Juarez Valley." "Juarez Valley Cotton Flows to U.S. Ports," *El Paso (TX) Herald-Post*, October 30, 1950, 1.

60. Dicken, "Cotton Regions of Mexico," 363–71; and Garloch, "Cotton in the Economy of Mexico," 70–77.

61. "Juarez Valley Does Not Fear Cotton Sale," *El Paso (TX) Herald-Post*, May 31, 1956, 17.

62. "CC Committee Encouraged by Nation's Chief," *El Paso (TX) Herald-Post*, May 18, 1939, 10.

63. J. T. Stovall to Dennis Chavez, March 5, 1947, folder 2, box 208, DCP; J. T. Stovall to Alton N. Porter, March 14, 1947, folder 2, box 208, DCP.

64. J. T. Stovall to Alton N. Porter, March 14, 1947, folder 2, box 208, DCP. Stovall explains in this letter that restrictions on export licenses could potentially mean that "only about one-third as much seed will move into the Juarez area *as normal*" (emphasis mine), indicating that the association had regularly sold planting seed to buyers in Mexico by this time.

4. Diversification

1. Ernie Pyle, "Dean [*sic*] Stahmann Farms Become Miracle of Mass Production," *El Paso (TX) Herald-Post*, December 13, 1939, 5.

2. Hanley, "The Stahmann Farms Migrant Community," 24–25.

3. "Valley Man Grows Cotton All Winter," *El Paso (TX) Herald-Post*, November 17, 1941, E-6.

4. Luis Sánchez, interview by Jane O'Cain, August 3, 2001, transcript, p. 4 [tape 1, side A], OHP-NMFRHM; Consuelo Márquez, interview by Jane O'Cain, December 12, 1997, and January 16 and March 17, 1998, transcript, p. 117, OHP-NMFRHM.

5. "Breeder Seeks Cotton Suited for Mill Needs," *Las Cruces (NM) Sun-News*, November 29, 1967, 8.

6. "Valley Man Grows Cotton All Winter," *El Paso (TX) Herald-Post*, November 17, 1941, E-6.

7. Smith and Cothren, *Cotton*, 150–51. The Del Cerro strain contained parentage from Watson Acala, Triple Hybrid, Hopi Acala, and Sealand. See "Breeder Seeks Cotton Suited for Mill Needs," *Las Cruces (NM) Sun-News*, November 29, 1967, 8.

8. "Valley Man Grows Cotton All Winter," *El Paso (TX) Herald-Post*, November 17, 1941, E-6.

9. "Breeder Seeks Cotton Suited for Mill Needs," *Las Cruces (NM) Sun-News*, November 29, 1967, 8.

10. "Stahmann Farms, Inc.: 'Diversified Farming,'" advertisement, *El Paso (TX) Herald-Post*, April 28, 1956, D-11.

11. "Irrigated 4000-acre N.M. Farm Demonstrates Values in Agricultural Diversion," *Albuquerque (NM) Journal*, October 6, 1965, D-4.

12. "Deane Stahmann Develops Better Variety of Cotton," *El Paso (TX) Herald-Post*, September 11, 1950. Stahmann told the paper: "I want to develop a cotton of high spinning and high yielding qualities so we can produce a cotton that will compete with synthetics and the foreign varieties." There was concern within the cotton industry that synthetics, such as rayon, represented an existential threat to the industry. The cotton industry has thus had to balance an embrace of modern technology with an insistence that the older technology of natural fiber remains superior.

13. García and Fite, *Preliminary Pecan Experiments*, 3–5; and García, *Pecan Experiments*. As horticulturalist at the New Mexico College of Agriculture and Mechanic Arts (NMAM), later New Mexico State University (NMSU), in Las Cruces, New Mexico, García researched many crops (perhaps most famously the chile pepper) and helped disseminate cultural and agricultural change throughout U.S.-Mexico borderlands in early twentieth-century New Mexico.

14. "Irrigated 4000-acre N.M. Farm Demonstrates Values in Agricultural Diversion," *Albuquerque (NM) Journal*, October 6, 1965, D-4; "Mesilla Valley Nuts Famous throughout Entire Country," *Albuquerque (NM) Tribune*, January 1, 1959, 6. For an in-depth discussion on the interconnections of agrarian reform policies between the United States and Mexico at this time, see Olsson, *Agrarian Crossings*.

15. Ernie Pyle, "Rambling Reporter," *Pittsburgh (PA) Press*, December 12, 1939, 25.

16. Ernie Pyle, "Rambling Reporter," *Pittsburgh (PA) Press*, December 12, 1939, 25.

17. "Irrigated 4000-acre N.M. Farm Demonstrates Values in Agricultural Diversion," *Albuquerque (NM) Journal*, October 6, 1965, D-4.

18. "The Man with a Hoe Gives Way to Geese in Nation's Cotton Fields," *Whitewright (TX) Sun*, March 7, 1963, 8; "Geese in Cotton Fields," *Alabama Journal* (Montgomery), March 5, 1963, 4.

19. "Cotton, Geese, Pecans Occupy Stahmann Farms," *El Paso (TX) Times*, April 29, 1956, reprinted May 4, 2012, in "Tales From the Morgue: El Paso History Is Never Dead," http://elpasotimes.typepad.com/morgue/2012/05/geese-cotton-pe.html.

20. Sanky Trimble, "Cooking Your Own Goose," *Mt. Vernon (IL) Register News*, November 24, 1954, 17.

21. "Cotton, Geese, Pecans Occupy Stahmann Farms," *El Paso (TX) Times*, April 29, 1956. See also John M. White, "Cotton, Geese, and Pecans," *New Mexico Magazine*, April 1960, 13.

22. Sánchez, August 15, 2001, transcript, p. 71 [tape 3, side B], and p. 60 [tape 3, side A], OHP-NMFRHM; Hanley, "The History of Stahmann Farms, 1926–1990," 40. A former bracero working on a 180-acre cotton farm in Fabens, Texas, for example, recalled how his farm began using geese as weeders after noticing the method developed at Stahmann's farms. See Richard Baquera, "Raymundo Villa," Item #81, BCA, http://braceroarchive.org/items/show/81 (accessed September 24, 2017). According to Sánchez, cotton growers from across the region, and even across the South, visited

Stahmann's farm specifically to buy goslings for their farms. Sánchez, August 15, 2001, transcript, pp. 67–68 [tape 3, side B], OHP-NMFRHM. Stahmann filled three railcars with goose down for pillow factories in 1955; "Cotton, Geese, Pecans Occupy Stahmann Farms," *El Paso (TX) Times*, April 29, 1956.

23. "The Shmoose," editorial, *Life*, February 16, 1953, 30.

24. "Irrigated 4000-acre N.M. Farm Demonstrates Values in Agricultural Diversion," *Albuquerque (NM) Journal*, October 6, 1965, D-4; "Unique Industrial Farm Attracts Many Visitors," *El Paso (TX) Herald-Post*, August 4, 1962, 2.

25. Hanley, "The Stahmann Farms Migrant Community," 31.

26. Hanley, "The Stahmann Farms Migrant Community," 33.

27. Sánchez, August 3, 2001, transcript, p. 6 [tape 1, side A], OHP-NMFRHM.

28. At a meeting of the Doña Ana County Agricultural Labor Committee at the Temple of Agriculture in 1945, Stahmann motioned that "a telegram be dispatched to 8th Corps Area Headquarters asking that the prisoner of war allotment be increased promptly to 1050 and that all prior promises made by the army regarding prisoners of war be carried out without delay. This motion was approved unanimously." Minutes of Meeting of the Doña Ana County Agricultural Labor Committee at the Temple of Agriculture, Las Cruces, New Mexico, May 31, 1945, folder 4, box 10, WPTP. A few months later Stahmann joined other cotton growers in a round of protests over restrictions on POW labor imposed by the army. The group of farmers also agreed to lobby the U.S. Congress to relax immigration laws "to the extent of providing a means of obtaining seasonal labor for this area from Mexico at appropriate times." All the growers got together to fix the wages for the year ($2.00 per pound in 1946). Minutes of Meeting of the Doña Ana County Agricultural Labor Committee at the Temple of Agriculture, August 17, 1945, folder 4, box 10, WPTP. Stahmann strongly supported the Anderson bill for a white crossing card for Mexican farmworkers in 1949 (April 5, 1949). The bill by New Mexico senator Clinton Anderson called for "'an open border' and virtually unrestricted recruitment from Mexico." Gutierrez, *Between Two Worlds*, 57.

29. Stahmann ran into trouble with the Department of Labor in the late fifties over "leasing" braceros from other farmers. When the pecans reached maturity and the farm phased out cotton in the late fifties, the farm no longer had an adequately large year-round workforce and had to rely more heavily on seasonal and migrant labor. In 1961 Stahmann hired 253 braceros during the pecan harvest. Stahmann faced scrutiny from the Department of Labor because he had hired workers loaned to him from other farms. Stahmann did not have adequate housing for the braceros. This lending of braceros, a violation of the law, illustrates the lack of legal protections braceros faced. See John E. Gross to Doña Ana County Farm and Livestock Bureau, August 24, 1961, Denver, Colorado, folder 4, box 168, DCP.

30. Flamming, *Creating the Modern South*, xxvii.

31. Hanley, "The Stahmann Farms Migrant Community," 29, 33, 57; Sánchez, August 15, 2001, transcript, p. 87 [tape 4, side A], OHP-NMFRHM.

32. "Irrigated 4000-acre N.M. Farm Demonstrates Values in Agricultural Diversion," *Albuquerque (NM) Journal*, October 6, 1965, D-4.

33. "JDLC Pension Plan," https://ufw.org/jdlc/ (accessed August 3, 2017).

34. Sánchez, August 3, 2001, transcript, p. 8 [tape 1, side A], OHP-NMFRHM.

35. For "upper management," see Sánchez, August 29, 2001, transcript, p. 131 [tape 5, side B], OHP-NMFRHM.

36. Sánchez, August 29, 2001, transcript, p. 153 [tape 6, side A], OHP-NMFRHM.

37. Hanley, "The Stahmann Farms Migrant Community," 82.

38. Born in the Sargasso Sea two hundred miles off the Atlantic Coast, American eels begin their lives traveling through the ocean to freshwater inlets where they swim upstream in search of food. From the rivers of Maine to the Rio Grande, the American eel was endemic throughout the United States east of the Continental Divide. The construction of Elephant Butte Dam in 1916, however, ended the historic migration of eels to the northern reaches of the Rio Grande in New Mexico and Colorado; the construction of Avalon Dam in 1954 and later the Amistad Dam in 1970 downstream in Texas signaled the end of the eel in the far western waters of the Atlantic watershed. Except for a few older adults, which could live up to fifty years, few eels were spotted in New Mexico in the sixties or thereafter. The American eel, a longtime western migrant and resident, became a victim of dams built for irrigation, flood control, and power. When farmworkers caught and ate the American eel, the world experienced the irony of one migrant of industrial agriculture gaining sustenance from the last generations of another migrant doomed not by farmworkers' hands but by the same industrial forces that had compelled farmers to seek workers from elsewhere. For more on the American eel in New Mexico, see Porpst, Burton, and Pridgeon, "Fishes of the Rio Grande," 408–11. There were at least two instances of eel sightings in New Mexico in the eighties, which were likely due to escape from an aquaculture facility in the upper Rio Grande watershed. See Pederson, "Return of the American Eel?," 16; Shepard, *American Eel Biological Species Report*, 46.

39. Consuelo Márquez, transcript, pp. 147–57, OHP-NMFRHM.

40. For mesquite worms, see Muñoz Zurita, *Larousse diccionario enciclipidico*, s.v. *Xamue*; for the culinary history of elvers, see Schweid, *Consider the Eel*, especially chap. 4.

41. Sánchez, August 3, 2001, tape 2, side A, OHP-NMFRHM.

42. Consuelo Márquez, transcript, pp. 125–26, OHP-NMFRHM.

43. Consuelo Márquez, transcript, pp. 125, 157, OHP-NMFRHM.

44. Sánchez, August 29, 2001, transcript, p. 162 [tape 6, side B], OHP-NMFRHM. See also C. Medina interview, quoted in Hanley, "The Stahmann Farms Migrant Community," 82–83.

45. Sánchez, August 29, 2001, transcript, p. 165 [tape 6, side B], OHP-NMFRHM.

46. C. Medina interview, quoted in Hanley, "The Stahmann Farms Migrant Community," 80.

47. Sánchez, August 29, 2001, transcript, p. 166 [tape 6, side B], OHP-NMFRHM.

48. Sánchez, August 29, 2001, transcript, p. 167 [tape 6, side B], OHP-NMFRHM.

49. "Unique Industrial Farm Attracts Many Visitors," *El Paso (TX) Herald-Post*, August 4, 1962, 2; "Irrigated 4000-acre N.M. Farm Demonstrates Values in Agricultural Diversion," *Albuquerque (NM) Journal*, October 6, 1965, D-4.

50. Stepp and Vise, "Stahmann Farms Produce Pecans," 9, 15.

51. While the agricultural fiestas that centered on *matachines* ceased by the end of the cotton era, smaller fiestas, largely created for the purpose of reunions with workers who had left the farm, continued on September 16 and July 4 after Stahmann's death. See Sánchez, August 29, 2001, transcript, p. 165 [tape 6, side B], OHP-NMFRHM; Márquez, transcript, p. 162, OHP-NMFRHM.

52. Ernie Pyle, "Rambling Reporter," *Pittsburgh (PA) Press*, December 11, 1939, 25.

5. Crossing Chiles, Crossing Borders

1. For examples of scholarship on race, modernity, and New Mexico statehood, see Montgomery, *Spanish Redemption*; Nieto-Phillips, *The Language of Blood*; Robert Larson, *New Mexico's Quest for Statehood*; and Holtby, *Forty-Seventh Star*.

2. "Biographical File," folder 1, box 1, and "Correspondence, 1940–1948," folder 3, box 5, FGP. For biographical sketches of Fabián García, see Paterson, *The Hot Empire of Chile*, 15–26; Padilla, *Chile Chronicles*, 6–7; and Rick Hendricks, "Fabián García, Biographical Sketch," http://newmexicohistory.org/2013/10/31/fabian-garcia-biographical-sketch/.

3. García, *Improved Variety No. 9 of Native Chile*, 3, 4, 16; García, *Chile Culture*, 12.

4. Emory, *Notes of a Military Reconnaissance*, 51.

5. Cabeza de Baca Gilbert, *The Good Life*, 45; Fabiola Cabeza de Baca Gilbert, "Chile," p. 1, folder 15, box 1, FCBGP. See also "Las Cruces: Manners and Customs of the Native Population as Described by Jimmy McCarthy in the Denver Tribune," *Rio Grande Republican* (Las Cruces NM), July 26, 1884, 4.

6. "New Mexico: End of the Chili Line," *Time*, September 15, 1941; "Embudo Rock Pile Monument to Old Chile Line," *Albuquerque (NM) Journal*, September 1, 1941, 8; and Fabián García, "Report on Horticulture," 1924, folder 4, box 5, FGP. Hugh G. Calkins, *Handling of a Cash Crop (Chili) in the Tewa Basin*, describes chile in northern New Mexico in the 1930s as a critical cash substitute in the region's economy, making it "the important commercial crop in the area . . . [and] the principal means by which flour, beans, lard, sugar, coffee, and clothing become available to the Spanish-American agriculturalist."

7. *Report of the Governor of New Mexico to the Secretary of the Interior*, 314–17; García, "Horticulture," 1908, and "Fruits and Vegetables in the Mesilla Valley," April 14, 1910, folder 4, box 5, FGP.

8. García, *Chile Culture*, 4. He uses the old agricultural use of the term *culture* here, which refers to the conditions and practices required for successful cultivation.

9. *Report of the Governor of New Mexico to the Secretary of the Interior*, 42.

10. Fabián García to Bonney Youngblood, January 10, 1934, 2, BYP.

11. The advent of widespread refrigeration and freezing in the 1950s helped make year-round green chile even more ubiquitous. The question of traditional or modern

along the lines of red and green chile remains relevant today. Most landrace chile in New Mexico continue to be grown in small acreages primarily to be dried and eaten as red chile; most green chile derives from meatier varieties developed by NMSU for industrial growing and processing.

12. García, *Improved Variety No. 9 of Native Chile*. Of the fourteen strains of chile García used, twelve were of the pasilla variety, one was colorado, and one negro.

13. García to Youngblood, January 10, 1934, 1–3, BYP.

14. Nieto-Phillips, *The Language of Blood*.

15. On La Alianza in New Mexico and its regional variations, see Arrieta, "La Alianza Hispano-americana, 1894–1965." On the La Alianza more broadly, see Cadava, *Standing on Common Ground*; Meeks, *Border Citizens*; and Gonzales, "Carlos I. Velasco," 265. Charles Montgomery argues that Hispano claims to whiteness in northern New Mexico differed from similar claims elsewhere in the U.S.-Mexico borderlands primarily due to class. While the White Legend extended to *paisanos* of all classes in northern New Mexico, elsewhere only wealthy Mexicans and Mexican-Americans (while still embracing a *mexicanidad*) tended to make this claim. See Montgomery, *Spanish Redemption*, 15–17.

16. Letter from Alfredo Levy, Apoderado Gereral en la Republica Mexicana de la Alianza Hispano Americana, to Jose Gonzales, presidente de la Logia #22 (AHA in Las Cruces), Mexico City, July 26, 1930. The original reads: "Efectivamente, hombres de la talla del hermano Fabián García, son un orgullo para nuestra raza y representan lo que el mexicano puede hacer cuando la voluntad y la cultura se unen en ellos." Also, Prof. R. Ramón Espinosa Villanueva to García, Ciudad Juárez, Chih., June 27, 1943, FGP. The original, in part, reads: "El Dr. García es un gran amigo de los mexicanos porque nació en México, de raza nuestra, que al oir español se emociona como un niño."

17. For claims of whiteness among members of La Alianza, see Meeks, *Border Citizens*, 97, 115. For quotation, see Fabián García, undated speech (pre-1912), p. 4, folder 1, box 6, FGP. García showed skepticism about the term *Spanish American*, at one point referring to the "Mexicans and the so-called Spanish Americans" of New Mexico. See García to Youngblood, January 10, 1934, 1, BYP.

18. Youngblood to García, Washington DC, September 26, 1944, FGP. See also García to A. J. Cook, March 7, 1913, folder 5, box 4, FGP.

19. Correia, *Properties of Violence*, 80.

20. John D. Tinsley to Frank Gardner, September 9, 1901, folder 5, box 4, FGP.

21. Youngblood to García, December 13, 1935, folder 1, box 2, FGP.

22. Youngblood to García, September 26, 1944, folder 3, box 5, FGP.

23. Fabián García, "The Value of an Education," May 24, 1928, folder 1, box 6, FGP.

24. "Member of A&M Staff since Graduation 52 Years Ago, Fabián García is Retired," *Las Cruces* (NM) *Sun-News*, April 22, 1945.

25. *Variedades de Arboles Frutales propios*, 9.

26. Governor to García, December 3, 1921, Chihuahua, Chih., folder 1, box 5, FGP.

27. Arnulfo Landaverde to Agricultural Experiment Station, December 24, 1925, San Francisco, Calif., folder 1, box 5, FGP.

28. Reynaldo Talavera to García, December 11, 1944, Chihuahua, Chih, folder 3, box 5, FGP; García to Talavera, November 25, 1944, Mesilla Park NM, folder 3, box 5, FGP.

29. "Mexican Land and Colonization Co. telegram," November 14, 1911, folder 4, box 1, FGP; William Myers to García, June 8, 1920, folder 1, box 5, FGP.

30. García, *Chile Culture*, 29–30.

31. For more on Ortega, see www.ortega.com/history; *Sunset*, vol. 6, Passenger Dept., Southern Pacific Co., 1901; "Fruit Interest," *Corona (CA) Currier*, December 16, 1899; and "Hundreds of People See Pure Food Display and Get Samples," *Oxnard (CA) Currier*, April 22, 1910, 7.

32. García bred onions, for example, with seed mostly supplied through seed companies such as W. A. Burpee in Philadelphia and Barteldes Seed Company in Lawrence, Kansas; the latter once provided him a particularly early maturing strain of Grano from Valencia, Spain. For examples of major university breeding projects involving foreign germplasm from the USDA introduction program, see Kingsbury, *Hybrid*, 148.

33. García, *Improved Variety Number 9 of Native Chile*, 16.

34. García, *Chile Culture*, 19.

35. García drew heavily from Swingle and Webber, "Hybrids and their Utilization in Plant Breeding." At times García lifts entire passages from this early resource on the science of hybridization. See Fabián García, "Variation and the Improvement of Agricultural Plants," undated lecture, folder 4, box 5, FGP.

36. Youngblood to García, April 27, 1934, BYP.

37. García to Youngblood, September 28, 1945, folder 2, box 2, FGP.

38. Youngblood to García, April 9, 1934, BYP.

39. "Club Work at the Taos Pueblo in Taos County for Year 1924," folder 4, box 5, FGP.

40. García to Youngblood, January 10, 1934, 4, BYP. See also Coon, Votava, and Bosland, *The Chile Cultivars of New Mexico State University Released from 1913 to 2008*. Youngblood alludes to García's work toward making the chile more appealing to non-Hispanic tastes when he states that García has "added vigor and *palatability* to the life-giving mais, chile, frijoles, and uvas" (emphasis mine) in Youngblood to García, December 13, 1935, FGP.

41. Percy W. Barker, Mesilla Park NM, in García, *Improved Variety No. 9 of Native Chile*, 15.

42. Fabiola Cabeza de Baca Gilbert, "Chile," folder 15, box 1, FCBGP.

43. See Cabeza de Baca Gilbert and Strong, *Boletín de Conservar*.

44. Scharff, *Twenty Thousand Roads*, 118. See also Rebolledo, "Narrative Strategies of Resistance in Hispana Writing," 142.

45. Cabeza de Baca to García, May 9, 1943, folder 2, box 2, FGP. In another example of their affectionate correspondence, García sent Cabeza de Baca lyrics to a song he wrote about their travels on the demonstration train in 1930. García to Cabeza de

Baca, May 1, 1930, folder 4, box 5, FGP. "Las recuerdos del tren agrícola me gustan mucho," she responded in Fabiola Cabeza de Baca to García, May 27, 1930, folder 1, box 2, FGP. A second letter attached from her adds, "Thanks a lot for the poem. It is very sweet and it brings back dear memories of you. I had not written because I wanted to try and write you an answer in poetry. No creo que jamás olvide aquello.—Fabiola."

46. Cabeza de Baca Gilbert, *The Good Life*, 45.

47. Padilla, *Chile Chronicles*, 7.

6. The Evolution of a Modern Pod

1. Denise Chávez, "Scenes of Home and a Dream in Green," *New Mexico Magazine*, February/March 1996, 38. In Doña Ana County, in southern New Mexico where the industry's growth was most concentrated, the number of acres in chile jumped roughly sixteenfold between 1949 and 1978. *United States Census of Agriculture: 1950*, vol. 1, pt. 30, New Mexico and Arizona, county table 5, chapter B, statistic for counties, p. 66; *United States Census of Agriculture: 1978*, vol. 1, pt. 31, New Mexico, county summary data, table 31, p. 145.

2. Paterson, *Hot Empire of Chile*, 5.

3. Harper, *An Improved Variety of Chile for New Mexico*, 1.

4. "Chile is 'Hot' on the National Market," Agri-Search pamphlet by the NMSU, Agricultural Experiment Station, Winter 1981, 2; Cotter, *A Review of Studies on Chile*, 4.

5. John Crenshaw, "Chile Man-Roy Nakayama," *New Mexico Magazine*, May 1976, 37; Cotter, "The Scientific Contribution of New Mexico to the Chile Pepper," 21; Coon, Votava, and Bosland, *The Chile Cultivars of New Mexico State University Released from 1913 to 2008*.

6. Carleton, "The Expansion of a Hot Commodity," 29.

7. Marvin Tessneer, "Producer Highlights Ag Labor Problems," *Las Cruces* (NM) *Sun-News*, December 15, 1974, 12.

8. Marvin Tessneer, "Louisiana Hot Peppers Tested Here," *Las Cruces* (NM) *Sun-News*, October 14, 1973, 11.

9. Jeanne Gleason, "Tabasco Thrives in Las Cruces," *Albuquerque* (NM) *Journal*, November 9, 1975, G-4.

10. Emma Jean Cervantes, interview by Jane O' Cain, July 9, 1996, tape 1, side B, and Emma Jean Cervantes, interview by Ashley Granados et al., July 23, 1997, OHP-NMFRHM.

11. Cotter, "The Scientific Contribution of New Mexico to the Chile Pepper," 20; Carleton, "The Expansion of a Hot Commodity."

12. Mountain Pass delivered a $5,884 grant to NMSU for chile research in 1976, for example, and in 1974 wrote a $1,000 personal check to Roy Nakayama, who commended the "industry's interest in chile research and that extra money has been added beyond state appropriations as incentives for researchers." "Grant Aids Chile Production," *Las Cruces* (NM) *Sun-News*, March 4, 1976, 19; "Society Given Promotion Check," *Las Cruces* (NM) *Sun-News*, December 25, 1977, 32.

13. House Bill 24 in the 1965 New Mexico state legislature was introduced by Arcenio Gonzales of San Miguel, New Mexico. A history teacher who had promised a former student, Helen Lueras, that he would follow her recommendation to propose the bill, Gonzales presciently noted that "chile has caught fire in the state of New Mexico." See "Chili Bill Passes," *Las Vegas (NM) Daily Optic*, February 3, 1965, 1; "Chili, Frijoles to Share State Vegetable Role," *Albuquerque (NM) Journal*, February 4, 1965, 2.

14. "This Week is Hatch Third Chile Festival," *Las Cruces (NM) Sun-News*, August 25, 1974, 9. Mountain Pass wrote a check to the group for $3,000 in 1974 and a $4,000 check in 1977. "Society Given Promotion Check," *Las Cruces (NM) Sun-News*, December 25, 1977, 32. See, too, Carleton, "The Expansion of a Hot Commodity."

15. International Connoisseurs of Green and Red Chile advertisement, *Las Cruces (NM) Sun-News*, July 29, 1977; "Last of the Red Hot Lovers? No Such Thing . . . ," *Las Cruces (NM) Sun-News*, August 11, 1977, 17; and "Society Enters 'Great Chile War,'" *Albuquerque (NM) Journal*, February 27, 1974, 22.

16. The Chile Institute Strategic Management Plan (draft), prepared by John R. Van Ness, October 11, 1995, pp. 2–3, 6, folder 19, box 23, DDC.

17. "Chile Growing Booms, Future Bright," *Las Cruces (NM) Sun-News*, February 22, 1976, 4.

18. In New Mexico, racialized and gendered connotations of the chile pepper have come in many forms. The term *chile* has long been a phallic symbol in parts of New Mexico. There is an old New Mexican joke, for example, about a cold evening at a crowded New Mexico bar. Two men, one Anglo and one Hispanic New Mexican, step outside to urinate. As they relieve themselves, the Anglo man says, "Pretty chilly, huh?" The other man responds, "Thank you." See Joe Davis, interview by Audilio Miranda, 1970, track 9, CD 182, box 2, RCC. For other phallic imagery and responses to it, see Bruce "Pacho" Lane, *The New Mexico Chile Film* (1989), http://docfilm.com/site/the-new-mexico-chile-film/ (accessed January 15, 2017). Gendered and racialized connotations abound in New Mexico cook-off culture. A chili cook-off in Socorro in 1979, for example, featured staged gunfights and "a lynching," and a Ute man from Gallup won the national chile competition with a recipe dubbed "Indian's revenge." "Chili Cook-off Slated," *Clovis (NM) News Journal*, May 20, 1979, 27; and "Gallup Indian Wins World Chili Contest," *Santa Fe New Mexican*, October 25, 1976, A12.

19. Smith, *The Great Chili Confrontation*, 42.

20. David Scofield Wilson, "Hot Peppers," in Wilson and Gillespie, *Rooted in America*, 106–8.

21. "*Martha Stewart Living* Gets a Taste of New Mexico," 3.

22. Dr. Benigno Villalon to Dave Dewitt, June 30, 1987, folder 4, box 1, DDC.

23. For *chili*, see, for example, New Mexico College of Agriculture and Mechanic Arts, *Fruits and Vegetables* (1917), 4; Fite and Hollinger, *Growing the Home Garden* (1928); Wetzel, *Judging for Home Economics 4-H Clubs* (1932), 22; and Wiltbank, *Home Vegetable Gardening* (1958).

24. New Mexico State University Alumni Association, *Green Chili Recipe Fiesta*.

25. For examples of insistence on spelling, see John Crenshaw, "New Mexico's Fiery Soul," *New Mexico Magazine*, May 1976, 34; Jeanne Croft, "Adoration of a Fiery God," *New Mexico Magazine*, October 1981, 67; and Jeanne Croft, "Chile!" *New Mexico Magazine*, March 1984, 40.

26. Dave Dewitt, interview by Donna Wojcik, May 20, 2016, New Mexico Farm and Ranch Heritage Museum Oral History Program, transcript, p. 33 [tape 1, side B], OHP-NMFRHM.

27. García, *Improved Variety No. 9 of Native Chile*, 4.

28. Sneed, *Chile*, 2. Several other historians repeated this fact. See, for example, Haverluk, "Chile Peppers and Identity Construction in Pueblo, Colorado," 46; Rick Hendricks, "New Mexico's Chile Kings: Fabián García and Roy Nakayama," *Tradición*, October 2012, 111.

29. Bosland, "Pepper Breeding and Genetics at New Mexico State University," 51; Dewitt and Bosland, *The Pepper Garden*, 15–16.

30. Bosland, "Capsicums: Innovative Uses of an Ancient Crop."

31. Bosland repeated this assertion in 2000, in Bosland and Votava, *Peppers*, 32–33, and again in 2009, stating that "the modern New Mexico pod type was developed beginning in 1894 when Fabián García at New Mexico State University started improving, through selection and crossbreeding, the local chile peppers grown by Hispanic gardeners around Las Cruces." See Bosland and Dewitt, *The Complete Chile Pepper Book*, 53. In 2015 Bosland repeated this claim, stating that "Fabián García began developing his new pod-type around 1894 by collecting 14 chile pepper accessions growing in backyards in the Las Cruces area. The chile pepper accessions belonged to three pre-Columbian pod-types, '*chile colorado*,' '*chile negro*,' and '*chile pasilla*.'" Bosland, "The History, Development, and Importance of the New Mexican Pod-Type Chile Pepper," 291. In a rare exception that only adds to the confusion, in 2008 Bosland in a published report on the chile cultivars of NMSU seems to imply García's initial experiments indeed began in 1907, when his report states that García's decision to use a *chile colorado* in his initial breeding experiments to develop a New Mexico pod type was "fortuitous to New Mexico, because 100 years later, chile (paprika) [. . .] has become an important part of the New Mexico chile industry." See Coon, Votava, and Bosland, *Chile Cultivars of New Mexico State University*, 1.

32. Rotary Club of Las Cruces, "2011-03-30, Danise Coon, NMSU Chile Pepper Institute," blog, March 30, 2011, http://www.lascrucesrotary.org/2011-03-30.

33. For an example of Bosland using the term *Anaheim-type*, see Bosland, "Pepper Breeding and Genetics at New Mexico State University," 51.

34. Bosland and Dewitt, *The Complete Chile Pepper Book*, 53; Bosland, "The History, Development, and Importance of the New Mexican Pod-Type Chile Pepper," 294.

35. Bosland writes that the seed Ortega brought back from New Mexico was the number 9 chile seed. Bosland, "The History, Development, and Importance of the New Mexican Pod-Type Chile Pepper," 294. For more on Ortega, see Andrews, *Peppers*, 93.

36. Stephanie J. Walker, "Chile-New Mexico's Hottest Harvest," YouTube video, 13:49, from a talk given to the Los Alamos History Society, November 2014, posted

by "LosAlamosHistory," November 17, 2014, https://www.youtube.com/watch?v=NJukFa8c1z4.

37. Croft, "Chile!," 40.

38. Margaret Page Hood, "Some Like it Hot," *New Mexico Magazine*, November 1958, 22.

39. Fray Angélico Chávez, "New Mexico's Bonnie Prince Chile," *New Mexico Magazine*, May/June 1974, 31.

40. Jim Sagel, "Chile del Norte," *New Mexico Magazine*, February/March 1996, 30–31; Padilla, *The Chile Chronicles*, 48.

41. Stanley Crawford, foreword to Padilla, *The Chile Chronicles*, vii.

42. Chávez, "Scenes of Home and a Dream in Green," 32, 35.

43. Gustavo Arellano, remarks from "The Big Debate: Local Ingredients, Foreign Chefs, and the Question of Culinary Cannibalism," panel presentation at FUZE.SW Food and Folklore Festival, November 2013, quoted in Rob DeWalt, "Chile Wars: Is That Green Chile On Your Plate from Hatch? And How Much Does It Matter?" *Santa Fe (NM) Reporter*, August 26, 2014.

44. Padilla, *The Chile Chronicles*, 110–11.

45. Dewitt, May 20, 2016, transcript, pp. 51–52 [tape 2, side A], OHP-NMFRHM.

46. Dewitt, May 20, 2016, transcript, p. 32 [tape 1, side B], OHP-NMFRHM.

47. See Walker and Havlik, *The Landrace Chiles of Northern New Mexico*, 1–8. See also, for an example of the Chimayó chile's fame, Nina Bunker Ruiz, "A Passion for Peppers: The Movement to Save New Mexico's Treasured Chiles," *Yes! Magazine*, February 14, 2014, http://www.yesmagazine.org/issues/education-uprising/a-passion-for-peppers-the-movement-to-save-new-mexico-s-treasured-chiles.

48. See "A Declaration of Seed Sovereignty: A Living Document for New Mexico," March 11, 2006, http://www.tnafa.org/uploads/6/6/3/4/66345041/seeddeclaration.pdf. A slimmed-down version of this declaration was passed in both the House and Senate of New Mexico in 2007. "A Joint Memorial Recognizing the Significance of Indigenous Agricultural Practice and Native Seeds to New Mexico's Cultural Heritage and Food Security," introduced by Carlos C. Cisneros, 2007, Senate Joint Memorial 38, 1st sess., 48th legislature, New Mexico.

49. Enrique Lamadrid, "*La guerra de los Chiles*: A Poetic Defense of Biodiversity, Seed Sovereignty, and Chile" (2009), http://www.savenmseeds.org/index.php/nm-chile-nativo (accessed July 20, 2017).

50. The first insect-resistant Bt Acala 1517 was developed by NMSU in 2005 and accounted for 14 percent of cotton acreage in New Mexico the following year. Chang, "Breeding and Genetics," 191.

51. One of the region's most successful growers in recent years, Matt Romero, for example, grows an "Alcalde Improved" variety, which derives from the Española Improved, an NMSU variety with genetic roots tracing back to the number 9. See Carlos Andres Lopez, "As Chile Season Reaches Its Peak, Culinary Pros Laud Heritage of State's Official Vegetable," *Santa Fe New Mexican*, September 20, 2011.

52. 2003 Chile Marketing Summit Draft, September 25, 2003, Las Cruces, New Mexico, p. 12, folder 10, box 8, DDC. The campaign against the GE chile took a variety of forms beyond the corrido, including the work by the Albuquerque-based nonprofit Save New Mexico Seeds and Christopher Dudley's documentary film *Genetic Chile* (2010). While GE chile has not been made commercially available, it has been researched. See Todd Myers, "Red and Green on the Border," in Evans, *Farming Across Borders*, 139.

53. Paul Romero, quoted in "Press Release to Oppose New Mexico Certified Chile Trademark Program," August 19, 2014, Save New Mexico Seeds, http://www.savenmseeds.org/index.php.

54. Chile production in New Mexico has generally declined in the twenty-first century. Acreage in chile dropped from nearly thirty thousand acres in 1990 to under ten thousand by 2016. See New Mexico Department of Agriculture, "2010 New Mexico Chile Production"; USDA National Agricultural Statistics Service, "2016 State Agricultural Overview: New Mexico."

55. See, for example, Joseph Kolb, "Imports, Small Harvest Hit Famed New Mexico Chile Peppers," *Reuters*, September 7, 2014, http://www.reuters.com/article/us-usa-new-mexico-chile-iduskbn0h20es20140908; Logan Hawkes, "Green Chile Competition Heats Up With New Colorado Peppers," *Southwest Farm Press*, September 4, 2015, http://www.southwestfarmpress.com/vegetables/green-chile-competition-heats-new-colorado-peppers.

56. Paterson, *The Hot Empire of Chile*, 4, 6.

57. Wilson, *The Myth of Santa Fe*, 4.

Conclusion

1. In 2018 chile brought in an estimated $53,766,000 total in revenue. The total revenue for cotton was not reported, but $45,858,000 was reported for upland and cottonseed sales. This total does not include the revenue for Pima cotton. While total revenue for the two crops is likely similar, the total acreage in cotton was 83,800 acres compared to 8,400 acres in chile peppers. USDA National Agricultural Statistics Service, "2018 State Agricultural Overview: New Mexico." The state produced 8,700 acres of chile in 2019, down from 17,500 acres in 2005 and from its all-time peak of 34,500 acres in 1992. USDA National Agricultural Statistics Service, "2019 New Mexico Chile Production"; USDA National Agricultural Statistics Service, "2005 New Mexico Chile Production"; and Skaggs, Decker, and VanLeeuwen, *A Survey of Southern New Mexico Chile Producers*.

2. See Walker and Havlik, *The Landrace Chiles of Northern New Mexico*.

3. Gustavo Arellano, remarks from "The Big Debate: Local Ingredients, Foreign Chefs, and the Question of Culinary Cannibalism," panel presentation at FUZE.SW Food and Folklore Festival, November 2013, quoted in Rob DeWalt, "Chile Wars: Is That Green Chile On Your Plate from Hatch? And How Much Does It Matter?" *Santa Fe (NM) Reporter*, August 26, 2014.

Bibliography

Archives

BCA. Bracero History Archive. Braceroarchive.org.

BKP-I. Governor Bruce King Papers, 1st Term. Collection no. 1972-009. State Records Center and Archives, Santa Fe NM.

BYP. Bonney Youngblood Papers. Herbert Hoover Presidential Library, West Branch IA.

DACNMR. Doña Ana County, N.M. Records, 1952–1946. Collection 1974-017. State Records Center and Archives, Santa Fe NM.

DCP. Dennis Chávez Papers. MS 394 BC. Center for Southwest Research, University Libraries, University of New Mexico, Albuquerque NM.

DDC. Dave Dewitt Collection. MS 484. Archives and Special Collections Department, New Mexico State University Library, Las Cruces NM.

DFCP. Governor David F. Cargo Papers. Collection no. 1969-001. State Records Center and Archives, Santa Fe NM.

EBIDR. Elephant Butte Irrigation District Records. MS 0325. Archives and Special Collections Department, New Mexico State University Library, Las Cruces NM.

FCBGP. Fabiola Cabeza de Baca Gilbert Papers. MSS 603 BC. Center for Southwest Research, University Libraries, University of New Mexico, Albuquerque NM.

FGP. Fabián García Papers. UA 011. Records of the College of Agriculture and Home Economics, Hobson-Huntsinger University Archives, New Mexico State University Library, Las Cruces NM.

FGTP. Francis G. Tracy Papers. Archives and Special Collections Department, New Mexico State University Library, Las Cruces NM.

FLQP. Frances Léon Quintana Papers. MSS 768 BC. Center for Southwest Research, University Libraries, University of New Mexico, Albuquerque NM.

MNP. Morgan Nelson Papers, 1951–1980. Archives and Special Collections Department, New Mexico State University Library, Las Cruces NM.

NMDC. New Mexico Digital Collections. University Libraries, University of New Mexico, Albuquerque NM.

NMSU LDC. NMSU Library Digital Collections. Archives and Special Collections Department, New Mexico State University Library, Las Cruces NM.

NMTBIR. New Mexico Territorial Bureau of Immigration Records, 1880–1911. Collection 1959-114. Center for Southwest Research, University Libraries, University of New Mexico, Albuquerque NM.

OHP-NMFRHM. Oral History Program transcripts. New Mexico Farm and Ranch Heritage Museum, Las Cruces NM.

RCC. Ruben Cobos Collection of Southwest Folklore and Folk Music. MSS 892 BC. Center for Southwest Research, University Libraries, University of New Mexico, Albuquerque NM.

TANM. Territorial Archives of New Mexico, 1846–1912. State Records Center and Archives, Santa Fe NM.

USSCSR-8. United States Soil Conservation Service Region Eight Records. MSS 289 BC. Center for Southwest Research, University Libraries, University of New Mexico, Albuquerque NM.

WPTP. Wendell Phillips Thorpe Papers, 1922–1963. MS 50. Archives and Special Collections Department, New Mexico State University Library, Las Cruces NM.

Published Works

Anderson, George B. *New Mexico: Its Resources and Its People.* Vol. 2. Los Angeles: Pacific States, 1907.

Andrews, Jean. *Peppers: The Domesticated Capsicums.* Austin: University of Texas Press, 1995.

Appelbaum, Robert. *Aguecheek's Beef, Belch's Hiccup, and Other Gastronomic Injections: Literature, Culture, and Food among the Early Moderns.* Chicago: University of Chicago Press, 2006.

Arellano, Gustavo. *Taco USA: How Mexican Food Conquered America.* New York: Scribner, 2013.

Arrieta, Olivia. "La Alianza Hispano-americana, 1894–1965: An Analysis of Collective Action and Cultural Adaption." In *Nuevomexicano Cultural Legacy*, edited by Francisco A. Lomelí, Genaro M. Padilla, and Victor A. Sorell, 109–26. Albuquerque: University of New Mexico Press, 2002.

Bailey, L. H., ed. *Cyclopedia of American Agriculture: 1909: A Popular Survey of Agricultural Conditions, Practices and Ideals in the United States and Canada.* New York: Macmillan, 1909.

Beckert, Sven. *Empire of Cotton: A Global History.* New York: Alfred A. Knopf, 2014.

Bendix, Reinhard. "Tradition and Modernity Reconsidered." *Comparative Studies in Society and History* 9, no. 3 (April 1967): 292–346.

Bennett, Jason Patrick. "Blossoms and Borders: Cultivating Apples and a Modern Countryside in the Pacific Northwest, 1890–2001." PhD diss., University of Victoria, 2008.

———. "'Nature's Garden and a Possible Utopia': Farming for Fruit and Industrious Men in the Transboundary Pacific Northwest, 1895–1914." In *The Borderlands of the American and Canadian Wests: Essays on Regional History of the Forty-Ninth Parallel*, edited by Sterling Evans, 222–40. Lincoln: University of Nebraska Press, 2006.

Berberich, Richard S. *Considerations in Establishing a Fruit Storage and Marketing Facility and a Chile Processing Plant in the Española Valley, New Mexico.* Report no. 70. Washington DC: USDA Farmer Cooperative Service, December 1964.

Bogener, Stephen. "Ditches across the Desert: A Story of Irrigation along New Mexico's Pecos River." PhD diss., Texas Tech University, 1997.

Bosland, Paul W. "Capsicums: Innovative Uses of an Ancient Crop." In *Progress in New Crops*, edited by J. Janick, 479–87. Arlington VA: ASHS Press, 1996.

———. "The History, Development, and Importance of the New Mexican Pod-Type Chile Pepper to the United States and World Food Industry." *Plant Breeding Reviews* 39 (2015): 283–324.

———. "Pepper Breeding and Genetics at New Mexico State University." In *Tomato and Pepper Production in the Tropics*, edited by Asian Vegetable Research and Development Center, 51–54. Tainan, Taiwan: December 1989. http://pdf.usaid .gov/pdf_docs/PNABG557.pdf.

Bosland, Paul W., and Dave W. Dewitt. *The Complete Chile Pepper Book: A Gardener's Guide to Choosing, Growing, Preserving, and Cooking.* Portland OR: Timber Press, 2009.

Bosland, Paul W., and Eric J. Votava. *Peppers: Vegetable and Spice Capsicums.* New York: CABI Publishing, 2000.

Botkin, C. W., and G. R. Hamiel. *Spray Residue on Apples in New Mexico.* New Mexico College of Agriculture and Mechanic Arts, Agricultural Experiment Station Bulletin 258. Las Cruces: May 1938.

Bowcutt, Frederica. *The Tanoak Tree: An Environmental History of a Pacific Coast Hardwood.* Seattle: University of Washington Press, 2015.

Bowman, Timothy P. *Blood Oranges: Colonialism and Agriculture in the South Texas Borderlands.* College Station: Texas A&M Press, 2016.

Bureau of Immigration of the Territory of New Mexico. *Eddy County, New Mexico.* Santa Fe: New Mexican Printing Company, 1901.

Burford, Thomas. "Apples." In *The Oxford Encyclopedia of Food and Drink in America*, vol. 1, A–J, edited by Andrew F. Smith, 78–80. Oxford: Oxford University Press, 2004.

Burke, Gerald M., Darrell T. Sullivan, and W. J. Vastine. *An Economic Base Report.* New Mexico State University Special Report. Las Cruces: Department of Agricultural Economics and Agricultural Business, Agricultural Experiment Station, New Mexico State University, July 15, 1969.

Cabeza de Baca Gilbert, Fabiola. *The Good Life*. 1949. Reprint, Santa Fe: Museum of New Mexico Press, 2005.

Cabeza de Baca Gilbert, Fabiola, and Veda A. Strong. *Boletín de Conservar*. New Mexico College of Agriculture and Mechanic Arts, Agricultural Experiment Station Extension Circular 135. Las Cruces: 1935.

Cadava, Eduardo. *Standing on Common Ground: The Making of a Sunbelt Borderland*. Cambridge MA: Harvard University Press, 2013.

Calhoun, Creighton Lee. *Old Southern Apples: A Comprehensive History and Description of Varieties for Collectors, Growers, and Fruit Enthusiasts*. Rev. ed. White River Junction VT: Chelsea Green, 2010.

Calkins, Hugh G. *Handling of a Cash Crop (Chili) in the Tewa Basin*. USDA Soil Conservation Service Southwest Region Bulletin 46. Conservation Economics Series no. 19. Washington DC: U.S. Department of Agriculture, July 1937.

Carleton, William. "The Expansion of a Hot Commodity." Master's thesis, University of New Mexico, 2011.

Chang, Jinfa. "Breeding and Genetics: History and Progress in Cotton Breeding, Genetics, and Genomics in New Mexico." *Journal of Cotton Science* 22 (2018): 191–210.

"The Chase Orchard: New Mexico's Famous Pioneer Orchard." *The Western Empire*, 1928. From the private collection of Gordon Tooley.

Cockerell, T. D. A. *Entomological Observations of 1894*. New Mexico College of Agriculture and Mechanic Arts, Agricultural Experiment Station Bulletin 15. Las Cruces: The Independent Democrat, 1896.

———. *Preliminary Notes on the Codling Moth*. New Mexico College of Agriculture and Mechanic Arts, Agricultural Experiment Station Bulletin 25. Mesilla Park: February 1898.

Cockerill, Percy Walter, and R. P. Callaway. *Economics of the Production and Marketing of Apples in New Mexico*. New Mexico College of Agriculture and Mechanic Arts, Agricultural Experiment Station Bulletin 242. State College: 1936.

Cook, O. F. *Cotton Improvement through Type Selection, with Special Reference to the Acala Variety*. USDA Technical Bulletin 302. Washington DC: U.S. Department of Agriculture, 1932.

Cook, O. F., and C. B. Doyle. *Acala Cotton: A Superior Upland Variety from Southern Mexico*. Washington DC: U.S. Department of Agriculture, 1927.

Coon, Danise, Eric Votava, and Paul W. Bosland. *The Chile Cultivars of New Mexico State University Released from 1913 to 2008*. Research Report 763. Las Cruces: NMSU Cooperative Extension Service, 2008.

Cooper, Frederick. *Colonialism in Question: Theory, Knowledge, History*. Berkeley: University of California Press, 2005.

Correia, David. *Properties of Violence: Law and Land Grant Struggle in Northern New Mexico*. Athens: University of Georgia Press, 2013.

Cotter, Donald. *A Review of Studies on Chile*. Bulletin 673. Las Cruces: NMSU Cooperative Extension Service, 1980.

———. "The Scientific Contribution of New Mexico to the Chile Pepper." In *Southwestern Agriculture: Pre-Columbian to Modern*, edited by Henry C. Dethloff and Irvin M. May Jr. College Station: Texas A&M Press, 1982.

Cox, Karen L. *Selling Dixie: How the South Was Created in American Popular Culture*. Chapel Hill: University of North Carolina Press, 2011.

Crawford, Dyvena. *Under the Apple Tree: A Personal History of Apple Growing in San Juan County*. Las Cruces NM: Sky Eagle Design, 2000.

Dewitt, Dave, and Paul W. Bosland. *The Pepper Garden: How to Grow Peppers from the Sweetest Bell to the Hottest Habanero*. Berkeley CA: Ten Speed Press, 1993.

Dicken, Samuel N. "Cotton Regions of Mexico." *Economic Geography* 14, no. 4 (October 1938): 363–71.

Emory, William Helmsley. *Notes of a Military Reconnaissance from Fort Leavenworth, in Missouri, to San Diego, in California, including Parts of the Arkansas, Del Norte, and Gila Rivers*. New York: H. Long and Brother, 1848.

Evans, Sterling, ed. *The Borderlands of the American and Canadian Wests: Essays on Regional History of the Forty-Ninth Parallel*. Lincoln: University of Nebraska Press, 2006.

———. *Bound in Twine: The History and Ecology of the Henequen-Wheat Complex for Mexico and the American and Canadian Plains, 1880–1950*. College Station: Texas A&M University Press, 2007.

———, ed. *Farming Across Borders: A Transnational History of the North American West*. College Station: Texas A&M University Press, 2017.

Eyer, John Robert. *Planting Corn as a Trap Crop to Protect Cotton against the Cotton Bollworm*. New Mexico College of Agriculture and Mechanic Arts, Agricultural Experiment Station Press Bulletin 598. Las Cruces: June 4, 1930.

Farmer, Jared. *Trees in Paradise: A California History*. New York: W. W. Norton and Company, 2013.

Faught, W. A. *The Operations of Local Cotton Marketing Agencies: Four Major Cotton Producing Regions, 1949–50 Season*. Southern Cooperative Series Bulletin no. 40. Auburn: Agricultural Experiment Stations of Alabama Publications, August 1954.

Fiege, Mark. *Irrigated Eden: The Making of an Agricultural Landscape in the American West*. Seattle: University of Washington Press, 1999.

Fite, A. B., and E. C. Hollinger. *Growing the Home Garden*. New Mexico College of Agriculture and Mechanic Arts, Agricultural Experiment Station Circular 96. Las Cruces: May 1928.

Fitzgerald, Deborah. *Every Farm a Factory: The Industrial Ideal in American Agriculture*. New Haven CT: Yale University Press, 2010.

Flamming, Douglas. *Creating the Modern South: Millhands & Managers in Dalton, Georgia, 1884–1984*. Chapel Hill: University of North Carolina Press, 1992.

Foley, Neil. *The White Scourge: Mexicans, Blacks, and Poor Whites in Texas Cotton Culture*. Berkeley: University of California Press, 1999.

Folger, John Clifford, and Samuel Mable Thomson. *The Commercial Apple Industry of North America*. New York: Macmillan, 1921.

Forde, Kate. "Celluloid Dreams: The Marketing of Cutex in America, 1916–1935." *Journal of Design History* 15, no. 3 (2002): 175–89.

Foscue, Edwin. "The Mesilla Valley of New Mexico: A Study in Aridity and Irrigation." *Economic Geography* 7, no. 1 (January 1931): 1–27.

Fullilove, Courtney. *The Profit of the Earth: The Global Seeds of American Agriculture*. Chicago: University of Chicago Press, 2017.

García, Fabián. *Apple Culture under Irrigation*. New Mexico College of Agriculture and Mechanic Arts, Experiment Station Bulletin 75. Santa Fe: New Mexican Printing Company, 1910.

———. *Chile Culture*. New Mexico College of Agriculture and Mechanic Arts, Agricultural Experiment Station Bulletin 67. Albuquerque: Albuquerque Morning Journal, 1908.

———. "History of Fruit Growing in New Mexico." In *Proceedings of the American Pomological Society*, vol. 29. Cleveland OH: The Society, 1905.

———. *Improved Variety No. 9 of Native Chile*. New Mexico College of Agriculture and Mechanic Arts, Agricultural Experiment Station Bulletin 124. Las Cruces: Rio Grande Republic, 1921.

———. *Pecan Experiments*. New Mexico College of Agriculture and Mechanic Arts, Agricultural Experiment Station Press Bulletin 467. Las Cruces: December 4, 1924.

———. *Proceedings of the Thirty-Eighth Convention of the American Pomological Society, Toledo, Ohio, December 7, 8, and 9, 1921*. Columbus OH: F. J. Herr, 1922.

———. "Report from the Horticulturalist." In *Eighteenth Annual Report of the College of Agriculture and Mechanic Arts Agricultural Experiment Station, 1906–1907*. Albuquerque NM: Albuquerque Morning Journal, 1908.

———. "Report from the Horticulturalist." In *Nineteenth Annual Report of the College of Agriculture and Mechanic Arts Agricultural Experiment Station, 1907–1908*. Santa Fe: New Mexican Printing Company, 1908.

———. *Spraying Orchards for the Codling Moth*. New Mexico College of Agriculture and Mechanic Arts, Agricultural Experiment Station Bulletin 41. Santa Fe: New Mexican Printing Company, 1902.

García, Fabián, and A. B. Fite. *Preliminary Pecan Experiments*. New Mexico College of Agriculture and Mechanic Arts, Agricultural Experiment Station Bulletin 145. Las Cruces: January 1945.

Garloch, Lorene A. "Cotton in the Economy of Mexico." *Economic Geography* 20, no. 1 (January 1944): 70–77.

Geiger, Roger L. *To Advance Knowledge: The Growth of American Research Universities, 1900–1940*. New York: Oxford University Press, 1986.

Giesen, James C. *Boll Weevil Blues: Cotton, Myth, and Power in the American South*. Chicago: University of Chicago Press, 2011.

———. "'The Truth about the Boll Weevil': The Nature of Planter Power in the Mississippi Delta." *Environmental History* 14, no. 4 (October 1, 2009): 683–704.

Gonzales, Manuel G. "Carlos I. Velasco." *Journal of Arizona History* 25 (Autumn 1984): 265–84.

Gray, James, and H. R. Stucky. *New Mexico Agriculture—1970.* Research Report 195. Las Cruces: NMSU Cooperative Extension Service, 1971.

Griffith, G. E., et al. "Ecoregions of New Mexico." Reston VA: U.S. Geological Survey, 2006.

Gutierrez, David Gregory, ed. *Between Two Worlds: Mexican Immigrants in the United States.* Wilmington DE: Scholarly Resources, 1996.

Hanley, Theresa. "The History of Stahmann Farms, 1926–1990." *Southern New Mexico Historical Review* 9, no. 1 (January 2002): 38–44.

———. "The Stahmann Farms Migrant Community." Master's thesis, New Mexico State University, 1991.

Harper, Roy E. *An Improved Variety of Chile for New Mexico.* New Mexico College of Agriculture and Mechanic Arts, Agricultural Experiment Station Press Bulletin 1041. Las Cruces: April 1950.

Haverluk, Terrence W. "Chile Peppers and Identity Construction in Pueblo, Colorado." *Journal for the Study of Food and Society* 6, no. 1 (Winter 2002): 45–59.

Hobsbawm, Eric, and T. O. Ranger, eds. *The Invention of Tradition.* New York: Cambridge University Press, 1983.

Holtby, David. *Forty-Seventh Star: New Mexico's Struggle for Statehood.* Norman: University of Oklahoma Press, 2012.

Johansen, Sigurd Arthur. *Migratory-Casual Workers in New Mexico.* New Mexico College of Agriculture and Mechanic Arts, Agricultural Experiment Station Press Bulletin 870. State College: 1941.

Keaton, Clyde Reece. "An Economic Analysis of Apple Marketing, Hondo Valley, New Mexico: A Comparison of Marketing Methods in an Area that Has Several Disadvantages but One Major Advantage—Early Maturity." PhD diss., University of Minnesota, 1955.

Keffer, Charles A. *Spray the Fruit Trees.* New Mexico College of Agriculture and Mechanic Arts, Agricultural Experiment Station Bulletin 10. Mesilla Park: May 17, 1899.

Kerrigan, William. *Johnny Appleseed and the American Orchard: A Cultural History.* Baltimore: Johns Hopkins University Press, 2012.

Kingsbury, Noel. *Hybrid: The History and Science of Plant Breeding.* Chicago: University of Chicago Press, 2009.

Kloppenburg, Jack. *First the Seed: The Political Economy of Plant Biotechnology.* 2nd ed. Madison: University of Wisconsin Press, 2004.

Knowlton, Clark S. *Some Observations about the Relative Lack of Success of Government Anti-Poverty Programs Among Mexican-Americans.* N.p.: [1970?].

Kurlansky, Mark. *Salt: A World History.* New York: Walker and Company, 2002.

Larson, Kenneth W., et al. *Comprehensive Plan, Espanola Planning Area, including Portions of Rio Arriba and Santa Fe Counties.* Albuquerque NM: Kenneth Larson and Associates, December 1971.

Larson, Robert. *New Mexico's Quest for Statehood.* 2nd ed. Albuquerque: University of New Mexico Press, 2013.

Leding, A. R. *Community Production of Acala Cotton in New Mexico.* USDA Circular 314. Washington DC: USDA, 1934.

Lomelí, Francisco A., Víctor A. Sorell, and Genaro M. Padilla, eds. *Nuevomexicano Cultural Legacy: Forms, Agencies, and Discourse.* Paso Por Aqui series. Albuquerque: University of New Mexico Press, 2002.

Magness, John Robert. *Apple Varieties and Important Producing Sections of the United States.* USDA Farmers' Bulletin no. 1883. Washington DC: Government Printing Office, 1941.

Manring, M. M. *Slave in a Box: The Strange Career of Aunt Jemima.* Charlottesville: University of Virginia Press, 1998.

Marcus, Alan I. *Agricultural Science and the Quest for Legitimacy: Farmers, Agricultural Colleges, and Experiment Stations, 1870–1890.* Ames: Iowa State University Press, 1985.

———, ed. *Engineering in a Land-Grant Context: The Past, Present, and Future of an Idea.* West Lafayette IN: Purdue University Press, 2005.

Marcus, Alan I., and Amy Sue Bix. *The Future Is Now: Science and Technology Policy in America since 1950.* Amherst NY: Humanity Books, 2007.

"*Martha Stewart Living* Gets a Taste of New Mexico." *Chile Pepper Institute Newsletter* 6, no. 2 (Summer 1997).

McWilliams, Carey. *Factories in the Field: The Story of Migratory Farm Labor in California.* Boston: Little Brown and Company, 1939.

———. *Ill Fares the Land: Migrants and Migratory Labor in the United States.* 1941. Reprint, New York: Barnes and Noble, 1967.

McWilliams, James E. *American Pests: The Losing War on Insects from Colonial Times to DDT.* New York: Columbia, 2008.

Meeks, Eric V. *Border Citizens: The Making of Indians, Mexicans, and Anglos in Arizona.* Austin: University of Texas Press, 2007.

Metz, Leon Claire. *Pat Garrett: The Story of a Western Lawman.* Norman: University of Oklahoma Press, 1974.

Mintz, Sidney. *Sweetness and Power: The Place of Sugar in Modern History.* New York: Viking, 1985.

Mitchell, Don. *Lie of the Land: Migrant Workers and the California Landscape.* Minneapolis: University of Minnesota Press, 1996.

Montgomery, Charles. *Spanish Redemption: Heritage, Power, and Loss on New Mexico's Upper Rio Grande.* Berkeley: University of California Press, 2002.

Muñoz Zurita, Ricardo, comp. *Larousse diccionario enciclipidico de la gastonomia mexicana.* México, D.F.: Larousse, 2012.

Musoke, Moses, and Alan Olmstead. "The Rise of the Cotton Industry in California: A Comparative Perspective." *Journal of Economic History* 42, no. 2 (1982): 385–412.

New Mexico College of Agriculture and Mechanic Arts. *Fruits and Vegetables*. New Mexico College of Agriculture and Mechanic Arts, Agricultural Experiment Station Circular 25. Las Cruces: November 1917.

New Mexico Department of Agriculture. "2010 New Mexico Chile Production." https://cpi.nmsu.edu/wp-content/uploads/sites/60/2016/06/nm_stats_2010.pdf.

New Mexico State University Alumni Association. *Green Chili Recipe Fiesta*. Las Cruces: NMSU Cooperative Extension Service, July 1973.

Nicholl, Edith M. *Observations of a Ranchwoman in New Mexico*. London: MacMillan and Co., 1898.

Nieto-Phillips, John. *The Language of Blood: The Making of Spanish-American Identity in New Mexico, 1880s–1930s*. Albuquerque: University of New Mexico Press, 2008.

Nostrand, Richard L. *The Hispano Homeland*. Norman: University of Oklahoma Press, 1992.

Novak, William. *The People's Welfare: Law and Regulation in Nineteenth-Century America*. Chapel Hill: University of North Carolina Press, 1996.

Okie, William Thomas. *The Georgia Peach: Culture, Agriculture, and Environment in the American South*. New York: Cambridge University Press, 2016.

Olmstead, Alan, and Paul Rhode. *Creating Abundance: Biological Innovation and American Agricultural Development*. Cambridge: Cambridge University Press, 2008.

Olsson, Tore C. *Agrarian Crossings: Reformers and the Remaking of the US and Mexican Countryside*. Princeton NJ: Princeton University Press, 2017.

Ott, Cindy. *Pumpkin: The Curious History of an American Icon*. Seattle: University of Washington Press, 2012.

Overpeck, John C., and William Thomas Conway. *Cotton*. New Mexico College of Agriculture and Mechanic Arts, Agricultural Experiment Station Bulletin 141. Las Cruces: January 1924.

Padilla, Carmella. *Chile Chronicles: Tales of a New Mexico Harvest*. Santa Fe: Museum of New Mexico Press, 1997.

Paterson, Kent. *The Hot Empire of Chile*. Tempe AZ: Bilingual Press, 2000.

Pauly, Philip. *Fruits and Plains: The Horticultural Transformation of America*. Cambridge: Harvard University Press, 2008.

The Pecos Valley: A Collection of Views in and about Roswell, New Mexico, Together with Appropriate Descriptions of Same, Also a Brief Statement of Facts concerning Lands Still Available in the Pecos Valley. Roswell NM: Trimble-Davisson Company, 1911.

Pederson, Jeff. "Return of the American Eel?" *New Mexico Wildlife*, vol. 30. Santa Fe NM: Public Affairs Division, Department of Game and Fish, 1985.

Pendleton, Granville. *San Juan County, New Mexico: An Ideal Agricultural Section with Plenty of Water and Land for Homeseekers*. Santa Fe: New Mexico Bureau of Immigration, 1906.

Phillips, Fred, G. Emlen Hall, and Mary Black. *Reining in the Rio Grande: People, Land, and Water*. Albuquerque: University of New Mexico Press, 2011.

Pilcher, Jeffrey. *Que Vivan Los Tomales!: Food and the Making of Mexican Identity*. Albuquerque: University of New Mexico Press, 1998.

———. "Tex-Mex, Cal-Mex, New Mex, or Whose Mex? Notes on the Historical Geography of Southwestern Cuisine." *Journal of the Southwest*, December 2001, 659–79.

Pollan, Michael. *The Botany of Desire: A Plant's Eye View of the World*. New York: Random House, 2002.

———. *The Omnivore's Dilemma: A Natural History of Four Meals*. New York: Penguin, 2006.

Proceedings of the Thirty-Eighth Convention of the American Pomological Society, Toledo, Ohio, December 7, 8, and 9, 1921. Columbus OH: F. J. Herr Printing Co., 1922.

Propst, David L., Gerald L. Burton, and Bryan H. Pridgeon. "Fishes of the Rio Grande between Elephant Butte and Caballo Resevoirs, New Mexico." *Southwestern Naturalist* 32, no. 3 (September 1987): 408–11.

Rebolledo, Tey Diana. "Narrative Strategies of Resistance in Hispana Writing." *Journal of Narrative Technique* 20 (Spring 1990): 142.

Report of the Governor of New Mexico to the Secretary of the Interior. Washington DC: Government Printing Office, 1902.

Report of the Governor of New Mexico to the Secretary of the Interior. Washington DC: Government Printing Office, 1903.

Rosaldo, Renato. "Imperialist Nostalgia." *Representations* 26 (Spring 1989): 107–22.

Routson, Kanin. "Genetic Diversity of Historic Apple Trees on the Colorado Plateau and Implications for its Preservation." Master's thesis, Northern Arizona University, 2007.

Sackman, Douglas Cazaux. *Orange Empire: California and the Fruits of Eden*. Berkeley: University of California, 2005.

Sandage, C. H., ed. *The Promise of Advertising*. Homewood IL: Richard D. Irwin, 1961.

Sandul, J. P. "The Agriburb: Recalling the Suburban Side of Ontario, California's Agricultural Colonization." *Agricultural History* 84, no. 2 (Spring 2010): 195–223.

Scharff, Virginia. *Twenty Thousand Roads: Women, Movement, and the West*. Berkeley: University of California Press, 2002.

Schönfeld La Mar, Bärbel Hannelore. "Water and Land in the Mesilla Valley, New Mexico: Reclamation and Its Effects on Property Ownership and Agricultural Land Use." PhD diss., New Mexico State University, 1984.

Schweid, Richard. *Consider the Eel*. Chapel Hill: University of North Carolina Press, 2002.

Shepard, S. L. *American Eel Biological Species Report*. Hadley MA: U.S. Fish and Wildlife Service, 2015.

Simpson, C. B., and L. O. Howard. *The Codling Moth*. USDA Bulletin 41. Washington DC: Government Printing Office, 1903.

Skaggs, R., M. Decker, and D. VanLeeuwen. *A Survey of Southern New Mexico Chile Producers: Production Practices and Problems*. College of Agricultural, Consumer and Environmental Sciences (ACES) Bulletin 782. Las Cruces: New Mexico State University, January 2000.

Smith, Andrew, ed. *The Oxford Encyclopedia of Food and Drink in America*. Vol. 1. New York: Oxford University Press, 2013.

Smith, C. Wayne, and J. Tom Cothren, eds. *Cotton: Origin, History, Technology, and Production*. New York: John Wiley and Sons, 1999.

Smith, H. Allen. *The Great Chili Confrontation: A Dramatic History of the Decade's Most Impassioned Culinary Embroilment, with Recipes*. New York: Trident, 1969.

Smith, Henry Nash. *Virgin Land: The American West as Symbol and Myth*. New York: Vintage, 1950.

Sneed, Ruth. *Chile*. Circular 309. Las Cruces: NMSU Cooperative Extension Service, August 1960.

Soluri, John. *Banana Cultures: Agriculture, Consumption and Environmental Change in Honduras and the United States*. Austin: University of Texas Press, 2005.

Stallings, James, and Jere Boyer. *Wholesale Fruit and Vegetable Markets in El Paso and Albuquerque*. Research Report 43. Las Cruces: NMSU Experiment Station, July 1960.

Stamen, Mark Lawrence. "Genetic Dreams: An Environmental History of the California Cotton Industry, 1902–1953." PhD diss., University of Iowa, 1999.

Starr, Kevin. *Inventing the Dream: California through the Progressive Era*. Oxford: Oxford University Press, 1985.

Steinbeck, John. *The Grapes of Wrath*. London: William Heinemann, 1939.

Stepp, Donald L., and Ruth Vise. "Stahmann Farms Produce Pecans on Two Hemispheres." *Borderlands* 28 (2010–11). https://epcc.libguides.com/c.php?g=754275&p=5406003.

Stewart, Rupert L. *Cotton Growing*. New Mexico College of Agriculture and Mechanic Arts, Agricultural Experiment Station Bulletin 120. Las Cruces: December 1919.

Stoll, Steven. *Fruits of Natural Advantage: Making the Industrial Countryside in California*. Berkeley: University of California Press, 1998.

Sumner, G. Lynn. *How I Learned the Secrets of Success in Advertising*. North Audley Media, 2009.

Swingle, Walter T., and Herbert J. Webber. "Hybrids and Their Utilization in Plant Breeding." In *Yearbook of United States Department of Agriculture. 1897*, 383–420. Washington DC: Government Printing Office, 1898.

Taylor, Paul. *Migratory Farm Labor in the United States*. Washington DC: Government Printing Office, 1937.

Townsend, C. H. Tyler. *Insecticides and Their Appliances*. New Mexico College of Agriculture and Mechanic Arts, Agricultural Experiment Station Bulletin 9. Las Cruces: Rio Grande Republican, 1892.

———. *Notices of Importance concerning Fruit Insects*. New Mexico College of Agriculture and Mechanic Arts, Agricultural Experiment Station Bulletin 5. Las Cruces: Rio Grande Republican, 1892.

———. *Scale-Insects in New Mexico*. New Mexico College of Agriculture and Mechanic Arts, Agricultural Experiment Station Bulletin 7. Las Cruces: Rio Grande Republican, 1892.

Traverso, Amy. *An Apple Lover's Cookbook*. New York: W. W. Norton, 2011.

Truett, Samuel. *Fugitive Landscapes: The Forgotten History of the U.S.-Mexico Borderlands*. New Haven: Yale University Press, 2008.

Truett, Samuel, and Elliott Young. *Continental Crossroads: Remapping U.S.-Mexico Borderlands History*. Durham NC: Duke University Press, 2004.

Trujillo, Phillip M., R. F. Hooks, and Darrell T. Sullivan. *Tree Fruit Variety Trials, Española Valley Branch Station, 1953 to 1968*. Bulletin 599. Las Cruces: NMSU Experiment Station, 1972.

Tyrell, Ian. *True Gardens of the Gods: Californian-Australian Environmental Reform, 1860–1930*. Berkeley: University of California Press, 1999.

United States Bureau of Plant Industry. *Seeds and Plants Imported during the Period from December, 1903, to December, 1905* . . . Washington DC: Government Printing Office, 1907. https://archive.org/stream/seedsplantsimpor97unit#page/128/mode/2up.

United States Census of Agriculture: 1935. Vol. 1, pt. 3. Washington DC: Government Printing Office, 1936.

United States Census of Agriculture: 1945. Vol. 1, pt. 30. Washington DC: Government Printing Office, 1946.

United States Census of Agriculture: 1950. Vol. 1, pt. 30. Washington DC: Government Printing Office, 1952.

United States Census of Agriculture: 1950. Vol. 1, pt. 33. Washington DC: Government Printing Office, 1952.

United States Census of Agriculture: 1959. Vol. 1, pt. 42. Washington DC: Government Printing Office, 1961.

United States Census of Agriculture: 1964. Vol. 1, pt. 42. Washington DC: Government Printing Office, 1966.

United States Census of Agriculture: 1978. Vol. 1, pt. 31. Washington DC: Government Printing Office, 1981.

United States Census of Agriculture: 1982. Washington DC: Government Printing Office, 1984.

USDA Agricultural Research Service, Farmer Cooperative Service, and Four Corners Regional Commission. *Appraisal of the Apple Industry in the Four Corners Region*. Washington DC: USDA Cooperative Service, June 1972.

USDA National Agricultural Statistics Service. "2005 New Mexico Chile Production." https://www.nass.usda.gov/Statistics_by_State/New_Mexico/Publications/Special_Interest_Reports/chile05.pdf.

———. "2016 State Agriculture Overview: New Mexico." (URL no longer available.)

———. "2018 State Agriculture Overview: New Mexico." (URL no longer available.)

——. "2019 New Mexico Chile Production." https://www.nass.usda.gov/Statistics_by _State/New_Mexico/Publications/Special_Interest_Reports/NM-2019-Chile -Production.pdf.

Van Dresser, Peter. *A Landscape for Humans.* Albuquerque NM: Biotechnic Press, 1972.

Variedades de Arboles Frutales propios para la parte norte de la mesa central. Boletín número 22. Ciudad Juárez, Chih.: Estación Agricola Experimental de Ciudad Juárez, 1906.

Wald, Sarah. *The Nature of California: Race, Citizenship, and Farming since the Dust Bowl.* Seattle: University of Washington Press, 2016.

Walker, A. L. *Farmers' Cooperation in New Mexico, 1925–1926.* New Mexico College of Agriculture and Mechanic Arts, Agricultural Experiment Station Bulletin 164. State College: July 1927.

Walker, Stephanie, and Charles Havlik. *The Landrace Chiles of Northern New Mexico.* Circular 679. Las Cruces: NMSU Cooperative Extension Service, June 2016.

Walsh, Casey. *Building the Borderlands: A Transnational History of Irrigated Cotton along the Texas-Mexico Border.* College Station: Texas A&M Press, 2008.

Weigle, Marta, and Peter White. *The Lore of New Mexico.* Abridged. Albuquerque: University of New Mexico Press, 2003.

Wetzel, Carolyn F. *Judging for Home Economics 4-H Clubs.* New Mexico College of Agriculture and Mechanic Arts, Agricultural Experiment Station Circular 11B. Las Cruces: May 1932.

Wilson, Chris. *The Myth of Santa Fe: Creating a Modern Regional Tradition.* Albuquerque: University of New Mexico, 1997.

Wilson, David Scofield, and Angus Kress Gillespie, eds. *Rooted in America: Foodlore of Popular Fruits and Vegetables.* Knoxville: University of Tennessee Press, 1999.

Wiltbank, W. J. *Home Vegetable Gardening.* Circular 287. Las Cruces: NMSU Cooperative Extension Service, December 1958.

Women's Auxiliary Committee, World's Columbian Exposition San Juan County, comp. *San Juan County, New Mexico.* Chicago: Rand McNally, 1893.

Young, James Webb. *The Compleat Angler.* Coapa [La Cañon de Cochiti] NM: Piñon Press, 1953.

——. *The Diary of an Ad Man.* Chicago: Advertising Publications, 1944.

——. *Ego-Biography.* Coapa [La Cañon de Cochiti] NM: Piñon Press, 1955.

——. *The Itch for Orders.* Coapa [La Cañon de Cochiti] NM: Piñon Press, 1957.

Index

Abert, James W., 38

Acala cotton, 93–96, 102, 181n56, 192n50. *See also* cotton

Ad Council, 52

advertising: for apples, 21, 28–29, 42, 51–60, 67; for chiles, 141–45, 154–55; for geese, 106; for pecans, 104. *See also* agrarian storytelling; boosterism

African American farmers and laborers, 81, 180n36, 180n39

agrarian storytelling, 2–5, 164–65; of Champagne apples, 50, 59–60; of chiles, 9–10, 121, 123–24, 126, 137–38, 147–49, 154–55, 160; of cotton, 81–82; by James Webb Young, 52–55; of yeoman myth, 50–51, 56–58, 88–91, 160, 164. *See also* advertising; boosterism; cultural symbols; nostalgia

agricultural fiestas, 114–15, 116, 117, 141, 178nn19–20, 186n51. *See also* harvest festivals

agricultural industries. *See* apples and apple orchards; chile pepper; cotton

agricultural laborers: apple orchards and, 58; cotton production and, 89–92, 97, 105; enslaved people as, 180n36; erasure and exploitation of, 4, 57–58, 61, 138; immigra-

tion laws and, 90, 184nn28–29; paternalism and, 83–85, 100, 107–11, 114–15, 116, 179n21; wage system of, 116. *See also* agricultural migrations; racism

agricultural migrations, 7–8, 21, 77–78, 97, 161–63, 173n84, 184nn28–29. *See also* settlement patterns

Ailes, Roger, 52

Albuquerque Journal, 54

alfalfa, 16, 25, 86, 101, 168n2

American Apple Exposition (1911), 39

Amistad Dam, 185n38

Anaheim pepper, 132, 147. *See also* chile pepper

Anglo culture. *See* whiteness

animal agriculture: cattle, 19, 101, 107; chickens, 101, 107, 115, 117; geese, 101, 105–7, 115, 183n22; goats, 24; sheep, 24, 101, 107, 130

Apple Congress, 39

An Apple Lovers Cookbook, 60

apples and apple orchards, 6–7, 72–73; advertising for, 21, 28–29, 42, 51–60, 67; in Colorado, 170n19, 170n31; cooperatives of, 7, 50–51, 62–73; as cultural symbol, 6, 16, 39, 45–47, 173n72; in Española, 175n29; Fred Dixon and, 49–50, 56, 58–60, 174n4,